The People Say Yes is the story of the making of Scotland's Parliament.

Returning to his native Scotland in the 1980s Kenyon Wright was deeply concerned by the affront to the nation's values of Thatcherite free market policies. And there was the democratic deficit where the majority consistently voted for parties that did not form their government.

Through his role as executive chair on the cross-party Constitutional Convention – a body widely credited with achieving minor miracles in the notoriously fragmented and factional world of Scottish politics – Kenyon Wright has done much to set the government of his country on the road to a positive and progressive future.

He gives an account also of the influences on a life that has sought to achieve peace, justice and a Christian respect for the integrity of creation.

"What happens when that other voice we know so well says, 'We say No, and We are the State.' Well, We say Yes and We are the People."

"We are the heirs of a nation that has always prized freedom above all else. We deserve something better than the secretive, centralised, self-serving superstate that the UK has become."

"My conversion to the Christian faith and my early political education went hand in hand and inoculated me against that kind of Christian faith which turns out people who are too heavenly-minded to be any earthly good."

"When the history of our time comes to be written the philosophy that we have called Thatcherism will be seen even by Conservatives as a temporary aberration, certainly from Scotland's tradition, history and instinctive feelings."

The *People* say YES

the making of Scotland's parliament

[signature]

KENYON WRIGHT

edited by
Harry Conroy

Argyll
publishing

© Kenyon Wright 1997

First Published 1997
Argyll Publishing
Glendaruel
Argyll PA22 3AE
Scotland

The author has asserted his moral rights.

British Library Cataloguing-in-Publication Data.
A catalogue record for this book is available from
the British Library.

ISBN 1 874640 92 0

Cover design Shane Connolly
Cover illustration Shaun McLaren

Typeset & Origination
Cordfall Ltd, Glasgow

Printing
ColourBooks Ltd, Dublin

to the memory of
John Smith whose vision
of Scotland's parliament
was never dimmed
and whose 'unfinished business'
is ours to finish

ACKNOWLEDGEMENTS

It would be impossible for me to acknowledge here all those involved in the Scottish Constitutional Convention who assisted me in my role as chair of the executive committee but I extend my thanks to everyone who supported our work in whatever way they could.

I wish to thank Harry Conroy for the manner in which he has edited this book and for suggesting it in the first place! Harry, of course, was campaign director of the Convention between 1990 and '92 and his prompting helped me to pull together the many aspects of this story. I wish to thank also Stuart Conroy and Lesley Sutter at Conroy Associates for valuable help in production, and my publisher for his useful capacity not to panic as deadlines loomed.

CONTENTS

Preface 9
1 A Series of Minor Miracles? 11
2 The Long March to Freedom 17
3 To Be or Not To Be 24
4 A Claim of Right 30
5 Learning 'to Live Dangerously' 39
6 We say Yes; We are the People 48
7 "Give me a child until he is five . . ." 59
8 "Learn Boy Or Get Out" 65
9 The God with Two Faces 72
10 The Tarnished Jewel 79
11 Healing the Wounds of History 90
12 Scotland the What? 105
13 Now for the Hard Bit 116
14 The Devil is in the Detail 124
15 Hope Springs Eternal 137
16 High Hopes and Disappointment 145
17 How Long, Oh Lord, How Long? 162
18 If You Can Keep Your Head . . . 181
19 'Further Steps' 197
20 Clearing the Highest Hurdles 207

21 The Final Doubts   217
22 Scotland's Parliament; Scotland's Right   221
23 Hurricane Referendum Strikes!   239
24 Forging 'Partnership for a Parliament'   257
25 Surprised by Joy   262
Appendix The Ten Commitments   270

PREFACE

"What does he think he's doing?"

"Who does he think he is?"

For eight years at least I have lived with this kind of question. When a churchman wearing a dog-collar is seen to be prominent in a movement for political change, even if it is not narrowly party political, it seems that people ask questions.

Writing in the *Scotsman*, outraged of Aberdeen asked, "Who does he think he is, this Canon who claims to speak for Scotland? He doesn't speak for me or for the 700,000 Scots like me who voted Tory!" A profile in the *Observer Scotland* quoted my words at the opening meeting of the Scottish Constitutional Convention and then said, "those less than sympathetic to the *Claim of Right* were snarling the question: who does he think he is?" The tone certainly varies from the snarling outrage suggested above to a mild interest or genuine surprise.

This book is written to answer both questions. In telling the exciting story of the Scottish Constitutional Convention and its search for the best way to a Scottish parliament, the following pages spell out what I think I have been doing.

It has however another dimension. I firmly believe that the leadership I have given to the Convention over the past years has sprung naturally and easily from all the experience of my life and the convictions I have learned over forty years of ministry. This book, I hope, answers the second question, Who does he think he is?

The question, Who am I? is never one we can fully answer for ourselves. At best we are all searching for our true identity.

Two things however, have become clear to me. The first is accessible to everyone whatever their faith or ideology; the second is probably only clear to those who share my Christian faith.

The first is that our identity, who we are, is fashioned by relationships past and present. I am truly myself in a community in relation to my family, my loved ones and all with whom I have any kind of relationship. I, of course, wear my masks. Different masks for different functions with different groups of people but underneath them all there is a reality taking shape. The man I am today, this complex mixture of grime and glory, of sublime vision and selfish motives, of good and ill, the man who has guided, persuaded, cajoled and bullied the Constitutional Convention into its achievements, can only be understood even partly by the stories that have made me what I am. In this book therefore, I have tried to tell some of these stories in a way that is not only accessible and coherent but that explains what it is that makes me tick.

The second answer is that this life on Earth makes sense only when it is understood as a journey to something beyond, as a time crucially important in itself precisely because it is set in the context of something greater that gives it full meaning and purpose. When life is understood as a journey, a pilgrimage to a destination in which our true human nature is to be perfected, a destination at which we are to be more truly ourselves as we were meant to be, then life itself is given a significance, a purpose, a meaning, a vision which makes it truly sacred.

Kenyon Wright
Glencarse, May 1997

CHAPTER I

A Series of Minor Miracles?

This is the story of the making of Scotland's Parliament.

It is a story which matters to every Scot. Indeed it is important for anyone who cares for the future of any part of the UK. Since the creation of Scotland's parliament is still very much part of contemporary events and is likely to be for some years to come, the truth is we are still too close to the events described in this book to put them in perspective and judge their ultimate significance. Some historian, well into the 21st century, will assess how important this was in the transformation of Scotland and Britain, but I am confident that the story of the Scottish Constitutional Convention will be seen as the turning point in the history of our nation.

It is certainly the story of an astonishing series of minor miracles. When I first agreed nearly ten years ago to join the steering committee that was then being set up, and thus took the first hesitant steps that led me to preside over the events that followed, I would simply not have believed that we could travel so far so fast. "Oh ye of little faith!"

Was it believable then that the political bodies in Scotland –

so renowned for their noble traditions of trenchant political analysis of events and their perhaps not so noble traditions of always falling out – would ever agree to differ while recognising common goals?

Was it credible that the Labour Party would abandon its traditional hesitation, commit itself to working with other parties, and nail its colours firmly to the mast of home-rule?

Was it credible that 80% of Scotland's Members of Parliament would line up to sign a Claim of Right which asserted the sovereignty of the Scottish people, and thus reject the claim of Westminster to absolute power?

Was it credible that two great political parties, which between them consistently commanded a majority of votes and seats both at local and national elections, would be prepared to join not only with each other, but with the broadest cross-section of Scottish civil society in living memory?

Was it credible that such a diverse body could work by genuine consensus – never imposing anything by majority voting, but always being ready to argue face-to-face until a way forward acceptable to everyone could be found?

Was it credible that the Scottish Labour Party would accept an electoral system which would ensure broad proportionality, and which would almost certainly deprive them of an automatic absolute majority in Scotland's parliament?

Was it credible, not only that these diverse forces would stay together for eight long years but would produce the most detailed, visionary and responsible scheme for a Scottish parliament within the UK?

I would not have set my hand to the plough from the beginning, had I not believed in my heart that these things were possible, that the people of Scotland could rise above their squabbles and their differences to present a common front at least long enough to achieve that parliament within which we could get back to our old divisions! I believed in my heart, but I admit my head told me otherwise. It would have been a brave man or woman who would have wagered in 1989 when the Convention began its work, that its historical achievement would be recognised throughout Europe and beyond. Malcolm Rifkind, then Secretary of State for Scotland, is reported as saying that if the Constitutional Convention was able to reach a common mind on the way forward for Scotland, he would jump off the roof of the Scottish Office. We will not hold him to that rash promise.

Even minor miracles are achieved not just by inspiration but by perspiration. Behind the Convention's success there is a long tale, if not of blood, certainly of sweat and tears! This book is the story of that process. I have tried to tell it honestly and as comprehensively as my memory and my extensive notes allow. If my hair is some what greyer now and my face perhaps more lined than it was at the beginning of the story it is largely because of those seven years of hard labour (though to be fair I would have to add 'hard Liberal Democrat', and the others were often hard too!)

The Convention has brought me into direct and regular contact with many of Scotland's leading politicians, both inside and outside the Scottish Constitutional Convention – and with some of the key movers and shakers in many other areas of life in Scotland. Many have impressed me; some disappointed me; a few disgusted me. Often my respect has been deepened for the integrity of many I have worked with. Sometimes my suspicions have been confirmed concerning the dishonesty of others.

Though I have tried to be frank and honest in my assessment of others, I do so humbly, for I make no claim for any special moral insight or holiness.

"Life," said the philosopher Kierkegaard, "must be lived forward but understood backwards." That is certainly true of the Convention. It is only now, as I look back, that it becomes clear how we have been able to overcome our differences, reach a consensus and present to the people of Scotland a scheme for a better government and a renewed nation – but above all remain firmly rooted in the moral and historic vision that was our inspiration and remains our foundation.

At that first meeting of the Convention in March 1989 in the historic setting of the General Assembly Hall of the Church of Scotland, I made that statement which was so widely reported as a gesture of defiance against the absolutism of the British State – "We say yes and we are the people." At the time I may not have been able to see where it was going to lead, but I did sense even then that it was the beginning of something significant that would change the face of Scotland and the United Kingdom for good.

In those uplifting moments, just before the Convention members lined up to sign that solemn *Claim of Right*, I remember – and indeed recorded privately at the time – feelings that I have not dared to speak of publicly until now.

I had a strange sense that I was surrounded, not just by the many hundreds present in the Assembly Hall, but by a "cloud of witnesses" from the past. On one side I felt the guardian presence of those Scots who in the 1320 Declaration, so far in advance of its time, told the King at Arbroath that he ruled "subject to the consent of the realm," and who pledged their lives "not for honour, glory or riches but for freedom alone."

I felt the presence of those who in the Claim of Right of 1689 had deposed the King for abusing his power and those who in 1842 had walked out of the General Assembly of the Church of Scotland in defiance of Westminster's right to impose patronage on Scotland.

To my other side I felt the presence of ghosts from my own past, those who had helped me in my pilgrimage and brought me to this time and to the convictions which I hold dear.

I have been asked to weave into this another story, much less important, much less historic but still, perhaps, not without interest. This is the story of my own life and how I came to this stage. Friends and enemies have called me many things over the past decade. These range from "a turbulent priest" and "the politicians' poodle" to "Scotland's Archbishop Tutu" and "Scotland's Makarios". Flattering or insulting, they all have one underlying question behind them: "Why are you, a minister of the Christian

Church, involved in such a political exercise?" The easiest way to answer that question and the way that might have the greatest effect in interesting, or perhaps annoying my readers, is to tell something of the story of my own life and how I believe I have been led to this moment.

It is not surprising therefore that this book will try to answer both questions. It is a personal and a political testimony. In the chapters that follow the two stories are closely interwoven. One I am convinced will one day change the course of Scotland's history and restore our nation at last to its true place in Britain and Europe. The other is of much less consequence but may still be of some interest.

The story of a glorious adventure alternates with some stories from an eventful life. The first matters to all of us and to our children. The second may at least entertain and perhaps explain and enlighten. The history of my life which is briefly told is not an attempt at a potted autobiography. Episodes are selected from my memories of a full life, for a specific purpose – to illustrate the experiences and the people who have influenced me in ways that I believe directly prepared me for this great task. You must decide whether I am right in that belief or simply deluded.

Everything that follows both about the Convention and my own life is as accurate as I can make it. In the case of the Convention I have been involved from the start probably more closely than any other individual. This story is therefore as near to the truth as any one person can get. As for my life it is not so much of a story as a few selected snippets. One thing I have learned both from my own experience of life and from my reading of how Jesus dealt with people. We are moved, influenced and even changed not just by theories or by philosophy but primarily by stories and by relationships. When I look back on my life I remember, not so much in great detail, but in snapshots and in stories – and above all through the people who feature in both. The stories of my life therefore are not the whole truth – that would be impossible and far too embarrassing for anyone involved!

I invite you to think back on your own early life and experience. What do you remember? I suspect it is the vivid mental picture or 'freeze frame', the story of something that happened, or the person who mattered to you. That is what gives all our lives their meaning and significance. Events alone are meaningless until they are part of a story. "Life must be lived forward and understood backwards."

Each episode, each encounter, each person – has its own autonomy, its own significance, its own internal logic. No part of our life exists merely for another part, as a preparation or a consequence. The tragedy for many lives is to live not in the present but in a remembered past or a hoped for future. Having said that, we *can* look back and see a pattern of meaning. All my stories have their own significance – but all have prepared me for this story – the story of Scotland's rebirth.

Someone once said, "We must listen to the music of the past if we are to sing in the present and dance into the future." A Scottish parliament speaking for a renewed nation within a reformed Union and a responsible Europe – that is our future.

CHAPTER 2

The Long March to Freedom

(1968-1985)

Scotland's parliament may at long last be a real prospect – yet most Scots will keep the champagne or whisky, both equally appropriate, on ice until we can be sure beyond doubt that in the wake of the Labour victory in the 1997 General Election, this time promises will be kept. Constant vigilance remains the price of freedom.

The road has been a long and hard one, littered with false starts and hopes betrayed. The all-party Scottish Home-Rule Movement was formed in 1886 and its history is well-documented. But for our purposes the modern story begins thirty years ago in 1968. It is important to understand that the desire for self-government has deep roots, long established in Scottish history.

In November 1967, Winnie Ewing won the Hamilton by-election for the Scottish National Party and such was the mood of the time, that the following year at the Scottish conference of the Conservative Party, then in opposition, Edward Heath made his famous Declaration of Perth. He formally endorsed the idea of an elected assembly for Scotland and, under the chairmanship of Sir Alec Douglas Home, set up a Scottish Constitutional Committee to plan in detail. It reported in March 1970, recommending a directly elected assembly with limited powers that did not include the enactment of legislation.

The Labour government meanwhile, set up a Royal Commission on the Constitution at the end of 1968. Its mandate was "to examine the present functions of the central legislature and government in relation to the several countries and regions of the UK." Lord Kilbrandon's commission reported in October 1973 and put forward six different alternative schemes, including the possibility of legislative assemblies for Scotland and Wales. Thus, even though they seemed to blow hotter or colder towards constitutional change according to the direction of the electoral wind, by 1973 both the Labour and Conservative parties were seriously occupied with the issue of devolving power from the Westminster Parliament. The Liberals too, remained firm in their support and indeed, confirmed their longstanding commitment to federalism.

In 1974 there were two General Elections and events gradually moved the Labour Government under Harold Wilson into firmer proposals for legislative devolution. A constitution unit was set up to translate the White Paper of 1974 into a Parliamentary Bill. The delay in doing this however, proved ultimately corrosive.

Harold Wilson was succeeded as Prime Minister in April 1976 by Jim Callaghan who had been very uncertain on the devolution issue. The main continuing enthusiasm and impetus came from the Minister of State in the Privy Council office, one John Smith! He at least, was faithful and consistent then and to the end of his life.

But the whole process took far too long, partly because of the government's faltering enthusiasm, running the country on a thin majority, but mainly due to the enormous technical and political difficulties caused by the method adopted. Every single government department was involved and details of what exactly had to be devolved and what retained by Westminster Ministries had to be negotiated.

Finally in November 1976 the Scotland and Wales Bill was presented to Parliament. There then began the tortuous path, laid with monstrous obstacles, put there by those who knew how to use complex and arcane Parliamentary processes, that was to lead to the referendum of 1979.

Why did this venture fail and how can we learn from it to ensure that the journey embarked on in 1997 does not fail, the momentum to self-government is not lost and history is not repeated?

Failure in 1979 happened for several reasons. The Bill itself was flawed and the arithmetic in Parliament made opinion lukewarm. In 1980 Gordon Brown, now MP and Chancellor of the Exchequer, an enthusiastic and committed member of the Scottish Constitutional Convention, considered the demise of the scheme in his *The Politics of Nationalism and Devolution*. The Scotland and Wales Bill was an *ad hoc* solution, he wrote, "which had precious little grounding in political principle or theory. All that supporters of the Act could argue was that (its proposals) were the best the House of Commons was capable of producing."

Comparison of 1997 with 1979 is instructive. The Scottish Constitutional Convention has provided just that deep grounding in political and constitutional principle and theory and the broad consensus of civil society that was lacking last time around. This time there is a stronger foundation of constitutional principle; a stronger sense of the "settled will" of our people; a stronger sense of outrage at the injustice and division the over-centralised Westminster Parliament has imposed on us against our will; and a stronger, ironclad promise from the Convention parties that this time they will not allow the machinations of Westminster nor Parliamentary manoeuvres to castrate, delay or disarm the parliament which is Scotland's Right.

Above all we have a Constitutional Convention and a Civic

Assembly that will insist on a participative future. We now know that politics is too important to be left to the politicians and that we, the people, must be the guardians of our own hopes.

In March 1979 the people of Scotland voted in the referendum on the plan put before them by Jim Callaghan's Labour Government for a Scottish Assembly. There is no doubt that the major blame for the failure to gain devolution was down to the last minute imposition of what has been called "the Forty Per Cent Rule". This device, unprecedented in democratic politics, was dreamt up as a wrecking procedure by George Cunningham, a backbench Labour MP, who although a Scot, represented an English constituency.

Cunningham proposed near the end of the Committee stage that at least 40 per cent of the registered electorate must vote Yes for the Scotland Act to be enacted. For the first time in British democratic history a simple majority of those voting on an issue, or Government election, would not be enough. The proposal was strongly opposed by the Labour Government but was passed by 166 votes to 151.

The result of the Forty Per Cent Rule was that although in the 1979 referendum, 51.6 per cent of voters cast in favour of the devolution proposals with 48.4 per cent against, the scheme fell. With a turnout of 63.3 per cent this meant that of the total electorate, only 33.9 per cent had actively voted YES.

There were many reasons for the low turnout. One was the fact that nine out of ten local councillors were against devolution as they believed it would take power from the councils. This meant, in particular that the Labour Party machine on the ground did not function. Voters were not encouraged to come out. There was also the confusion caused by the fact that all political parties were divided with activists on both sides of the debate. None of this helped mobilise a positive campaign.

Opponents of devolution have since then referred to devolution being rejected by the Scottish people, or the proposals having failed. They rarely mention the unique hurdle, foreign to British politics, which was imposed by Westminster, a hurdle which if present in our General Elections would ensure that few if any Governments would be elected. I have not carried out detailed research back into history, but in living memory all British Governments have been elected by a minority even of those voting.

It also has to be admitted that the scheme was undoubtedly flawed and inadequate, and was opposed by many individuals on these grounds. It is significant the Conservative Party which in the run-up to the 1997 General Election constantly repeated the naive slogan of the Tartan Tax, actually condemned the 1979 scheme precisely because it gave no fiscal powers to the proposed Assembly, leaving it at the financial mercy of Westminster.

The former Conservative Prime Minister, the late Sir Alec Douglas Home, called for a No vote on the grounds that he would remain committed to devolution, and that if elected a Conservative Government would produce a better scheme. Few supporters of devolution will forget his words, "I would hesitate to vote against this Bill if I did not believe that devolution will remain at the top of the political agenda."

A third, and important reason, was simply that the time was not ripe. There was no strong feeling of alienation and the power of the centralised British State, however unacceptable in principle, was broadly tolerable. The Scottish electorate had become accustomed to the fact that governments, whether Conservative or Labour, used their powers towards Scotland moderately, reflecting a broad national consensus.

For these reasons, good or bad, the referendum of 1979 failed. It was probably a blessing in disguise that it did, for the Scottish Assembly it would have put in place would have been one with limited powers and entirely subject to Westminster. It would have been a weak and sickly body compared to what is now planned.

The failure to win the referendum meant that Jim Callaghan's Government had to repeal the Scotland Act, and his minority Government then lost a No Confidence motion with the SNP voting against the Government. This led to a General Election in June which resulted in the Conservatives led by Margaret Thatcher gaining power for a generation.

Once in power, Margaret Thatcher who during the referendum campaign had said that a No vote did not mean a person was voting against the principle of devolution, quickly turned cold on the question. She introduced what she described as "conviction politics" and compromise and consensus became notions to be scorned.

The years that followed witnessed the gradual emergence of a new political and governing philosophy in British life. The growth of what came to be called Thatcherism, marked the end of the broad consensus in our politics which had, since 1945, included the concept of the Welfare State, full employment and a mixed economy.

From Scotland's position they were years of gathering gloom as the growing centralisation of government, the cancerous spread of unelected quangos with enormous spending powers, and the imposition on Scotland of policies that were opposed with rapidly growing vehemence seemed to mark not just changes in policy but the imposition of something like an alien ideology. Certainly they marked a growing divergence of political development between Scotland and the rest of the United Kingdom.

Thatcherism was seen to be a kind of extreme English nationalism that neither heard nor cared for Scotland. The competitive market ideology together with the obsessive centralisation of power and the persona of Margaret Thatcher herself combined to offend something deep in Scotland's collective psyche – a profound if inarticulate sense of the values of community, of caring, and of democratic control of limited power.

Paradoxically the result of this was that in many ways Thatcherism was the midwife for a rebirth of a clear feeling of Scottish identity. Scotland and England diverged politically with growing decisiveness. Our country rejected Thatcherism and all its works. The stage was set for a new initiative.

Following the failure of the referendum and the election of a Government which quickly displayed its rejection of devolution, many pro-devolutionists had given up and gone back, literally or metaphorically to "cultivate their gardens." The flame of democracy in Scotland burned low. That it was not entirely extinguished is largely due to the stamina of a small band of Scots, led and inspired by the late Jim Boyack.

As the feeling of helplessness grew Jim Boyack, a Labour Party grassroots activist helped found, in March 1980, on the first anniversary of the ill-fated referendum, the Campaign for a Scottish Assembly. On the fourth anniversary in March 1983, Boyack along with five others kept a cold all-night vigil outside the Parliament Building, and were joined in the morning by 140 others, including ten MPs.

They handed into the Scottish Office the following declaration:

> "We, symbolically representing the members of a Scottish Assembly, do bring to the notice of Her Majesty's Government that a question of democracy is at stake, and we must ask the question 'When are you going to fulfil the constitutional wish of the Scottish people to have a democratically elected Assembly?' "

Theirs was a voice still crying in the darkness – but the first glimmer of dawn was about to break.

CHAPTER 3

To Be or Not To Be

(1985–87)

In May 1985, the Campaign for a Scottish Assembly thought that the time was ripe to issue a consultative paper entitled *The Scottish Constitutional Convention*. This, as far as I am aware, was the start of the process which was to lead eventually to where we stand today. The CSA led by Jim Boyack as Convener asked interested parties to respond to secretary Hugh Miller by the end of September of that year.

The paper began by setting out the problem:

"Repeatedly down the years a great volume of Scottish opinion has been expressed in favour of an elected assembly to deal at least with all those aspects of government which concern Scotland only. An assembly still has not been achieved, and this is the clearest evidence that Scottish opinion cannot be effectively registered in the British Parliament.

"This situation must not be allowed to continue much longer. A political climate has be to be created in which a Scottish Assembly becomes inevitable whichever party is in power. We see a Constitutional Convention as means of so registering Scottish opinion as to make an assembly inevitable and to ensure that the assembly created is an effective one."

The paper went on to call for such a Convention which would

"provide a representative Scottish body through which particular Scottish interests could be expressed and coordinated, and with which British government would have to deal openly. The real arguments for and against particular features of an assembly would not be hidden in the Cabinet Room."

Interestingly the paper set out the possible task of such a Convention in words which have largely been fulfilled.

"The case for the Constitutional Convention lies in the right of self determination of the people of Scotland. Acceptance of this democratic and constitutional principle in no way compromises the specific political principles of any individual or organisation. In the Scottish context a Constitutional Convention would:

a. Articulate and represent the Scottish demand for an assembly.

b. Draft the provisions of an assembly scheme setting out the powers, the sources of finance and relationships with British Government.

c. Negotiate with British Government the timetable and implementation of that scheme.

d. Arrange any necessary test of Scottish support, e.g. by referendum."

The paper also stated that any such Constitutional Convention had to be representative if it was to speak with authority for Scotland.

After a period of some eighteen months of consultation and gestation around the consultative paper, the CSA organised a Declaration Dinner in an Edinburgh hotel at the end of February 1987. Representatives of many facets of Scottish life were invited to attend and to align themselves with the following declaration:

> "We believe that the time has come when Scotland must assume control over her own affairs through a democratically elected assembly. Only by so doing can we properly develop our skills and our resources, safeguard our national culture and identity, and restore a proper sense of dignity to our people. We therefore believe that the Scottish Assembly should be set up by the next Government as an immediate priority."

The organisers had chosen three "prominent Scots" none of them politicians, to speak at that dinner, which was to have results greater than they could have hoped for. The three were Prof Christopher Harvie of Tübingen University, Kay Carmichael, a well-known social activist in Scotland, and myself. Since I suppose it was my presence, and speech, at this Declaration Dinner, that set my feet firmly on the path that would lead to play such a seminal role in the making of Scotland's parliament, I have been asked "why me?" Why was I asked to be one of these three who shared these hopes and aspirations for Scotland that frosty February night in Edinburgh?

The answer must, I presume, lie in the way I had developed my role as general secretary of the Scottish Churches Council and thus become reasonably well-known at least in the circle of those who were the likely believers in (and readers of) the magazine *Radical Scotland*.

Though I had not, up to that time, been especially active in the Home Rule movement or in the Campaign for a Scottish Assembly, I had greatly raised the profile of the Churches Council since I took over in 1981 and in particular had been active in ensuring the Churches were seen to be acting together for social justice and world peace. When the peace movement arranged the highly successful "arms around Scotland" and managed to organise an unbroken human chain from the Clyde to the Forth, across central Scotland, I persuaded the leaders of all the main Churches to stand together and form part of the chain in central Glasgow, near the Cathedral. The impact was considerable and widely reported.

Again, during the grim days of the miners' strike, I organised all the main Church leaders to spend a day together, visiting the main mining centres and talking to all concerned. This was not only given wide coverage, it drew strong condemnation from the Government and their business supporters. It was a day never to be forgotten, as we stood on the picket lines, watched the police at work, and talked to those brave and committed miners and to the courageous wives who so staunchly, and at such cost to their families, stood by them. My wife Betty later arranged for a day at Scottish Churches House in Dunblane for some of the miners' wives to meet women from the Scottish Churches. It was a moving and unforgettable meeting, which resulted in contacts and friendships that are still strong today. Certainly these ordinary men and women, struggling to save their jobs and the communities that meant so much to them, did not deserve the cruelty of a powerful state that used every means at its disposal to discredit and defeat them. Still less was there any excuse for a Prime Minister who so shamefully branded them "the enemy within".

Through these and other commitments, I suppose it was true, as the chairman of a meeting once said of me, that "his face is becoming increasingly common!" No doubt that may have led Alan Lawson, editor of *Radical Scotland* and organiser of the Declaration Dinner, to conclude that I might have something intelligent, or at least provocative, to say about Scotland's future.

I have been told that what finally convinced Alan Lawson that I would be a suitable speaker for such a dinner was when we were both on a delegation to London when the 1986 Commonwealth Games was being threatened by a boycott by the New Commonwealth countries who were unhappy at Thatcher's refusal to impose sanctions on apartheid South Africa. We had gone to the Indian High Commission and because of the time I had spent in India, I knew the officials personally and we explained why Scotland was different and did not share the Thatcher government's views on apartheid. It appears that my arguing a case for Scotland's own identity convinced Alan Lawson that I should be invited as a speaker to a Declaration Dinner. It was an invite which was to change the course of my life.

I spoke at the dinner of my return to Scotland in 1981 after many years spent both abroad and in England, and of the "perceptible recovery of national cohesion and consciousness" that I found. Our nation, I said, is deeply threatened by industrial decline and social collapse and only the decentralisation and the development of more effective national institutions will enable Scotland to work.

I referred to two fundamental convictions, one negative and one positive which were not party political but deeply moral in their basis. The negative conviction was that we had come to the end of the road, the feeling that this can't go on. We were not ready any longer to acquiesce in a Scotland which was being impoverished, divided and militarised against her will. I said that those present at the dinner were giving notice to the next government whatever its complexion that the time had come to listen, that the time had come for a Scottish Assembly with real powers. I predicted that if such an Assembly was not established that I believed that the Scottish people would accelerate a process already begun to form social, political and economic coalitions with real authority to speak for the people of Scotland and safeguard our nation.

On that night in February 1987, I declared:

"Our nation is without hope and our world is doomed
unless we can find a new moral basis for human
relationships. The policy of a Scottish Assembly must
be a policy of life; fully based on a vision of a new
moral order both within the nation and among the
nations. This is not Utopia. It is the starkest realism,
for in this age with all its related threats to the very
integrity of life itself, only relationships based on a
new political morality will work. We must be seen
clearly to put human and not purely economic goals at
the centre of our policy. That is not piety, it is
common sense.

"A Scottish Assembly could actually show a better
way; even within its limited powers it can align itself
with the vast majority of the world nations and
peoples who now see clearly that only new thinking
will do for a new age."

Despite the passing of time I still believe that my opinions hold
good. Since then we have had the Rio Summit in 1992 and the
dangers of global warming are commonly known. Europe has
recognised the need to decentralise and the philosophy of
subsidiarity is commonly held in most European countries with
the exception of our own which sadly remains the most centralised
governed country in Western Europe. Just weeks after that
Declaration Dinner, the 1987 General Election was to be upon us
and the political scenario was to become even darker.

CHAPTER 4

A Claim of Right

(1987–89)

The widening of the political rift between Scotland and England was heightened only a few weeks after the Declaration Dinner when Margaret Thatcher's Conservative government swept to a second General Election victory in June 1987.

The Thatcher government triumphed in England – that is if a large majority of seats supported by a minority of votes can be counted as a triumph – but at the same time was humiliated in Scotland. Once all the results were in, the Conservatives had 375 seats compared to Labour's 229, yet in Scotland the Scottish Conservatives lost more than half of their MPs, including two Scottish Office Ministers and the Solicitor General for Scotland. Of Scotland's 72 MPs, Labour now had 50 and the Conservatives 10 with the SNP and the Scottish Liberal Democrats sharing the rest. Scotland had again voted Labour but to no avail.

This near-doomsday scenario helped to stiffen the resolve of the Scottish Home Rule movement. The Campaign for a Scottish Assembly reacted by appointing a sixteen-strong constitutional steering committee which was chaired by Professor Sir Robert Grieve. The other members of the committee included WR Anderson, Ian Barr, Rev Maxwell Craig, Sandra Farquhar, Professor Nigel Grant, Joy Hendry, John Hendry, Pat Kelly, Isobel Lindsay, Una Maclean Mackintosh, Professor D Neil MacCormick, Paul H Scott, Judy Steel, myself and Jim Ross.

Readers who are sharp observers of Scotland's politics may have spotted that there were no professional politicians on this committee. The grouping did cover a wide spectrum of Scottish life including the churches, trade unions, business, and academics.

Two others were appointed to the committee but had to resign because of other commitments. They were Bishop Joseph Devine representing the Roman Catholic Church and Councillor Derek Barrie.

The Campaign for a Scottish Assembly asked the committee to report on:

a. All aspects of the case for forcing Parliamentary action by setting up a Scottish Constitutional Convention for the express purpose of creating a Scottish Assembly;
b. The practical steps required to set up such a Convention on an effectively representative basis;
c. The tasks it should be prepared to undertake in order to achieve an Assembly.

It was Jim Ross who put together the final document *A Claim of Right for Scotland*. Jim Ross had been a senior civil servant who had served in the Scottish Office at St Andrews House and who had been responsible for the proposed parliamentary legislation in 1979. The document was written in a highly effective and readable style making it a powerful paper which was described by one journalist as "the dynamite which finally shifted the logjam of Scottish politics."

With hindsight, it may have been better and certainly more

accurate if this document had been entitled *Towards* a Claim of Right for Scotland. As it clearly recognised, the true equivalent of previous such Claims in Scottish history could only be made by a larger body and was in fact made at the inaugural meeting of the Constitutional Convention in 1989, which began with the true *Claim of Right for Scotland*, namely the recognition of the people's sovereign right to decide. There is always some risk of confusion here. It is helpful to distinguish clearly between the constitutional steering committee's final document which was a closely and cogently argued case for Scotland to issue a Claim of Right and form a Constitutional Convention, and the actual Claim of Right which became the starting point and foundation of the Convention itself. The first is a long and closely argued document. The second is a brief and challenging statement of principle.

The constitutional steering committee met seven times between February 15th and June 22nd, 1988. However when the document was launched at a press conference in the George Hotel in Edinburgh with the entire steering committee in attendance, commentators would have been entitled to remark that if it was dynamite, it was rather like that small charge which almost unnoticed cracks the dam and allows through the first trickle of water. The flood would come later.

The prologue to the *Claim of Right for Scotland* reads:

"Twice previously Scots have acted against
misgovernment by issuing a Claim of Right: in 1689
and 1842. Circumstances now may be though less
stark and dramatic than on these previous occasions.
But they are none the less serious.

"Now, as then, vital questions arise about the
constitution and powers of the state. Then it was
clearly understood that constitution and powers were
the issue. Now there is a danger that this will not be
fully recognised; that symptoms, such as the Poll Tax,
the Health Service, Education and the Economy, are

mistaken for causes, which lie in the way in which Scotland is governed.

"It is for a larger body than ourselves to set out in full the constitutional rights Scotland expects within the United Kingdom. That would be the true equivalent of the Claims made in 1689 and 1842. But we hold ourselves fully justified in registering a general Claim of Right on behalf of Scotland, namely that Scotland has the right to insist on articulating its own demands and grievances, rather than have them articulated for it by a Government utterly unrepresentative of Scots."

The report recognised that the failure to provide good government for Scotland was a product, not merely of faulty British policy in relation to Scotland but was a result of a fundamental flaw in the British constitution. The committee claimed that rectifying these defects would improve the government of the whole of the UK.

The *Claim of Right* identified one of the fundamental flaws as the fact that Scotland was governed by a team of Ministers and an administration who were supposed to provide Scotland with a distinctive government as provided for in the Act of Union. Yet the steering committee pointed out that the Scottish Office Ministers could not possibly provide this distinctive government. The document put its finger unerringly on the fundamental democratic deficit which Scotland experiences.

"We are not aware of any other instance at least in what is regarded as the democratic world, of a territory which has a distinctive corpus of law and acknowledged right to distinctive policies but yet has no body expressly elected to safeguard and supervise these. The existing machinery of Scottish Government is an attempt either to create an illusion or to achieve the impossible."

The committee concluded that the erosion of Scottish government through the centralisation of powers in Westminster was bound to continue unless it was "decisively reversed through a Scottish assembly." Thereafter followed a devastating analysis of the English Constitution and its single source of power – the Crown in Parliament.

We stated that power is embodied in the Prime Minister who has effectively appropriated almost all the former Royal Prerogatives with the power to appoint and dismiss Ministers as well as other formidable powers of patronage. In effect this means that the Prime Minister controls Parliament which effectively means that a British Prime Minister has a degree of arbitrary power which few, if any, English, and no Scottish monarchs have rivalled. This power is hidden behind the fiction of Royal sanction, and the pretence of deference to Parliament to give legitimacy to a concentration of power without parallel in Western society. We stated,

> "The American constitution was framed largely with a view to making such a development impossible. Even the centralised and executive-biased French constitution distributes power, demonstrated by the recent balance between the President and Prime Minister there. Against all this there is in the United Kingdom not a single alternative source of secure constitutional power at any level."

Our report clearly pointed out that a situation which was never really acceptable to Scotland in theory, could be lived with – could be tolerated in practice – so long as there was on the one hand a broad consensus between Scottish and English politics, and on the other hand, a government at Westminster that did not misuse its powers under the Royal Prerogative.

There can be no doubt that Mrs Thatcher's government misused these centralising powers and created a gulf between Scottish and English politics. She must be seen as one of the primary midwives of the Scottish parliament We illustrated this from the single painful example of the Poll Tax. The report made no moral judgement on the legislation itself but said,

> "Whatever the arguments for or against, its unpopularity is beyond dispute. It is attracting greater resistance and creating a more serious risk of disobedience to the Law than any other issue in living memory. Now that it is being enacted for England and Wales, its defects are being highlighted by the Government's own backbenchers, though nothing was heard from them when it was forced through for Scotland against the opposition of six sevenths of the Scottish MPs. No legislation at once so fundamental and so lacking in popular support would have been initiated other than in a territory within which the Government was unrepresentative of, and out of touch with, the electorate."

I commend anyone concerned for the future of Scotland to read *A Claim of Right for Scotland* in its entirety. On the basis of a very carefully argued case for Scottish democracy, it called for the establishment of a Scottish Constitutional Convention. The *Claim of Right* recognised that it was impossible to expect or hope that such a Convention would be established by the Thatcher Government.

The report recognised that notwithstanding this, the Convention could be composed simply of Scottish MPs providing that an overwhelming majority took part. But we recommended that it would have added authority if it also consisted of representatives from local government providing greater room for political groups who strongly support an assembly but who were under-represented in the Parliament of that time. We also suggested that room could be made for non-political interests who support an assembly. That these views carried some weight can be seen in the make-up the Convention was to have with representatives from the trade union movement and churches as well as local authorities and political parties.

The steering committee recommended that a Scottish Constitutional Convention should have three tasks:

1. to draw up a scheme for a Scottish Assembly;
2. to mobilise Scottish opinion behind that scheme;
3. to deal with the government in securing approval of the scheme or an acceptable modification of it.

I believe it is significant that the only changes made when the Convention was actually established was the addition of the words "or Parliament" to the first task above and to change the third in an important respect which now reads: "to assert the Right of the Scottish people to implementation of that scheme."

It should be remembered that while the 1988 *Claim of Right* report consistently used the word Assembly, it also pointed out in parenthesis that "All previous proposals for Scottish self government have preferred the historical term, Parliament, used in Scotland for many centuries. We believe that there are good arguments for returning to the traditional usage of Parliament rather than Assembly, but this is a matter which should be considered by the Scottish Constitutional Convention."

Indeed one of the first acts of the Convention was to agree with this opinion. It is now generally recognised in the usage of all political parties and other groups, that we are talking about a parliament for Scotland.

I believe that what we said then has stood the test of time, and the fact that in the intervening years we had the 1992 General Election in which the Conservatives were again returned to power while the vast majority of the Scottish electorate continued to vote for other parties, only added weight to the views we expressed then.

We said then that Scotland was facing a crisis of identity and survival as it continued to be governed without consent. We recognised that Scotland was not alone in suffering from the absence of consent in government. The problem we said afflicted the United Kingdom as a whole, but Scotland we contended was unique both in its title to complain, and its awareness of what is being done to it.

I am sure we reflected what many Scots have said to themselves and friends when Government spokesman appear to say that Scottish election results were not a true reflection on how Scots felt about what the Government was doing. We are told that we secretly love what we constantly vote against.

In 1988 we said that, "Scotland if it is to remain Scotland can no longer live with such a constitution, and has nothing to hope from it." Nothing that has happened since then has encouraged me to change my views which are expressed in the *Claim of Right* document.

Up until the end of its life on May 1st, 1997 the Conservative Government was as determined as ever to ignore the wishes of the majority of Scots for devolution, and a Parliament in Scotland to deal with internal Scottish affairs. John Major claimed when he took over from Margaret Thatcher that he would be a "listening Prime Minister." There was no evidence to support this.

Indeed at a Press Fund lunch in Glasgow's Marriot Hotel in September 1996 he had the audacity to tell his audience of several hundred, mostly journalists, that he accepted that his view on the Union was a minority view in Scotland, but that he believed he was right. Where does that leave democracy? Such a statement merely highlights the democratic deficit Scotland suffers from.

The committee of sixteen said that if the Scottish people showed the enterprise to reform their own government they would also start the process of reform of the English constitution. As the epilogue put it very eloquently, the move to set up a Scottish parliament would "serve as the grit in the oyster which produces the pearl."

There can be little doubt that this prediction is already proving itself to be accurate. Does anyone believe, to take one example, that without the Scottish Labour Party and the Liberal

Democrats agreeing that proportional representation would be used in electing a Scottish parliament that the two parties at UK level would have found the stimulus or the will to come together to discuss this issue in relation to Westminster elections?

The committee's final conclusion was crystal clear:

> "Setting up a Scottish Constitutional Convention and subsequently establishing a Scottish Assembly cannot themselves achieve the essential reforms of British Government, but they are essential if any remnant of distinctive Scottish Government is to be saved and they could create the groundswell necessary to set the British reform process on its way."

These were the ringing and inspiring words that successfully conceived the Scottish Constitutional Convention. A long hard road lay ahead of us through the winter of 1988-89 if we hoped to bring it to a healthy birth.

The report as I said earlier was treated with some scepticism by the media and you could understand their standpoint. Why should the Labour Party for one, with its commanding lead at the ballot box, and its army of Scottish MPs agree to sit round the table with other parties? After all, what importance should be given to a steering committee who although many of them were talented, they were not professional politicians with a mandate from the electorate? And the Campaign for a Scottish Assembly until then had been a fringe pressure group which, as it was cross-party, carried no great influence with any political party.

A Claim of Right for Scotland has however proved to be an historic document which acted as a catalyst and from which the events which have dominated Scottish politics for the past decade have flowed. It articulated with clarity and conviction the central claim for the democratic right of the people and gave that a historic perspective and depth. It shifted at last the logjam that had paralysed Scotland since the aborted hopes of 1979.

CHAPTER 5

Learning 'to Live Dangerously'

Whether or not *A Claim of Right for Scotland* bore fruit or merely gathered dust as a theoretical piece of paper with no practical value depended to a great extent to the Labour Party's reaction to it.

From the mid-sixties onwards the Labour Party had become the focus of popular support over large tracts of Scotland, especially the heavily populated Central Belt. Labour had become almost the establishment party in Scotland and the party of Scottish opposition to Tory Westminster rule. Repeated overruling of Scotland's vast Labour majority of Scottish MPs by almost total Conservative dominance in the south of England left feelings of national disenfranchisement. With such a strong electoral support in Scotland Labour therefore played a pivotal role in deciding the fate of the suggestion in *A Claim of Right for Scotland* that a Scottish Constitutional Convention be formed to study the way forward.

In July 1988, few people would have forecast that the Labour Party would by that autumn make a firm decision to join a Scottish Constitutional Convention. It was commonly felt that they had various reasons not to.

That they did so is largely due to one man who undoubtedly influenced the Labour Party's decision very greatly. That man is Donald Dewar, then Shadow Secretary of State for Scotland and leader of the Scottish Labour Party, who after an initial hesitation became convinced of the case for a Convention in early autumn.

Speaking at Stirling University in October 1988 he made it clear that Labour intended to take part in the Convention. For a politician respected and recognised for his careful responsibility, and his abhorrence of what he calls gesture politics, Donald Dewar spoke with remarkable boldness. He told his audience – "Scots are going to have to learn to live dangerously for a while." The Convention and its subsequent success owes much to that declaration.

Despite the fact that Donald Dewar's statement is a matter of public record, a myth has grown up that the result of the Govan by-election on November 10th 1988, which saw Labour's candidate Bob Gillespie suffer a humiliating defeat at the hands of Jim Sillars for the Scottish National Party spurred Labour into joining the Convention. This was not the case. The Labour Party's decision had been made well before the by-election. Indeed the consultation exercise carried out among their party members regarding their participation in any Convention had already been completed by October and had resulted in a firm support for the Convention proposal. No one would deny however that the Govan result no doubt strongly underlined the conviction that there was really no other way to go.

Indeed the victor at Govan, Jim Sillars made a statement which reads strangely in the light of his party's later negative attitude to the Convention. Sillars said that his victory underlined the need for cross-party cooperation and actually called for a dialogue in the belief that Scotland could really only move forward by united action rather than by inter-party squabbles.

Meanwhile the Liberal Democrats, then the Scottish Liberal and Social Democrats reaffirmed their consistent support for Home Rule. Malcolm Bruce MP, their leader in Scotland, said that "devolution is dead" and commended the way forward through a cross-party Constitutional Convention.

Media interest in the creation of a Convention was growing, fuelled by the fact that the major political parties were showing a serious interest in taking part. The *Herald* of December 14th, 1988 reported that "a discreet struggle is taking place within the Campaign for a Scottish Assembly over the prospective chairman for the proposed Scottish Constitutional Convention." The *Herald* speculated that the favourite was David Steel with others backing John Pollock, the retired general secretary of the Educational Institute of Scotland. My own name was mentioned as "being mooted as a compromise candidate."

In the first three months of 1989 events moved rapidly but often with many twists and turns. On January 27th the first formal cross-party talks took place in Edinburgh chaired by Sir Robert Grieve. All the political parties were invited to attend by the Campaign for a Scottish Assembly. The Scottish political scene had been galvanised by Thatcher's third general election victory which saw Scotland again vote by a substantial majority against Thatcherism but end up being ruled by a party which could only gain 10 out of Scotland's 72 Westminster Parliamentary seats.

Twenty six prominent Scottish leaders turned up at the meeting in the COSLA headquarters in Edinburgh, among them Donald Dewar, Malcolm Bruce and SNP chairman, Gordon Wilson. STUC general secretary Campbell Christie was present as was Edinburgh councillor Eric Milligan who represented the Convention of Scottish Local Authorities; Margaret Ewing MP; Alan Armstrong, convener of the CSA; Ray Michie MP; Ron Waddell, secretary of the LibDems; Murray Elder, secretary of the Scottish Labour Party and Bruce Black, a deputy general secretary of COSLA who acted as secretary to the Convention.

On this occasion there was much more media attention and both the Liberal Democrats and the Labour Party expressed their commitment to the proposed Convention idea. Malcolm Bruce, the LibDem leader described the day as an historic event and said, "if the same spirit can be carried forward we have very solid grounds for optimism."

Donald Dewar was typically realistic and hardheaded when he said, "It will be a fairly long and hard road but everyone has now got started." Unfortunately this was to turn out not to be quite accurate as although the SNP chairman attended the meeting and expressed guarded optimism, he refused to speculate on what the SNP's final decision was likely to be.

The next two months were to be dominated by determined attempts to keep the SNP on board. The first cross-party meeting had appointed a smaller business committee to get on with the task of preparing for the first Convention. I was asked to chair this committee, but its success in preparing so thoroughly for the first ever meeting of the Convention was largely due to the secretarial services provided by COSLA through Bruce Black. His administrative and reporting skills ensured that our plans were well laid. However neither his skills not my persuasion were sufficient to secure the SNP's support or membership of the Convention.

Unlike the other two political parties the SNP presented demands which they wished to be satisfied before they joined. They believed that they were entitled to a larger representation than they had been allocated by the meeting. They insisted on an assurance on the sovereignty issue, i.e. that the Convention would not simply endorse devolution but would commit itself to the sovereignty of the Scottish people, which was seen as an implicit rejection of Westminster's sovereignty in Scotland. Their third and final demand was what they called "legitimisation". This amounted to the proposal that the Convention should be elected rather than simply appointed and more important, that whatever the Convention put to the people of Scotland should be tested in a multi-option referendum in which the option of Independence in Europe would be included with the *status quo* and Home Rule.

To the astonishment of many observers, and I suspect to the SNP itself, the new Convention partners including the Labour Party more or less accepted their first two demands. The agreement that the Convention should start with a formal Claim of Right as a declaration of the 'sovereign right' of the Scottish people was a particularly important and astonishing agreement.

The final demand of the SNP concerning a multi-option referendum was more difficult since the whole point of the Convention was to achieve some kind of consensus in a scheme that everyone would endorse and campaign for. Indeed, we tried to meet this SNP demand by building in a safeguard against any party or group being steamrollered into anything to which they could not at least consent. Alan Armstrong, the convener of the Campaign for a Scottish Assembly, pointed out after the cross-party talks on 27th January,

> "On the question of decision-taking in the
> Convention, it was agreed that it should normally
> proceed by consensus . . . It would be open to any of
> the major political groupings to indicate an issue was
> of such fundamental importance to them, that they
> could not be bound by an adverse vote, and in such
> circumstances no vote would be taken."

That decision, though it did not succeed in its aim of keeping the SNP in the fold, was nevertheless of crucial importance. In practice, it meant that we had to struggle through to reach consensus – a hard but richly rewarding process, strangely foreign to our usual adversarial or Ya-Boo politics. In all my years chairing the executive, I do not remember that we ever had to vote on any major question. God knows, I sometimes wished we could. It would have cut short long and convoluted negotiations, but it would have prevented some of us from 'owning' what was decided. This decision to insist on consensus made possible that astonishing series of minor miracles to which this book bears witness.

What we could not accept – and this became the sticking point (many argued, the excuse) for the SNP – was that in the end we should offer options for a referendum, since this would have destroyed the whole purpose of our search for a single commonly accepted way forward. Donald Dewar pointed out that it would be self-defeating to have a Convention produce options on which the parties would then campaign against each other. He said, "If you are going to produce a series of options, you remove the incentive to agree, and I believe a great deal of confusion would result."

Let me make this clear, for many people have failed to understand the true meaning of consensus. From the beginning we understood that consensus did not imply total agreement, and that every party would be able to reserve its position, or go further than the Convention's scheme. However we did see the aim of the Convention as producing a scheme which everyone could accept as at least the first step. The proposal of a referendum that presented three options was a difficult one but further discussion could certainly have taken place and the business committee was asked to pursue these matters. The door was not closed on the SNP.

Immediately after the first cross-party meeting the SNP negotiators, Jim Sillars, Margaret Ewing and Gordon Wilson, came under immense pressure from angry supporters who accused them of either selling the party out, or of being naive. The result was that on Monday, January 31st the SNP announced that it would not take part in what they described as "Labour's rigged Convention". It was a decision that the business committee strove hard and long to change. I can bear personal witness to the sincerity and vigour with which we tried to persuade the SNP to reconsider and to remain open to the Convention proposal and work with others in Scotland.

I called a private meeting in a committee room in the Commons on the last day of February 1989 which was attended by Margaret Ewing and Jim Sillars for the SNP, Donald Dewar for Labour and Malcolm Bruce for the Scottish Liberal Democrats. It became clear that our genuine efforts to keep the SNP on board were doomed to failure. We had to go ahead without them.

Earlier in February the business committee had decided that

the first meeting of the Convention should take place on March 30th. The committee decided that the venue should be the Church of Scotland's Assembly Hall in Edinburgh as this would "express the aspirations of the Scottish people in the best possible way." In announcing this decision I denied that the absence of the SNP would in any way invalidate the Convention but I had appealed to them not to break "the kind of unity that is within our grasp as probably never before in recent history." This plea brought no results. On March 4th, the National Council of the SNP decided by a large majority but with opposition from some of its more articulate members to boycott the Convention.

Looking back at those events it is difficult not to agree with those who have suggested in the past that the SNP had already decided not to participate on party political grounds, and that the conditions being put forward were merely a face-saving formula deliberately designed to be unacceptable.

I must however make clear that on our part that we tried sincerely and tirelessly to keep the unity that we believed would be the strongest basis for the Convention. The SNP decision undoubtedly made the Convention less representative than it would otherwise have been. However I believe their decision to stay away damaged the SNP more than any damage done to the Convention. The fact that most of their conditions were met, including their central condition about the sovereignty of the people leads me to my belief that minds had already been closed before we started the discussions. It may be that the SNP was riding high after the Govan by-election victory and saw itself as being able to go it alone.

From a nationalist party political standpoint it may have seemed better to sustain a 'pure' position which continued to maintain (in a strange alliance with the Conservative Party) that the real and only choice before the Scottish people was between independence and the *status quo*.

With the benefit of hindsight I have to confess to mixed feelings about the SNP's decision. On the one hand part of me has always regretted their refusal to take part, and indeed I am on record as saying repeatedly over the last seven years that the door has remained open for them to join the Convention. On the other hand I recognise that the work of the Convention in seeking a consensus around a single acceptable scheme for a Scottish parliament would have been much harder, and perhaps nigh impossible, had the SNP been part of our deliberations.

God knows it has been difficult enough as it is, with the broad spectrum of politics and social concern which existed in the Convention. With a nationalist view present, consensus might have been impossible. The result we have managed to achieve means that the Scottish people now have before them, three distinct options: the *status quo*, which I personally believe has been thoroughly discredited; the option of a nation state independence; and the Convention's scheme which is similar to the model of autonomous government that exists in virtually every other European democracy.

From the SNP's own point of view it would probably have been wiser never to have been involved at all. From the Convention's point of view however it is good that they were there, even if only for some of the preparatory stages. Their presence and their demands propelled the Labour Party and other partners into concessions which they might not otherwise have been prepared to offer or accept. The whole idea of sovereignty, and of real progress by consensus, were matters which the Churches had certainly proposed from the start in the Convention, but which the SNP's brief flirtation reinforced.

In contrast to the SNP taking a backward step away from consensus, the Labour Party in those early months of 1989 were confirming their strong commitment. Political reality had certainly moved far and fast. Just twelve months before in March 1988 Neil Kinnock speaking at the Scottish Labour Party conference had made no mention of the issue of devolution. Questioned on this that same evening on TV he responded somewhat testily and with a demeanour expressing some scorn that there were several other issues he had not mentioned such as "environmental conditions in the Himalayas."

The next question asked him whether there was any possibility of supporting a Constitutional Convention which at that time had been floated in the public arena as an idea. Kinnock responded that he would find it very hard to imagine there being much support for such an idea.

By the March 1989 party conference the political position had changed dramatically. One leading member of the Scottish Labour executive wrote, "by the March 1989 Party Conference the party leader had come to Inverness via Damascus. In stark contrast to his previous visit Neil Kinnock embraced the project with an enthusiasm which has to be seen to be believed and offered his most far-reaching and forthright support ever for the concept of Scottish Home Rule."

By this time the stage had been finally set for the birth of the Convention. Many had forecast, indeed no doubt hoped, that it would be stillborn, a mere talking shop, a flop, a headless chicken. It certainly fitted none of these descriptions. Indeed the first Convention exceeded even its supporters' best dreams. The meeting on March 30th was almost universally judged to be an occasion that genuinely deserved to have the term 'historic' attached to it.

We had come a long and sometimes weary way. An even longer way, had we known it, lay ahead. However on that windy March day in the Assembly Halls of the Church of Scotland we crossed the Rubicon. There was no way back.

CHAPTER 6

We say Yes; We are the People

*"You must listen to the music of the past
if you are to sing in the present
and dance into the future."*

The General Assembly Hall of the Church of Scotland in Edinburgh has been commonly described as "austerely impressive". Situated near the top of the Mound, that man-made hill in Edinburgh, scooped from earth and silt at the bottom of the ancient Nor Loch, the present day site of Princes Street Gardens, its main function now is to house the General Assembly, the governing body of the Church of Scotland. For one week in May each year 1,200 or so ministers and elders meet and deliberate.

It is an imposing sombre and articulate gathering – recognised as such even by former Prime Minister Margaret Thatcher, who while she was still in power, chose the General Assembly in 1988 as the most appropriate audience before whom to reveal her own basic values of Christian individualism. Her address came to be called the Sermon on the Mound.

Her lecture was not universally well received. The Moderator, the elected Chair of the assembly and the recognised 'leader' of the Church of Scotland, presented the Prime Minister with two Church reports, on housing and poverty, both highly critical of Government policies – and suggested that she read them carefully! Commenting later on her 'sermon', the Moderator, Professor James Whyte of St Andrews University, pointed to two yawning gaps in her theology or ideology. First, she recognised no valid power between the individual (or family) and the State. She clearly still believed "there was no such thing as community". Second, she failed to recognise any moral imperative in the actual creation of wealth, as opposed to its distribution through charity.

The Assembly Hall had thus been accustomed to hosting the great and the good but those who assembled there on March 30th, 1989, represented certainly one of the broadest cross-sections of Scottish society ever to gather.

The General Assembly has often been called "the nearest thing we have in Scotland to a Parliament," but that mantle on that day clearly fell on the Scottish Constitutional Convention. We had the major political parties – Labour and the Cooperative Party, Scottish Liberal Democrats and Social Democratic Party. Smaller political parties representing a broad spectrum of views were also present with the Communist Party, Scottish Green Party and the Orkney & Shetland Movement playing their part. Over sixty Scottish MPs were present along with MEPs and the vast majority of Regional, Islands and District Councils.

Other major Scottish institutions who had agreed to join the Convention were the Scottish Trade Union Congress, the Scottish Churches including representatives from the Catholic Church as well as the Church of Scotland. The world of commerce was also present with the Scottish Council Development & Industry and the Scottish section of the National Federation of Self-Employed & Small Business which is now known as the Federation of Small Businesses.

The reality that the Convention represented a wide spectrum

of Scottish society was further borne out by the fact that both *An Comunn Gaidhealach* and *Comunn Na Gaidhlig* gave their support as did representatives of a number of ethnic minority communities who reflected the diversity of Scottish society.

The coming together of such a gathering lead the *Scotsman's* correspondent to write:

> "Convention organisers stress that the MPs, MEPs, Councillors and miscellaneous high heidyins who make up the Convention are not intended to be any kind of surrogate Scottish Parliament. But the venerable timbers of the Assembly Hall, already used to the lively annual debates of the Church of Scotland, and the sermons of the occasional visiting English Woman, have an unmistakeable parliamentary air."

The word 'historic' tends to be over used, but both the Scottish and London-based media seemed near unanimous in using that word to describe the first meeting of the Convention. The *Times* spoke of "an historic declaration," and of the Convention as "the country's most significant political initiative since the Act of Union in 1707."

However Peter Jones, then the Scottish political correspondent of the *Scotsman*, was rather more sceptical, and displayed his usual questioning style when he wondered whether the inaugural meeting of the Convention would "be a date to remember or just another footnote in history? Scottish history, especially the ebbing and flowing tides of moves for self government, abounds with such footnotes!"

Time has yet to decree whether the Convention will be a major chapter in Scotland's history, or a footnote. I am sure that Mr Jones would agree with me, that we have come a long way since that day on March 30th, 1989. The Convention has put together proposals for a Scottish Parliament which have at the very least given the Scottish people the opportunity to express their views on a devolved parliament for Scotland firstly in a General Election and then in a referendum. I remain convinced that March 30, 1989 is a date which will be remembered as the turning point, the seminal event, in the fortune and history of Scotland.

Since I had chaired the business committee which has prepared for the Convention, I was asked to set the tone by giving the introductory address. My life had certainly taken a new path in the previous two years. Until I was invited by the Campaign for a Scottish Assembly to address the Declaration Dinner in Edinburgh only a few weeks before the 1987 General Election, my life had revolved around Church work as General Secretary of the Scottish Council of Churches. I never for a moment though that my agreeing to be one of sixteen members of the constitutional steering committee which drew up *A Claim of Right for Scotland* would lead me to address such a gathering in the Assembly Hall. It was a daunting task. I was faced with the most representative and most distinguished audience I had ever spoken to, the serried ranks of 80 per cent of Scotland's MPs and MEPs among them such politicians and speakers as the late John Smith of the Labour Party and David Steel of the Liberal Democrats.

Also before me would be representatives of virtually every Scottish local authority as well as church, trade union and many people from the world of business. I was determined to raise the moral tone of the day. While preparing my speech I resolved not to make it part of the knockabout of party politics. Certainly the occasion would be highly political if only because of the array of Scottish politicians present, but I believed that the day did not belong to the politicians but to the people of Scotland.

We live in the time of sound-bites, an age in which most television news reporting is so brief that we are heard only if we are able to encapsulate what we want to say in a single sentence. Anyone who has been interviewed by a television reporter will tell you that if you are considered a newcomer to the process it is explained to you that you have to keep your replies short, and we are talking here of seconds. This manner of speaking was, of course, not what I had been accustomed to. One of the privileges of being a minister is that when delivering a sermon you are allowed to develop your point. After all, the congregation is not going anywhere until you are finished. Not so with television. If you cannot get your point over very quickly then what you had to say will not be used. At the time when I was preparing my speech for that first Convention meeting, Mrs Thatcher had been widely reported rejoicing at the birth of a grandchild, as saying, "We are a grandmother." Playing on that apparent delusion of grandeur, I used a phrase which certainly has become the most widely quoted words I have ever said in public. I said:

> "What if that other single voice we all know so well
> responds by saying, 'We say No, We are the State.'
> Well We say Yes and We are the People."

The well-known reporter, Iain MacWhirter was kind enough to write later that this was "a marvellously crafted soundbite" and it apparently found its way onto prime time television news in the United States. It was effective because it succeeded in encapsulating the central challenge that the Convention was making to the authority of the British State.

Apart from being a marvellous demonstration of widespread unity and the existence of a Scottish consensus, what did the first meeting of the Convention actually succeed in doing? The truthful answer has to be at least partly that its importance was symbolic. As Iain MacWhirter commented, "to get all the Labour MPs and Council leaders to line up before the Moderator's chair, like school children at assembly, and to sign a declaration of the sovereignty of the Scottish people was marvellous political theatre."

The Claim of Right which was signed by all members of the Convention present and is held by the Constitutional Convention as guardians, reads:

> "We, gathered as a Scottish Constitutional

Convention, do hereby acknowledge the sovereign
right of the Scottish people to determine the form of
government best suited to their needs and do hereby
declare and pledge that in all our actions and
deliberations their interests shall be paramount."

It was indeed a defining moment in Scotland's history. When, there
on the Mound, one by one, so many of Scotland's political, cultural,
religious and business leaders put their names to a declaration of
popular sovereignty, and putting the will of the Scottish people
first, they did indeed cross the Rubicon. There was no retreating.

In my speech I made a number of points which opponents
have since described as arrogant but which I believe to be nothing
more than the simple truth. I said quite clearly that, despite the
absence of both the Conservative and Scottish National Party, both
at opposite ends of the constitutional spectrum, that the
Convention in a very real sense represented Scotland. "At the risk
of offending some of my political friends," I said, "I dare to say
that by any standard of measurement we are much more
representative of Scotland than the Westminster Parliament is of
the United Kingdom."

I set out the basic difference in constitutional tradition which
separates Scotland and England, a difference which many in
Westminster still do not realise to this day. This is quite simply
that in Scotland, power is passed to the rulers by the Scottish people,
and it is the people who are sovereign. In England, Parliament
claims to be sovereign, not the people. I explained to the audience
in the Assembly Room that day that our Claim of Right was rooted
in Scottish history based on the unique and wholly democratic
character of Scotland's traditional understanding of sovereignty
and power. My words were:

"When we pass together the declaration then we will
represent Scotland in an even deeper and important
sense. We are not met here to make claims for

The People Say Yes

ourselves. We are met to make a claim for Scotland
and to set our hands to the task of giving substance to
that claim."

Drawing attention to the fact that the Convention was meeting
exactly 300 years since the Scottish Parliament passed the first Claim
of Right in Scottish history in 1689, not far from the spot where
we were gathered, the modern Convention I explained was firmly
in the mainstream of Scottish constitutional history.

The Claim of Right of 1689 had stated that King James VII
was deposed because he violated, "the fundamental constitution
of this Kingdom and altered it from a legal limited monarchy to
an arbitrary despotic power." It was directed against the despotic
abuse of power by an arbitrary monarch who claimed for the Crown
absolute authority. Our Claim 300 years later was not so very
different. We directed our Claim of Right against the despotic
abuse of power by an arbitrary government which claimed for the
Crown in Parliament absolute unlimited authority which goes
against the basis of the Scottish constitutional understanding of
power set out as long ago as 1320 in the Declaration of Arbroath.
This asserted that the King of Scots rules "subject to the assent of
the community of the realm."

I take quiet satisfaction in the fact that the Scottish Churches
have always been part of the formation of the Scottish
understanding of power, and I told my audience that I took even
greater pleasure from the fact that senior representatives of the
Scottish Churches were members of the Convention. I also
reminded those present that the second Claim of Right in Scottish
history was made by the General Assembly of the Church of
Scotland in 1842 which questioned the right of a British Parliament
to meddle in the Churches affairs.

Although I did not wish in any way to make a party political
speech or to descend into a political slanging match I could not
address such a gathering without acknowledging that the arch of
the Convention which spanned Scottish society rested on two pillars

– the historic claim, already made, and the contemporary sense of outrage at the Scotland was being treated.

"There can be no doubt," I said, "that one of the primary midwives of Scotland's movement to Home Rule today, was Mrs Thatcher and the ideology which she, thank God with so little success, attempted to impose on Scotland." I drew on Gladstone's speech in 1886 during the Irish Home Rule debate in Parliament to illustrate the problem facing Scotland. Gladstone had said:

> "The passing of many good laws is not enough in
> cases where the strong permanent interest of the
> people, their distinctive marks of character, the
> situation in history of the country require not only
> that these laws should be good but that they should
> proceed from a congenial and native source, and
> besides being good should be their own laws."

The Convention was meeting on the eve of the imposition of the Poll Tax which had been described by the leaders of the three largest Scottish Churches as "undemocratic, unjust, socially divisive and destructive of community and family life." But the Poll Tax was a symptom, the most painful and the most obvious of a whole series of symptoms. It was our purpose to look beyond the symptoms to the constitutional disease.

On something like thirty-three different occasions in the life of the Parliament then sitting, measures had been debated which quite fundamentally affected Scotland's national institutions and the quality of life of our people. Again and again and again the elected representatives of the Scottish people have voted by a margin of 6 to 1 against these damaging policies.

Yet again and again and again Parliament had imposed these on Scotland. Had they been marginal questions or had we still been living with the political consensus of the past, these constitutional anomalies and these violations of the spirit of the Treaty of Union might have been just tolerable. They were now no longer tolerable. Like Gandhi "our task is to make injustice visible even if it be by our suffering."

Certainly the first meeting of the Convention was partly symbolic. It seized the moral high ground by focusing the sense of deep resentment at the imposition on Scotland of policies so vehemently rejected by our people. The meeting, however, was not only symbolic. The *Claim of Right* included a firm commitment to do three things: to agree a scheme for an assembly or parliament for Scotland; to mobilise Scottish opinion and ensure the approval of the Scottish people for that scheme; and to assert the Right of the Scottish people to secure the implementation of that scheme.

In the three hour debate following my introductory speech there was a recognition that we faced an enormous task. Labour Shadow Secretary of State for Scotland Donald Dewar called for "independence for Scotland, independence of action, the reality of power, the control of our own affairs, our relations and continuing links with the rest of the United Kingdom." It was significant that the world devolution was seldom if ever used. Donald Dewar spoke of "independence in the United Kingdom," others spoke of Home Rule or autonomy, or simply as I did, of a Scottish parliament.

This of course was fitting, as the Convention did not begin with any fixed scheme. Its task was to come forward with a scheme through a process of genuine and open debate. We were committed only to agree a scheme for the parliament of Scotland. I explained it this way:

> "It will certainly be no easy task but two things are
> clear. First any scheme we put forward must be by
> consensus, the highest common factor of our common
> thinking which gives no political grouping or party
> everything it wants but which the Scottish people,
> whatever their many differing views, can see as a real

and viable proposal for at least the next step. Second we have a lot of hard work before us for any scheme must not just be a general idea, it must be carefully worked out in detail."

We must admit that we never fully succeeded in delivering the second part of our remit which was to "mobilise Scottish opinion and secure the approval of the people." Our failure to deliver fully on this was due largely to a lack of resources. Our hands were also partly tied by Conservative legislation which prevented local authorities from spending money on party political campaigning.

The Scottish media almost unanimously greeted the Convention as the beginning of something important. Writing in the *Scotsman* under the headline, A Douce Start to the Revolution, Ruth Wishart described the meeting as "a solemn affair, very different from the Westminster way of doing things." She further wrote:

> "House of Commons warriors studiously applauded the contributions of those they routinely jeer in another place and harmony threatened to break out unchecked, as the Communist Party warmly applauded the acumen of the Church. Many of the speakers, overwhelmingly male, repeatedly called for a greater gender balance. Truly this was a day of Scottish firsts. Different too was the tone shorn of its customary party political stridency."

Perhaps Ruth Wishart was right when she ended her article by describing the activities of the Convention as being "a douce way to bring a revolution." In my dictionary, Revolution is defined as "a great change" or "a fundamental reconstruction". What we began that far off day in 1989 will change Scotland one way or another.

Yes, the first meeting of the Convention was certainly hailed as a success. Symbolically it succeeded in establishing the Convention's credentials to speak meaningfully for Scotland. It grounded our work firmly in the historic view of power. It effectively claimed the middle ground of Scottish politics, leaving the Conservatives and the SNP, albeit at opposite ends of the spectrum, on the margins. In practical terms it set an ambitious programme for the Convention which we then believed was to occupy the next three years. Perhaps we would have been less bright-eyed and eager to go, had we known it was not to be three but many more years!

At that first meeting, Donald Dewar proposed and Malcolm Bruce seconded my election as chair of the executive. I am not sure I would have started the race had I known it was to be such a marathon! Was I prepared for the uncharted task I undertook that day?

CHAPTER 7

"Give me a child until he is five . . ."

– learning about prejudice

The preceding chapters should, I hope, explain where the Convention came from. Where did I come from? If are to believe the saying often attributed to the Jesuits – "Give me a child until he is five and I have him for life" – the early years are formative and even decisive in shaping the whole of life's pattern and journey.

The most readable way of describing my birth is probably to record a few lines of doggerel which I wrote on the occasion of my twenty-first birthday in 1953 to amuse, or perhaps to embarrass, my friends and family.

> "T'was on a moonlit August night
> At the hour of half past one
> That a tale is told of a drama bold
> In a little street called Dunn.
>
> From a dim lit close a man sped forth
> And made his hasty way

To number five in Greenlaw Drive
Where dwelt physician Hay.

Come forth, come forth physician good
And do your duty plain
The world awaits with bated breath
Deliver me a wean.

So forth they sped with hasty tread
Two men with aim but one
Through the dark night they took their flight
To the little street called Dunn.

And there at last the deed was done
An infant handsome, fair
To honour him the lights were dim
In every close-mooth there."

Allowing for poetic licence and youthful vanity, anyone who knows
Scotland and who is addicted to Trivial Pursuit or the gathering of
useless information will be able to work out not only where and
when my birth took place but even the name and address of the
attending doctor. I am told I was a restless child, never wishing to
sleep but always ready to be up and going. This was no doubt
reinforced greatly by my father's peripatetic profession. He gave
his working life to 'dyeing', like my grandfather, after whom I was
named, and great-grandfather who bore the same name as my
father, Charles James Wright. My great-grandfather was universally
known as Charlie Blue because he was responsible for the
development of a particular kind of blue dye. It was this colourful
discovery that brought him at the end of the nineteenth century
from Lancashire to Scotland to the thread mills of J & P Coats in
Paisley.

All these generations were dyers. Indeed one of the earliest verses I recall my father teaching me was apparently current in Paisley at that time. It ran:

"My wee lad's a dyer,
He work's in Coatses Mill,
He gets his pay on Saturday
And has a half a gill.
He goes to Kirk on Sunday
Half an hour late,
He pulls the buttons off his shirt
And puts them in the plate."

Whether this latter revelation of the religious customs of dyers was to have an unexpected influence on my infant mind and was to lead me away from yet another generation of care of textiles to the care of souls, I can only guess! I learned early, to my great delight, that the Wrights in Scotland were of the Clan McIntyre. Many of my forbears of Glen Noe were 'out of the '45' – that is, they had fought for the lost cause of Bonnie Prince Charlie in the romantic but ill-fated Jacobite Rising of 1745 and '46. Later, for safety's sake, they had anglicised their names to Wright. The family's Lancashire interlude has never, of course, deterred me from being proudly Scots.

Before I was aware of any of this, when I was still trying to take my first faltering steps, my parents joined that great army of Scots who restlessly roam, and often settle, throughout he world, yet who remain fiercely loyal to the land of their birth. They left the backstreets of the industrial town of Paisley for the decadent and darkening lands of Eastern and Central Europe. My father was appointed the chief chemist of J & P Coats for the vast area in which they had mills at that time – every country from the dominant German *Reich* to the struggling democracies of Czechoslovakia and Poland to the corrupt little kingdoms farther east.

My earliest conscious picture memories are of the large and

pretentious house which was our base at Lodz in Poland, and a series of vivid mental 'snapshots' of some of the great cities of Europe, round which I was dragged, often literally I am told, kicking and screaming. The restlessness of my babyhood flowered into a precocious infancy. My parents had, to the end of their lives, a deeply loving, committed and faithful relationship, and hardly deserved to be embarrassed in public all over Europe by a little boy who, I am told, always got his own way by the simple expedient of screaming lustily and irrepressibly. My inward eye can still see some of the scenes, which I can only, self-charitably put down to a strident but natural demand for attention and stability.

I see myself standing looking up at the great wheel in the Prater in Vienna – later to be made famous by Orson Welles looking down from its height, as he described the "little dots" below, to the strains of the Harry Lime theme on the haunting zither. I was screaming in terror at the suggestion that we went up on it because – and I only confessed this to my parents years later – I was convinced that the carriages must turn upside down at the top! Surely a perfectly logical assumption for a child to make.

I see myself again in Vienna but this time in the opulent hushed magnificence of the great ballroom of the Schonbrunn Palace of the Habsburgs, with its glorious chandeliers and its palpable atmosphere of nostalgia for a lost empire – for a 'city that had no longer a country'. It must have been the year in which Austria lost its independence and became part of the growing monster that was the greater German *Reich* – but that meant nothing to me. I simply decided that I was tired of palaces and wanted to get out. Naturally I used my successful technique. I screamed and my parents tell me the chandeliers tinkled as they picked me up bodily and rushed out of the building.

This time I see myself in Budapest, coming down some eight flights of stairs from the room in the city's most luxurious hotel in which my parents had assumed me to be safely asleep. Clad only in a pair of fetching Mickey Mouse pyjamas I squirmed out of the restraining arms of a well-meaning *concierge* to run – yes, screaming

– into the opulent lounge in which my parents were drinking coffee with the flower of Hungarian high society.

There are many such stories – and I can only assume that the patience I needed to guide the work of the Constitutional Convention over the past years must have been a determined reaction to the impatience of my infancy!

At the time I was, of course, blissfully unaware of the gathering storm clouds that were so soon to plunge Europe into war, to ruin so many of the cities in which I walked and to condemn so many millions to torture, pain and death. My father told me that we had once passed by train through a small and insignificant little Polish village called Oswiecim. Some forty years later I was to return to that place which had by then become an eternal symbol of horror under its German name – Auschwitz.

Unaware I may have been, but my young life was not untouched. I was to be infected by prejudice in a way that has, I believe, effectively inoculated me against it for the rest of my life.

The city of Lodz, though Polish, was home to a large number of people of German origin, who maintained their own institutions and whose loyalty to the Third Reich was increasing. My father spoke fluent German, as the *lingua franca* of the area he covered, and I too was fluent as only a small child could be. Consequently I was sent to the local German kindergarten to start my education at the age of four.

After two months however, I was suddenly removed! One day, as my mother and father were walking me home, for some reason they took an unaccustomed route. As we went to enter a particular street, I piped up "*Gehen Wir nicht durch diese Strasse. Hier leben viele schmutzige Juden.*" ("Don't go through this street. Many dirty Jews live here.") My kindergarten days ended abruptly – and I was not allowed to forget!

It was however, another more poignant incident that was to bring home to me, in later years, the waste, loss and human tragedy that was nationalism and prejudice. During our stay in Vienna, my parents had become friendly with a gentle and distinguished man whom I called Uncle, and who grew fond of me despite my faults! He was a musician and composer – not widely known, but celebrated in his own community. He was to give me one of the most precious gifts I have ever received. I have it before me now as I am writing – four faded and yellowing sheets of music. At the bottom is handwritten: "Composed by Mr Nohrig – Harland – Austria – February 1935 for Kenyon Wright (age 3 years)."

It is the tune composed by Richard Nohrig, to the lovely words of a lullaby (*Wiegenlied*) by one Detler Von Liliecran. I wish that books could sing so that all who read these words could hear the beauty of the haunting melody my 'Uncle' wrote for me in an Austria that was part of a different world.

It is, of course, in German but the words of the last verse can be roughly translated as . . .

"Sleep my little one, the time is coming,
When the rain will fall, storm and snow will come.
Sleep while you may, in peace without care,
While you still can know rest and security."

As he composed the music to these words, the storm that was to blow away the security of Europe, and destroy that old world forever, was growing ever darker and more menacing.

The Uncle who gave me such a unique gift of undying beauty perished in one of Hitler's concentration camps – probably in the gas chambers of Auschwitz. I was to pray for him there one day nearly half a century later. His lovely music is for me a constant reminder that our common humanity is greater and infinitely more important than any nationality, race, colour or ideology. One day, when I too have finished my course, I hope to be able to thank him for that.

CHAPTER 8

"Learn Boy Or Get Out"

– learning about power and piety

That first frantic year of the Convention's life, threw me in at the deep end of Scottish politics. If I was able, in the end, after much struggling to swim and not drown it is, I believe, because I was able to combine a religious faith with a degree of political common sense and wisdom, both of which I trace right back to my days at school. From being the relatively obscure general secretary of the Scottish Churches Council, I suddenly found myself in the eye of a political storm.

Jesus once said that his followers must be "as wise as serpents and as harmless as doves". I have always taken that to mean that we must be in the world but not of it. That is we must share fully in the struggles, the pain and the striving for a better society and a fairer world but that we do not share the false values, assumptions and motivations of the society in which we live. Fortunately, the fact that my conversion to the Christian faith and my early political education went hand in hand effectively, and permanently, inoculated me against that kind of Christian faith which turns out people who are "too heavenly-minded to be any earthly good".

If my early years in a Europe darkened by the menacing clouds of Nazism helped to set me against the evil of prejudice, then I look back to my school years as the period that taught me both about power and about piety. I have no difficulty in understanding the contemporary debate about the moral values that must be expressed in politics – for I have always believed that the art to real politics is to maintain a clear and single minded moral purpose and vision, while at the same time recognising the world of compromise, negotiation and give and take, through which all real political or social advance is achieved. When a journalist calls me a "cleverer than he lets on" clergyman, I protest only to the extent that I honestly believe my motives remain clear and firm. Both my political education – my sense of how power really works – and my religious education – my certainty that at the very core of the universe there is not just meaning and unity but actually personality – I can trace back to my years at school. It was then that I began to learn both about power and about prophecy.

When my mother and I returned from a war-threatened Europe, we left my father still circulating in the capital cities of central and eastern Europe and, though he never spoke much of it, I have reason to believe that his work during this period was as much for the British Secret Service as for the textile industry.

I feel sure I was a somewhat precious, precocious and pampered child. My fluency in German was matched, I am told, by the precise and prim way in which I spoke my native tongue. Not to put too fine a point on it I spoke with what in Scotland is described as "having a bool in the mooth". All this was to change in one brief month.

Having been diagnosed as suffering from diphtheria, I was incarcerated in Hawkhead Infectious Diseases Hospital, Paisley in a ward filled with my exuberant contemporaries. In that brief month I not only apparently forgot my German – though I am told that the ease and fluency with which I relearned it later was proof that no child ever truly forgets anything he has learned in infancy – I compensated by learning a new language – Hospital Talk. The main dish served to us was, I told my parents, "tatties and munsh" and if you wanted some reading material all you had to do was yell "haw nurse, gizza comic". Thus the smooth edges of my sheltered infancy roughened up a little in preparation for the experience of school.

Paisley Grammar School – the only school I ever attended apart from the German Kindergarten – has a proud historic tradition. The foundation charter given by King James VI of Scotland in 1576 stated its objectives as "that the youth mey be instructed in good morals and the knowledge of letters and virtue and may be qualified not only for serving God in the ministry of the Word, but also for being able and useful members of the community in our said Burgh." I hope the good King Jamie will feel that his aims have been at least partly successful in my case.

Someone once said that education should provide Greek, grace and gumption. My Greek is certainly very rusty and the experience of the Constitutional Convention has put a great strain on the other two qualities! I hope however, I have still a trace of them.

I owe much to Paisley Grammar School & William B Barbour Academy, to give it the honour of its full name. The school gave me the love for words, in prose and poetry, for which I have a photographic memory. It led me through the school dances (Slow-Slow, Quick-Quick, Slow to the velvet tones of Victor Sylvester, and the Eightsome Reel and Dashing White Sergeant) to my first innocent romances. What happened I wonder to Evelyn Craig or Joan Sutherland?

The school also encouraged the budding actor in me and I took the lead for several years in the annual school play under the watchful eye of 'Curly' Campbell (so called, no doubt, because he was largely bald). The parts ranged from a comic king through some heavy stuff in which the local paper commended me for playing a old man, to the Mad Hatter presiding over the Wonderland Tea Party.

I may have some Scottish gene missing but from schooldays on I have never been able to share even slightly, the obsession of my contemporaries with football. This is a serious confession for a Scot, and one likely to lose me much sympathy, but I must be honest and admit that I have always found politics much more interesting than sport. I was dragooned of course into the compulsory weekly sessions at the Penilee Road sports field, but the PT teachers soon found it was much easier just to leave me to my thoughts in a corner of the field.

The debating society and the drama club were the places where I shone, but I was certainly no swot. I had a reputation of being one of those who prepared everything at the last minute, who never actually failed but "could do better". Since the motto of the school, roughly translated in the title to this chapter, was *Disce Puer Aut Abi*, I can only assume that I did enough to be tolerated! Two stands interwove in those school years – my own growing convictions and the background, at least for six of those formative years, of the ever present and yet strangely distant war.

I have a vivid picture of the war – my mother, baby brother and myself squatting in the middle of the night in the cramped space under our floorboards which had been made into an air-raid shelter. I do not remember any fear. The feeling was rather one of interest and even a kind of excitement as we heard the bombs explode on nearby Clydebank. Even when my father, by this time an air-raid warden, brought home those twisted and jagged pieces of metal which we all collected as 'shrapnel' and regularly exchanged, the war still seemed like a kind of extension to the adventure films we paid sixpence to see every Saturday. A piece of torn silk from the parachute of a land-mine still did not make it seem any more real, even though the mine killed several people in the west end of Paisley.

My perception changed, I believe, only when my father volunteered for the army and was allocated, because of his fluency in German and his knowledge of eastern Europe, to the intelligence corps. His training led him to be suited, we learned later, for being parachuted into Yugoslavia, no doubt to join the legendary Fitzroy McLean and the partisans under Tito. A terrible accident may well have saved his life. While training on the remote Hebridean island of Benbecula, my father had a horrendous motorcycle crash which left him with the bones in his arm and leg shattered. For months I remember visiting him with my mother in the military hospitals in Glencorse and Hairmyres. His fingers were held in a frame with wires through each one. Somehow the war came closer, to us though his injuries ensured that his duties were restricted to the interrogation of prisoners of war and others.

In the months immediately following the end of the hostilities my father became a field security officer in the Löben area of Austria. He uncovered the mass grave of Jewish and other prisoners massacred during a forced march and helped bring the perpetrators to justice. When he died I found the gruesome pictures of the opening of that grave and the transcript of the evidence he had given to the War Crimes Tribunal amongst his possessions. Somehow I felt it was a kind of justice for the murder of my 'uncle' Richard Nohrig, whose story I told earlier and who died in Hitler's concentration camps. Also among my father's papers I found not only one of the final editions of the Austrian Nazi paper in which the death of Hitler was announced in black border, but also a fascinating copy of the *Daily Express* of Wednesday 16th October 1946, the headline on which read, "Göring first to hang at 1am today." It went on to describe how the execution of the Nazi war criminals had been over in 90 minutes and how "Göring was first to walk to the scaffold."

These must be collector's items now, especially since Göring actually committed suicide in his cell! Possibly an early lesson, not to take the headlines too seriously.

As the war ended my own growing convictions crystallised. It was in 1945 that I became both a committed Christian and a convinced socialist. Like most good evangelicals I can remember the day of my 'second-birth'. It was at a scripture union camp near Turnberry that the influence of my fellow campers led me to make a decision for Christ that I have certainly developed, and may often have failed in, but that I have never renounced. I was not tempted into that 'pietism' or world renouncing dualism which many evangelicals unfortunately display. My mind was always too logical for that. I have since come to believe, ever more firmly, that not only is Christianity actually true but that it explains and enlightens our human condition and sheds light on the dilemmas we face in our world, all in a unique way. Nothing surprising in that. After all, if these are the Maker's instructions, we should not be surprised that they work!

My political conversion was perhaps more gradual but certainly came to a head before that watershed general election of 1945, which so changed the entire direction of our society. Recently I came across the speech – probably the first of that kind I ever made – in which I stood as the Labour candidate in a mock election in our senior school. These were the distant days when a school like Paisley Grammar, with its middle class emphasis, would naturally be strongly Conservative, even in Scotland. The fact that I almost won them over most have been a tribute to my moving eloquence! I stressed the importance of cooperation rather than competition and ended by quoting the last line from a hymn that stated "tis the people marching on, marching on" to which I added "and we must march with them or we will be swept relentlessly aside before them." I like to think, though it may be something of a conceit, that even then I believed in the sovereignty in the people not the state.

By 1950, the mid century year, I was a prefect in the sixth form and was asked to edit the school magazine *The Grammarian*. As I look at my rather tattered yellowing copy nearly fifty years later I can see changes. It cost one shilling. The evidence of the normality of corporal punishment is there. One pupil from the first form writes in it: "Teachers terrible creatures/ Weary us all to the core;/ And some have thoughts and deadly plots/ To give you the strap (which is sore)."

When I come to the editorial for which I was of course directly responsible I find ample evidence that my views and perhaps my prejudices were already well-formed and not fundamentally changed over the long years since. Today my language might be a little less flowery, but the convictions remain. I urged my peers to build the world of tomorrow from the ruins of the world today. It should be a world of justice and equality, a world in which all nations may live in permanent peace as equal participants in the greatest social change of all time. The editorial ends with a quotation from the *Rubaiyat* of Omar Khayyam which means as much to me now as it did then:

> "Ah love! Could thou and I with fate conspire
> To grasp this sorry scheme of things entire
> Would we not shatter it to bits – and then
> Remould it nearer to the heart's desire!"

I did not, of course, then know what life held for me. To what extent have I been able to make even the smallest contribution to the remoulding of the scheme of things? Others must judge that. I do believe, however, that the Scottish Constitutional Convention is part of that remoulding. It is more than simply a minor adjustment of our political system. It is an attempt to create a new kind of democracy capable of carrying us with confidence and hope into a new millennium. The words I wrote as a tender youth in that mid-century year remain my hope for a new century.

Chapter 9

The God with Two Faces

– learning about politics

My lifelong commitment both to political justice and to the truth and relevance of the Christian faith were born and nurtured during my days at school. It was however, at university that they reached maturity and eventually led me to the day when I had to choose.

There are, I suppose, two decisions that all of us have to take which determine the very course of our lives. One is the choice of a partner for life and the other the choice of a career or as I prefer to say, a calling. Certainly for me the college years were the decisive period in the choosing of my way for the future.

In 1950 I turned my faltering steps away from the security of Paisley Grammar School to the excitement of a Glasgow University that was then in the throes of a great celebration. Five hundred years before, in 1450, a Papal Bull had established the University, the oldest in Scotland but for St Andrews by a few years. 1950 was therefore a great excuse for celebration. One of my earliest mental pictures of the University is of the Hall of the Union, later the site of many of the political debates that I took part in, but at that time it was the venue for the University's great celebratory ball. I can still see the banner which ran like a frieze around the balconies. It read, in increasingly large letters:

"1450 – uno. 1550 – duo. 1650 – trio. 1750 – quatro. 1850 – quinto. 1950 – SEX SEX SEX SEX SEX."

What a promising welcome for an eighteen year old beginning his university years. The promise however, was more exciting than the reality. The swinging sixties were far ahead of us – we were still locked in the postwar austerity of the somewhat fearful fifties.

Another event of that year, which seemed to confirm my initial impression that university life was a combination of parties and riots, was the installation of our new Rector. Dr John McCormick was a highly controversial figure, the leader of the Covenant Movement and a staunch Scottish Nationalist. His Rectorial address was totally inaudible over the cacophony of sound, as a student attempted to walk on a tightrope from one balcony to another. The magazine *Picture Post* managed to photograph the scene – a hall filled with a mist of flour bags – just as I stood up and turned round to see what was happening. The result was the clear impression that I was in some way the ringleader and inspiration of this riotous anarchy. Nothing could have been further from the truth. I was, in fact, the most innocent of bystanders gradually learning the ways of the wicked world but it gave my friends many hours of merriment at my expense.

Forty-five years later, Scottish Secretary Michael Forsyth was to accuse me with total, but typical inaccuracy, of having been a leader of CND in Scotland, and implied that I was a dyed-in-the-wool trouble maker. I am glad he never saw that photograph in the *Picture Post!*

I was soon to learn that student life was not all fun, frolic and frivolity. I cannot however, resist a mention of the student songs, which we seemed to sing on every possible occasion, appropriate or not. They ranged from the irreverent to the inept, from the hilarious to the downright silly, from the beautiful to the bawdy – such classics as *Harry was a Bolshi, Goliath of Gath, Green Grow the Rushes Oh* and *The Darkies' Sunday School* (the latter being of course so politically incorrect that I am sure it has been altered!). They have remained with me for the rest of my life.

I have never been quite sure whether to be grateful or envious that I largely missed the swinging sixties! Certainly the nearest we came to debauchery was the occasional session of heavy petting during or after a university ball or dance – normally in the dimly lit upstairs lounge of the students' union. This lounge was fitted with ancient couches – leather I think – which had been deeply and permanently moulded by generations of couples in passionate clinches. We called these couches 'divinities' on the Shakespearean ground that "there is a divinity that shapes our ends". I suppose though, that it would be more truthful to say that our ends (or at least those of our illustrious predecessors) had shaped the 'divinities'. There must be a profound thought or at least a sermon there somewhere.

Any encounters I had in that lounge – and there were a few – were innocent enough for I had already met the love of my life and my heart had been captured permanently. It was not at university that this momentous event occurred but at the Church at Paisley Methodist Central Halls, where I shared the teaching of a Sunday School class with Betty Robinson, who moved me as no other woman had done before or since. We were married in 1955 at the end of my university career.

Looking back over these years which were filled with excitement, incident and I hope achievement, Betty has been at my side. The nature of love changes but true love deepens as we discover more about one another. A poem which I sent to her before our marriage tells nothing but the truth:

> So take me dear and understand my worst
> And freely pardon it, being confessed
> And let me find in loving thee, my best.

However, if my pursuit of the woman who was to be my wife and the mother of our children was single-minded, the other great decision – the choice of a profession or calling in life – was a much more arduous and difficult path. It was natural for me to join the student Christian movement, but also to be active in student politics. My second home was the Labour Club, at that time dominated by the figure of Dr Dick Mabon, later to become Secretary of State for Scotland and then lose his way in the political wilderness of the Social Democratic Party for which he could not hold his Greenock seat. The Glasgow University Union was very much a hothouse for the nurturing of political ambition, and I rubbed shoulders there, in many debates with at least a dozen personalities who were later to become well known politicians of all shades – people like Teddy Taylor of the Conservatives and Menzies Campbell of the Liberal Democrats.

Of these Union debates I can remember comparatively little but I must have played a reasonably effective role in them for, in 1953, I was elected Chair of the Labour Club in succession to Dick Mabon and therefore would, had I continued at the University, have been 'Prime Minister' in one of the 'Governments' of the following session.

Through the three years in which I read for my degree at Glasgow, my ambition remained clear, constant and unambiguous. I wanted to become a politician and one day to be Prime Minister of this country. None of us is ever told what might have been. There is a passage in one of CS Lewis' *Narnia* books where Aslan, the great lion (the godhead figure in these children's stories), says in answer to a question from one of the children as to what might have been, "no one is ever told what might have been – but we can all find out what will be." A poet once wrote:

> The saddest words of tongue or pen
> Are just these four – It might have been.

From my knowledge of the characters and abilities of my friends who went on to become party politicians, and from my own confidence – I hope without false pride or modesty – in my own God-given abilities, I still believe that I might have made it! It might have been. I do not, however, find these words sad or disappointing. I look back with some curiosity but not nostalgia. My intention had been to take my MA and go on to do law and gain an LLB, which was for many the most obvious path to political engagement. Towards the end of my third year at the University something happened. In circumstances which I will not describe, I went through what amounted to a second conversion experience. I became convinced that, although there was nothing wrong with political ambition, I was called to travel a different way – to full-time service of the church.

The title of this chapter, The God With Two Faces, is a way of saying that either choice could have been the will of God. I am not one of those who argues that to serve the Church is somehow any better than any other job. If God calls a man or woman to the ministry of the Church and he or she insists on going into politics for power or into business for money, then he or she is simply disobedient to the heavenly vision. Having said that though, it is just as true the other way around. If any man or woman being genuinely called by God to a political life or any other human endeavour decides instead, for whatever reason, to go into full-time service of the Church then that is equally disobedient. In other words one is not intrinsically better than the other.

Often through the years when I have been interviewing candidates for the ministry and asked their motives I have received the reply, " I want to serve God full-time." It is a response that has always angered me – for I have always said to them every Christian serves God full-time. Do not confuse direct service of the Church with the service of God.

I remain convinced that every politician who shares the Christian faith which I hold, and many who do not, are equally serving God full-time whichever party he or she belongs to. The real choice in life, in whatever profession or calling we chose, is to be "in the world but not of it", that is to be fully part of the struggle to be human, but not to share the false values and assumptions of a world interested primarily in money and power.

Having already been elected Chair of the Labour Club and with my feet firmly on the path which has led many others into political prominence, I turned round, and offered myself to the Methodist church. My friends in Glasgow were by and large amazed and frequently appalled by my decision. The church however, possibly motivated by the traditional welcome for the sinner who repents, oiled the wheels and made it possible for me to be put through the necessary processes, so that my theological training could begin at Cambridge University in October 1953.

Cambridge was wonderful. Two glorious years in which my appreciation of the Christian faith grew were interrupted by exploring its colleges and punting on the river Cam. Above all my relationship with the woman I loved deepened.

During the long summer holiday between the two years I spent at Cambridge, the opportunity to broaden my political knowledge arose – I was invited to join a delegation travelling to China. The journey was unforgettable. A small group of us flew from London to Prague and then continued by train to Moscow. The journey from Moscow to Peking was broken up every two hours or so because the plane could only manage to fly 500 miles at a time. It did give me the opportunity to see places like Kazan, Omsk and Ulan Bator. The journey was well worth it for the thrill a young man experienced at seeing Tienamin Square, the Gates of Heavenly Peace and the Great Wall of China.

Five years later, in 1960, my student career had an Indian Summer. On returning from my first term as a missionary in India, I attended Glasgow University yet again. This time I was studying for a Master of Theology Degree under the guidance of the late and highly revered Dr William Benely. I threw myself back into the world of student politics at the age of 28 as though I had never been away. The only difference was that I was now fully committed to the Christian Church. During that second spell at

Glasgow the president of the Labour Club, and Prime Minister at the appropriate Union debate, was a slim and articulate youth with the rather plain name of John Smith. I cannot claim to have been a close friend but remember several conversations with him and my feeling then was that he would probably have a distinguished political career.

While I have no regrets on a personal level, and indeed looking back over my life I can see how I have been led forward phase by phase, if I am honest there is one lingering regret in the background. It is that – just possibly – I might have played some part, large or small, in making the difference that might have prevented or cut short the worst excesses of the Thatcherite agenda. If that sounds impossibly bigheaded so be it! I might perhaps have made some difference to an era which has caused such pain, such division, such increase in poverty, homelessness, violence and greed. I am convinced that when the history of our time comes to be written the philosophy that we have called Thatcherism will be seen even by Conservatives as a temporary aberration, certainly from Scotland's tradition, history and instinctive feelings. It was a period of an assault on our fundamental principles, which we resisted to a remarkable degree.

In choosing the ministry of the Church did I choose Life? God alone knows the answer and perhaps the reader may judge from this account. Certainly if Scotland not only gets the democratic parliament which is her right, but more importantly uses it to create a healthier and more sustainable society for the new millennium, that would crown all that I have tried to be and to do through the years.

CHAPTER 10

The Tarnished Jewel

– learning about poverty

The Indian Empire was called the jewel in the British crown. When my wife, Betty and I sailed towards the Gateway of India at Bombay as newly weds in 1955, the jewel had been somewhat tarnished. The gruesome massacres and mob violence which tore the old British India apart had muted the joy of freedom in the newly established republic. It was still a place echoing with the voices of empire, and trailing the glory of a proud history.

I went to India with not just a missionary zeal but a well-tuned sensitivity to the need for political justice and freedom. I left India fifteen years later with my faith strengthened and refined by the experience of the ancient religions of the East; and with my sense of justice defined and given clearer shape and deeper understanding by my contact with the patient and dignified poor.

I learned my chief lesson by experience not theory or study. This was that abject poverty existed side by side with ostentatious wealth not by accident or by the just desserts of either, but through a global economic and political system that created and perpetuated both beneficiaries and victims. In short I came to understand how it was that, by and large, the rich got richer and the poorer got poorer and that the key was not just wealth but power – not just deprivation but powerlessness and marginalisation. And I became convinced that this was true both internationally between North and South and, in varying degrees, also within all nations. My political convictions and my sense that these were moral issues and, therefore, related to my faith were both confirmed.

While in my final year of theological studies at Cambridge I was asked, as all budding Methodist Ministers then were, to opt either for Home or Overseas. Home meant a posting by the Conference to any church in Britain. Overseas meant being freely available, to what was then the Methodist Missionary Society, for allocation to any of their far-flung missions in Asia, Africa and the Caribbean. The Methodist system stressed obedience and you were obliged, under oath, to go wherever you were sent.

I chose Overseas and to this day I am still not certain why. Maybe it was a subconscious attempt to get far away from the political scene that was so likely to have a seductive influence. If so, in the light of what has since happened to me, it sure failed! Maybe it was just the wanderlust imbued in me from my peripatetic infancy already described in an earlier chapter. Whatever the reason I have never regretted it. I feel a deep and permanent love for India and her peoples who taught me so much and helped, for better or worse, to make me what I am now.

The *bon mot* of the philosopher Kierkegaard, which I quoted earlier, that "life must be lived forwards but understood backwards", has, in my life, been experienced in a particular way. At each major turning point, the new challenge has always come to me unexpectedly and usually unsought – but when it came, I had to work hard to seize the opportunity to turn it into a chance for real change and achievement. I suppose that has led to an activist kind of Christianity, in contrast to the pietism or quietism that simply leaves things to God. Like the gardener who was complimented with the words, "Well, between you and God you've made a lovely place" and replied, "Yes, but you should have seen it when it was left to God!"

I have always felt that God offers partnerships and trust not ready-made answers. He gives us talents and opportunities beyond our control – and, at least in my case, leads us into places we never chose. Quite simply, He expects us then to get on with the job of ensuring that His will is "done on earth as it is in Heaven". In the end, nothing else really matters.

So I chose overseas and the Missionary Society determined that it was to be West Bengal, in the North East corner of India. Thus it was that on 16th October 1955 just a month after our wedding in Paisley, Betty and I boarded the P&O liner *Carthage*. The ship was old and tired and was on its last voyage. It carried with it a proud tradition of travelling to the Orient that has since died. Generations of Empire-builders had written on their Passage Forms the evocative formula POSH, which meant "Port Out Starboard Home". In the era before air-conditioning these were the important shaded sides of the ship and therefore were the privilege of the rich and influential. We were, of course, outward bound in a starboard cabin. I suppose the opposite of POSH must be SOPH, these cabins being allocated to missionaries and other lesser mortals. I certainly recall the journey as hot, airless and uncomfortable but fascinating, especially through the Suez Canal and the Red Sea.

After eighteen days at sea, landing briefly at Gibraltar, Suez and Aden – ports over which the Union Jack still flew, and a further two days in a slow train crossing the Indian plains, we arrived in the chaos and cacophony of Howrah Station in Calcutta. It is tempting to be self-indulgent and tell the story of these years in graphic detail but that is another book. I must be disciplined and stick, as promised, only to a few people and events that have a direct bearing on my character and views as they affect what is happening in Scotland today. All of those I am about to introduce are, to me, 'saints'. Each of them taught me at least one, and in most cases both, of life's two great lessons.

First, the people that influenced me were always those marked by a quiet sense of what was really important in life and detached from the endless frenetic search for more possessions and power that most of us regard as life's purpose. I often envied, but was seldom able to emulate, their careless unconcern for their own selfish gain and fame.

Second, they taught me the lesson already spelt out, that poverty and need are neither God-given nor inevitable, and that political change, rather than charitable giving, offers the only permanent cure.

My first 'saint' is Saroda. In 1956, I took charge (along with two schools and six churches, sixty miles apart) of a small Leprosy Home in a town called Raniganj. Raniganj, or Queenstown in English translation, was long ago a major junction of the great railway network, on the edge of the Bengal coalfields. It had long since become yet another rail stop *en route* to Calcutta and beyond. The Leprosy Home was built on a pleasant place on the river bank, well beyond the limits of the town, in a spacious compound providing a self-contained village set apart and secure from society.

Most mornings I would cycle there to meet the patients and talk with the doctor and staff. The discovery that leprosy could be easily cured with regular medication had only just been made and the new policy of treating only outpatients on a weekly basis recently instituted. However the Home was still full of people who, over the years, had been banished by their frightened families and communities. Many of them, in the days before treatment, had lost limbs through ulceration or had faces ravaged by the disease.

Saroda (if she had another name, I never knew it, and I don't believe she did either) was in her mid-fifties when we first met. Nearly half a century before, she had been brought into the Home as a little girl whom a missionary had found abandoned and alone, with the first signs of the terrifying disease. She had spent most of her life since then in the Home and long ago had lost both of her legs below the knees and both her hands. She moved around on a small platform fitted with tiny wheels. Her hair was always shorn and worn close to her head in what my wife told me was an 'urchin cut'. A daily ritual for the women was to bathe mid-morning, and then meet to comb each other's long hair, enjoying the warm sun. Long hair is a prized possession and an important part of Indian womanhood. Although Saroda couldn't take part in this ritual, she was always there in the middle, conducting operations. Often the women would meet on her verandah where she held court, with loud discussion or uproarious laughter. She must have seen most of the women arrive in the Home – some young girls, some mothers, some wives – all of them with their own story to tell of pain and rejection. Saroda was both mother and sister combined, offering hope and love. The discovery of leprosy meant immediate rejection from home. Such abandonment by a loved one was too much to bear by the afflicted, and the shame it brought on the family concerned. She held the group together by sheer force of personality. Her eyes shown like two pieces of ebony, intent on comforting and supporting "her family". In spite of her mutilated body and inability to use her hands and feet, she could outrun them all in her little platform cart, made for her by one of the men patients. (The men lived in a separate part of the village, in accordance with the strict rules that were the norm for Indian society outside.)

When I think of Saroda I do not see her disfigured body but the beauty, serenity and sheer happiness of her face. As I write this now the tears are unashamedly in my eyes – not out of pity, but of gratitude for what she was. When I visited her, as I did at least twice a week for some years, she was always humorous, cheerful and a joy to know. I know that I got so much more from our meetings than she did, for I always left her with a deep and humbling sense that I had been with one for whom the bells of Heaven would ring.

One day Betty and I managed to persuade her to come out with us in the car for a few hours. Her childlike wonder and pleasure at all she saw was infectious. That day she saw her first train with all the excitement and innocence of a young child. She was captivated by the teeming life of the villages and the ordinary daily doings – small children at play, women working in the rice fields, the busy bazaar in town, all the everyday things we take for granted. Her delight was akin to the child in each of us that says 'aah' at the first sight of Christmas lights. There was no regret or envy in her for all that she herself had missed in life. She could only rejoice in the rich tapestry before her. She had probably never known such freedom, probably born to a mother living on the streets and she looked on the 'outside' world as being for others. This was not her life, and she went home to tell the story of her adventure to the other women, with no regrets for the society that had rejected her and continued to reject people with leprosy.

She once asked me about our journey to India. Her reaction to my attempt to describe an eighteen day sea voyage was to ask my wife very confidentially so none of the others nearby could hear, how we managed to go to the toilet. The only boats she had ever seen were the little open craft that sailed up and down the river near the Home.

My most precious memory of Saroda is more personal. By 1959 we had been friends for well over three years and she told me one day, in no uncertain terms, that it was high time my wife was pregnant! Moreover, she informed me that she was now praying earnestly for just such a development and her air made it clear that, as far as she was concerned, that was the end of the matter – the outcome was no longer in doubt.

When, shortly after this conversation we discovered we were expecting a baby, Saroda was convinced she was solely responsible, notwithstanding nature's more usual and enjoyable method. She declared constantly that it was a boy my wife was carrying and wasn't a bit phased when it turned out to be a girl. Lindsey Jane – the first of our three daughters – was baptised in the Leprosy Home Church, the only place where Saroda could easily attend. I see her now beaming with proprietorial pride in the front row.

Saroda died a few years later. If there is anyone I confidently expect to greet in Heaven it is Saroda. That is, of course, assuming

I get there. But I am comforted by the thought that, like the importunate widow in the parable, Saroda would give the celestial powers no peace until they let me in, deserving or otherwise.

Incidentally , that summer before Lindsey was born, we spent some time in the hill station of Mussoorie. The Dalai Lama had just escaped from Tibet and Betty had witnessed the procession of his retinue coming across the mountains into Mussoorie, and the pageantry of his reception, before I arrived. His court was set up in the mansion house of India's best-known industrialist family, the Birlas. We, along with others, were received by him in formal audience, blessed and each presented with the traditional white scarf. I take great delight in the fact that our unborn child was blessed, not only by the saint called Saroda, but by the Dalai Lama, spiritual head of Tibetan Buddhism. Lindsey Jane, our first born, has long displayed an attractive serenity! Perhaps that blessing had an effect! It was a new and moving experience for us, and possibly also for the Dalai Lama so soon after his arrival into a strange new country, to meet so many non-Tibetans anxious to bid him welcome and to show respect. Our fifteen years in India continued to show a constant pattern of surprise and adventure – but, as I say, that is another book.

My second 'saint' may seem an unlikely candidate for the title. Indeed, he would certainly find the accusation both amusing and totally incredible. K.C. Shivaramakrishnan was a devout Hindu of high caste. His very name is an invocation to three Gods in the Hindu Pantheon. He was also something unusual in a civil servant and an officer of the Indian Administration Service – he combined organisational brilliance with vision and integrity.

Our first meeting was when he was in charge of the Development Authority in the new steel and industrial township of Durgapur, where he had the task of allocating all land in a custom-built town of 300,000 people which had previously only been jungle. Within the space of a month, he was approached by the representatives of five different Churches, including myself, asking for land to build a place of worship. He made no answer but summoned us all together to his office to deliver a rebuke that I have never forgotten. This is what he said:

> "Durgapur is a new place. We have people from all over India and all over the world. They have different languages, different religions, different customs. My task is to build a harmonious community. Go away and come back only when you are ready to be part of the answer, not part of the problem!"

There have been many times in the life of the Constitutional Convention when I have longed to say that to the leaders of the political parties. Indeed, in different words, I did say it and, to a surprising degree, it was heard.

Certainly, that day long ago in Durgapur, I learned a lesson about reconciliation. A divided Church proclaiming a message of reconciliation is like a bald man selling hair restorer. It fails to convince.

We listened and we took heed. I became pastor for a united church in that town and later founded the Ecumenical Social and Industrial Institute, working with industry and also training church workers from all over India to work in urban and industrial situations. Shivaramakrishnan, or Shiv as we came to know him, became a friend and advisor. When he later became Director of the Calcutta Metropolitan Development Authority he took on perhaps the most difficult job in India, that of saving this "marvellous and monstrous city" from collapse and decay. An Indian newspaper asked the question, "Can India survive Calcutta?" Some three million people lived in abject poverty – in the 'bustees' (slums without sewage electricity or water) – as squatters, in huts of tin and cardboard, or as street-dwellers.

With help from the IMF, Shiv carried through a Bustee Improvement Programme which brought water, sanitation and paved pathways to millions. I recall him once explaining wearily that he could only improve matters, to go further and actually rehouse three million people was a pipe-dream, far away from political reality. He added, cryptically, "to rehouse all these people would cost as much as is spent in two hours in the Arms Race, as much as three nuclear bombers. That is, of course, away beyond the means of the human race to achieve."

Shiv understood what few bureaucrats do, that physical improvement is not enough, that people must be enabled to free themselves through education, economic activity and common sense. I was asked, with his full support, to channel the work of voluntary agencies, like Christian Aid, into an integrated programme in Calcutta which came to be known as Calcutta Urban Service. This worked with local slum communities to establish simple schools, clinics, economic activities and community development. Together we achieved no miracles but, I believe, we made a difference. That is perhaps all we can ever claim.

If we did indeed make a difference it was, in large measure, due to my third 'saint', Canon Subir Biswas of Calcutta, who became my closest friend and colleague in India. He too was an unlikely saint, a cultivated handsome young priest with a rich and cultured speaking voice who, as curate at St Paul's Cathedral in Calcutta, had become the darling of the affluent expatriate community and was in constant demand for a round of parties and social engagements.

He was, I think, devastated when his Bishop, Metropolitan Lakdasa de Mel, who was a patron of our work in Durgapur, confided in me that Subir would be spoiled if he stayed on in Calcutta, and that he was to be sent to work with me in the new town a hundred miles away. Both of us were apprehensive, but a firm friendship was soon cemented. Beneath his softness and easy humour, he proved to have a heart of gold and a will of steel.

When Subir came back to Calcutta, a changed man after the years in Durgapur, his return was timely and fortuitous. In 1970 and '71, the people of East Bengal, just across the border, tried to throw off the oppressive mantle of the Pakistani army and were met with brutality, rape and murder that amounted to genocide.

Millions of refugees fled across the border into an already poverty-stricken West Bengal and Subir Biswas gave all his energies to feeding, housing and helping these wretched families in the ramshackle refugee camps all along the border area. Day after day he was out from early morning to late at night, exhausted and often ill. The venerable ancient cathedral was turned into something resembling a massive warehouse, storing food, tents, clothing and medicines on their way to the front line. The services were held in the midst of it all but few objected in the face of the sacrifices being made by Subir and others.

By this time I was already back in Britain, at Coventry Cathedral, but I kept in close touch. In August 1971, I spoke at a mass rally in Trafalgar Square to "Stop Genocide – Recognise Bangladesh". Sharing the platform were such luminaries as David Kossoff, Reg Pentice MP and Justice Abu Syed Chowdhury, a former Judge of Dacca High Court and Vice Chancellor of Dacca University, who was now the official representative of the nascent Bangladesh abroad.

When patience finally snapped and the Indian army entered Bangladesh to be welcomed as liberators by a suffering people, Justice Chowdhury returned to be the first President of a free Bangladesh. When I visited him in 1972, the Government House still bore the scars of war.

The liberation of Bangladesh however, made even greater demands on Subir Biswas and the organisation he had built up. Village after village had been destroyed by the retreating Pakistani army and Subir helped to rebuild some 50,000 houses as well as providing wells, education, tools, seeds and clothing to thousands.

When, at last, the need of Bangladesh became less acute, Subir turned what was now a large and impressive organisation to the needs of Calcutta itself and I undertook at the European end to establish the Europa-Calcutta Consortium. This was a network of organisations in Britain, Germany and the Netherlands that agreed to work together for the renewal of Calcutta and channelled funds for development to Subir and his team.

Exhausted by his Herculean efforts, Subir developed a heart condition and finally a brain tumour. He died prematurely in 1977. All Calcutta and many beyond mourned his passing. Mother Teresa, with whom he worked closely, spoke movingly of how his work was complementary to hers, she directly with the dying destitutes and he in an attempt to help people change their lives and communities. I will always be grateful for having known and worked with this great man. He must have saved hundreds of lives and brought relief and justice to thousands. I am proud to have been able to share, however humbly, in his life and work.

Like many great men, he was somewhat autocratic. He got things done and did not easily suffer fools gladly. To come to the Cathedral in the seventies, as I often did, was to find him at the hub of frantic and constant activity. He surrounded the Cathedral with billboards that carried messages reflecting his philosophy, which I wholeheartedly share. One was: "The greatest thing you can do for another is not only to share with him your wealth, but to reveal to him his own."

Another: "The only thing necessary for evil to triumph is for good men to do nothing."

Then there was: "The one thing needed is the realisation that my own welfare is bound up with that of all others."

And "You are not making a gift of our wealth to the poor. You are giving him what is his own. What has been given for the good of all, you have allocated to yourself. The world is given to all, not just to the rich."

Let Subir Biswas have the last word from India. When we were about to leave for the new post at Coventry Cathedral, his last words to me were these: "The greatest thing you can do now for India, is to change Britain!"

Well Subir, you have to admit, I'm trying.

CHAPTER 11

Healing the Wounds of History

– learning about peace

By the end of the sixties, my education and development were ready, though I probably did not know it at the time, to take another great leap forward. In 1970 I accepted an invitation to join the staff of Coventry Cathedral and we sailed from India for the last time with our three beautiful daughters, Lindsay, Shona and Shelagh then aged eleven, nine and six.

It was no coincidence that the one place in Britain that wanted to know more about and develop links with our pioneering work in India was Coventry. The great new cathedral there, the vision of Basil Spence is, I believe, one of the few modern buildings that will survive the test of time. It is a symbolic statement in stone and glass and it became, through the vision of leaders, not just a building but the centre of the most visionary and exciting experiment in contemporary forms of ministry in Britain.

On the 14th of November 1940, German bombers had attempted to destroy Coventry. Some 1,400 people died and much of the city centre was burned to the ground. The fourteenth century

Gothic cathedral was reduced to a smouldering pile of rubble within ruined and windowless walls. The devastation and death were by later standards actually very limited, certainly compared with the later atrocities at Hamburg, Dresden and especially Hiroshima, where one hundred people died for every one at Coventry.

The significance of Coventry's destruction lay, not in its size but, in its purpose. It was the first major attempt, in modern warfare, to destroy a city totally as a means of attacking the morale of the people. Hitler spoke openly on German radio of his determination to 'Coventrate' all major cities in Britain. That intention gave added symbolic power to the acts of the cathedral's main priest, Provost Howard. Standing the next day in the ruins, he solemnly vowed that the cathedral would rise again. With a workman, he took three of the medieval nails, which had held the roof together and were now littering the floor, and formed them into a cross. The Coventry Cross of Nails was then placed on to the ruined altar. This cross has now become a symbol of worldwide reconciliation. On the wall behind the ruined altar are inscribed the words "Father forgive", taken from Christ's statement on the Cross. Beside them is the Old Testament quote from the rebuilding of the Temple: "the latter glory of this house shall be greater than the former says the Lord, and in this place will I give peace."

Bishop Cuthbert Bardsley, a man of transparent godliness, used to say with delight that he was the first bishop in history to have been able to be present both at the laying of the foundation stone and the consecration of his completed cathedral. It was, however, Bishop Bardsley's appointment of Bill Williams (officially the Very Reverend H.C.N. Williams) to be the Provost of this new cathedral, that was really an enormous leap of faith. Bill Williams was very different from the traditional mould of Anglican church leaders. He did not come from a public school and Oxbridge but was, in fact, brought up and educated in the divided South African society. Though a hard man to live with, as I was to discover during my years at Coventry, he was, beyond doubt, the right man for the job for he had the imagination, insight and drive to make Coventry, not just a significant building, but a place of experiment and excitement unparalleled in Britain.

Certainly, I can think of no other Anglican Church leader who would have taken the risk of inviting me, a comparatively unknown Methodist minister from a far away project in India, to come to Coventry Cathedral to take charge of its urban ministry and later of its widespread and challenging ministry of international contacts.

By the time I joined the cathedral staff in 1970, they had already developed an unique international mission and a team working with every aspect of life in the city itself. Each Monday morning we gathered early for Communion, breakfast and then a staff meeting at which each member of the team reported on the work done and the problems faced by their group in the last week. To listen and join in that meeting was to catch a glimpse of what the Church was meant to be. One by one we heard from the industrial mission on the state of the car industry; from those working with the city council on the urban problems; on race relations and related issues; on the arts and culture; on youth affairs and on the widespread international ministry, as well as the more traditional aspects one would expect in any church. To sit through that staff meeting was to be conscious of a church at the heart of its community, exercising a ministry of reconciliation that went far beyond the religious or personal lives of its members and stretched out into every part of the community of Coventry and indeed far beyond.

Due to my experience in India, my first years there were as director of urban ministry but I continued to return to Calcutta at least once a year. I became secretary of a group called the Europa Calcutta Consortium which was a coalition of voluntary agencies from Germany, the Netherlands and Britain, including Christian Aid, coordinating their help for the city of Calcutta and its three million slum dwellers.

By 1974, the Church of England had come into full communion with the newly formed Church of North India, of which I was a minister or priest. The result was that I found myself in a unique position. Without ceasing to be a Methodist minister, I was able to be licensed by the Bishop of Coventry and therefore to become an Anglican priest. As far as I know, I was then, and am still, the only person able to combine the two. I often joked that in order to be fully accepted by my Christian brothers and sisters next door, I had to go via Calcutta.

That year, the Bishop of Coventry took another step in the history of the Anglican Church by appointing me as a Canon of the Cathedral. I began seven years in possibly the best job in the British churches.

To be director of international ministry at Coventry Cathedral, with its worldwide contacts and its vision of reconciliation and healing the wounds of history, was not only the best job, it was truly unique. Two years later, one of the church papers called me "the farthest travelled clergyman in the Kingdom". For one with a wanderlust already evident, I found myself quite wonderfully able to combine my joy in travelling with a sense that I was contributing to a process of healing and reconciliation. Indeed I have always had an instinctive reaction of sympathy to a few lines of verse I once heard Ludovic Kennedy recite:

> My heart is warm with the friends I make
> And better friends I'll not be knowing
> But there isn't one train I wouldn't take
> No matter where it's going!

I like that, especially if we extend train to include plane and maybe other forms of transport.

Shortly after I took over the international ministry, a visitor arrived at my office. I must confess that when this rather shabby looking elderly man took his seat opposite me I had no idea that it was to be the beginning of a great adventure. I probably assumed that, like most of my visitors, he was a religious crank or that he was after money. My guest introduced himself as Joseph Abileah, and began to tell me of the Society for Middle East Confederation in Israel of which he was co-president. His story gripped me from the start. Here was a man, clearly a pious and faithful Jew, who had committed his life to reconciling the Palestinian and Arab neighbours and to the political confederation involving Israel, Palestine and Jordan. It sounded, as a political solution, impossibly naive and utopian but, like so many enthusiasts, his commitment was infectious. I found myself promising to visit him at his home in Hypha in Israel as soon as possible.

The following year I was able to arrange to break my journey to Calcutta at Tel Aviv airport. Joseph Abileah met me at the airport and took me on a fascinating pilgrimage through the Arab West Bank, which had been annexed by Israel in the Six Day War of 1966. I remember we drove from Jerusalem through Ramallah and Nablus and then along the valley of the River Jordan. At every town he was greeted as a friend and was able to introduce me to those who were, at that time, the leaders of Arab opinion. Gradually, I understood the pain and resentment that was later to explode into the so-called Intifada, the revolt of the Palestinians against their Israeli occupiers.

The climax of our visit, however, was when he took me to a small community occupying a few Nissan huts and a derelict bus on a barren hillside just opposite an old Crusader fort half way between Jerusalem and Tel Aviv. The community brought together Jews, Arab Moslems and Arab Christians, thus spanning the enormous divisions both ethnic and religious. The founder, an ethnic Jew and now a Dominican priest, was introduced to me as Father Bruno. I remember him taking me out onto the hillside and waving his arms across the landscape. "This," he said, "is a hill soaked in blood."

During the conflict that led to the setting up of the state of Israel, that hillside commanded the road to Jerusalem. It was of vital strategic importance and was fought over repeatedly, changing hands several times between the Jewish and Arab forces. My host was not exaggerating. It was indeed a hillside soaked in blood and now the home of this community of reconciliation. The fellowship called itself Neve Shalom, which means Oasis of Peace and is a direct quote from the scriptures of the Old Testament. When I said farewell to the Community of Neve Shalom and later to Joseph Abileah and continued eastwards to India, I was determined that Coventry Cathedral must link with these courageous people.

About a year later I received a phone call from Germany. The caller introduced himself as Elias Jabbour, an Israeli Arab from the town of Shfar Am near Nazareth. He was leading a youth delegation, comprising both Arabs and Jews, under the auspices of Neve Shalom. They were in Germany but wondered if we would welcome them in Coventry – at two days notice! One thing I have noticed down the years is how easy it is to find ways to say no. Part of my philosophy has always been to find ways to yes wherever possible, so I agreed at once and set about trying to accommodate thirty young Israeli Jews and Arabs. In the end we had to put them up in a church hall but to this day many of them remember the hospitality they were given by that local church. They spent a few days with us in the Cathedral, meeting youth groups from Coventry.

The most memorable moment came at the end of their stay when we gathered around the baptism font in Coventry Cathedral. When the Cathedral was being built, the architect had approached the governments of Israel and Jordan to ask whether a massive boulder from the hillside at Jerusalem might be donated to the Cathedral. Since Bethlehem at the time was still part of Jordanian territory, it took an unusual act of cooperation between Jordan and Israel, then bitter enemies, to allow that massive stone to be transported to Coventry where it became the baptismal font of the new Cathedral. It is lit by the sun's rays being filtered through the golden stained glass of the massive baptistry window, symbolising the Holy Spirit breaking through over so many years to a successful conclusion.

Later I visited Shfar Am as Elias Jabbour's guest and learnt something of the warmth and lavishness of Arab hospitality. I remember meeting his father who was to die not long after my visit. He was bedridden but clearly one of the leading figures of the town, a place in which Arab Christian, Jew and Druze lived in harmony. He had served his time in the forces of the Ottoman Empire and told stories of the Turkish, British and Israeli occupations. Like his son Elias, who had come to be my close friend, he remained committed to peace and his reaction to the actions of Israel was one more of sadness than of bitterness.

One of the results of this hospitality offered to me was a first hand experience of the humiliation that Israel's Arab citizens regularly suffer. Normally, on entering or leaving Israel, as a foreigner, I was at most subjected to some close questioning and an occasional luggage examination. This time, however, on admitting that my residence for several days had been with a distinguished Arab family in Shafa Am, I was subjected to the most intensive and embarrassing physical examination by two Israeli officials.

The positive result of these contacts was the setting up in the town of Shafa Am of what came to be called the House of Hope. Supported by Coventry Cathedral and by groups related to Coventry through the Community of the Cross of Nails in the USA and elsewhere, this House of Hope was set up as a meeting place where Arab and Jew and people of different faiths could come together regularly both socially and for honest debate and discussion.

Through those years of close and recurring contact with both Jew and Arab in Palestine and Israel, my views on the Middle East conflict were turned round completely. Like many in the West, I began with enormous sympathy for a brave little country that seemed to be struggling against the concerted might of bullying Arab neighbours massively bigger than herself. Here it seemed was a people who had been the victims of attempted genocide and now the clear underdog and threatened with extinction.

That has changed. Israel seems to have been unable to learn

the real lesson of the terrible experience of her people. Yad Vashem, the memorial to the holocaust, never lets us forget the obscene horror that was perpetrated on this nation by so-called Christian and cultured nations. The Israeli response to that cruelty seemed to be not the resolve "this will never happen again" but "this will not happen *to us* again." The result is that many of the methods of false appropriation, marginalisation, denial of rights and even torture that were the start of Europe's humiliation of the Jews are now being used by the modern state of Israel against those they count as enemies or by whom she feels threatened.

In 1979, the German group with young volunteers at Coventry, Action Atonement made a risky proposal. They suggested to me that a group of young people from Coventry might be joined by a similar group from West Germany and that they might go for three weeks of work and experience to the former concentration and extermination camp of Auschwitz. That summer twelve young people from Coventry Cathedral, including my daughter Lindsey, travelled by coach to Berlin. Once there, we and the twelve Germans spent three days studying the facts of the Nazi period. Our study included a visit to a house on the Wannsee, Berlin's great lake, in which the decision was made to go for what was called the Final Solution of the Jewish question. That Final Solution was in practice a decision to exterminate every Jew in Europe. The house is now unmarked but I have never forgotten its innocent appearance by the side of a beautiful lake.

All our study however, could not have prepared us for what we were to experience when we at last journeyed across Poland and reached Auschwitz. We stayed in a small hostel just beside Auschwitz One, the original labour camp with its grim huts and death cells. We were joined there by a group of young Poles and our entire company was divided into three sections, each of them spending two days of the week on one of a list of tasks.

The growing horror that crept in on the group I was with is something I will remember until I die. Our first task was comparatively easy and undemanding. We were simply to weed the area between the barbed wire fences. On either side of the gate with its iron motto *Arbeit Macht Frei* (Work Brings Freedom) stretched two layers of barbed wire. To touch the inner electrified wires had meant instant death. For prisoners who had reached the point of utter despair, the common practice was to rush up to the fence and throw themselves onto the wire. Indeed, the last thing one sees on leaving the Museum of the Holocaust at Auschwitz is a life-sized figure of a prisoner draped in death over the wires and, above him, the two words, Never Forget.

Weeding the section between the wires may seem a boring task but, the very fact that we were in an area normally inaccessible to the public meant that there was the possibility of unusual discoveries. I myself found a small coin of the Nazi period and, much more significantly, a small piece of metal that was later identified as the valve of a wind instrument. It was the habit of the SS guards, with their strange mixture of cruelty and culture, to have the camp orchestra play each day as prisoners went out on their enforced labour and again on their return.

The reality of Auschwitz was brought home to us much more however, when at our second task we were taken to Auschwitz Two. That area, called Birkenau, which had been a labour camp and latterly the extermination camp, housed the gas chambers which had disposed each day of at least 10,000 people. Here we were given the task of sorting out rooms full of artifacts left behind by those who had gone to their deaths. In one room, I recall, piles of battered old suitcases. Our job was to put them into some kind of order so that they could become part of a travelling exhibition to allow the message of Auschwitz never to be forgotten. Many of the suitcases bore the names and addresses of Jewish families from all parts of Europe who had gone, in most cases unsuspectingly, to their deaths. Yet another room was filled with prison clothing, much of it now in tatters. In its midst, we discovered something even more gruesome. It was a suit made entirely of human hair, shaven from the heads of female prisoners.

In that room also stood a filing cabinet that still contained hundreds of the triangular patches used to identify the nature of each inmates 'crime'. Yellow for Jews, red for political, pink for homosexual, green for gypsies and so on. I may have got the colours wrong but the principle remains.

A survivor of the camp, Herr Franz Huber, who still lived in a small house within sight of the camp, seemed unable to tear himself away from all of his experiences. He told us a story about the filing cabinet. He was an accomplished artist and had been commissioned to prepare and paint the patches for use by the prisoners. He had been asked to take charge of a tiny plate and chalice that were used among the Christian prisoners for their communion services, an activity strictly forbidden under pain of death. He had hidden these in the midst of the patches since normally he was the only one to be instructed by the SS guards to bring them out. He told us, in broken tones that showed he was remembering the incident vividly, how an SS guard called Müller came in and started rifling through the files. Our friend watched him closely since the discovery of the tiny communion vessels would have meant instant execution. Fortunately, Müller found what he was looking for before reaching the hidden vessels.

An even more significant experience awaited us on our third task. It was, in some ways, the simplest of all. We had access to the camp records and files. We were allowed to spend time going through the inventories of the number of prisoners received, those who had died and those expected. For the gas chambers the numbers were given simply in round figures, with no dignity at all. For others, however, the figures tell their own story. Two hundred and fifty Russian prisoners were brought in one week. Four weeks later, one hundred and twelve of them were still alive and at work. There had been some attempt to destroy these records but this had only been partially successful and this grim evidence remained of the efficiency with which the machine of death operated.

One day after we had finished work, I came across a young German girl sobbing uncontrollably, the tears appearing to well from the depths of her soul. It was a long time before she could tell me what was the cause of her grief. At last she regained some composure and told me that among the records the SS guards had left was a name she dreaded seeing – her father's. "I feel dirty. I will never be clean again." Her words have haunted me ever since. What could I, a minister of the Christian Church say to her? I could only say, with the sincerity of all my heart, that in the infamy, selfishness and sin of the human race all of us are dirty. None of us will ever be clean again except by the forgiveness and cleansing offered by God. The promise made to Jew, Muslim and Christian in the Old Testament stands, "Though your sins be as scarlet, saith the Lord, I will wash them whiter than snow."

Though that German girl was an extreme case, none of us were unaffected. The lesson we learned was not totally what might have been expected. Our first reaction was, of course, to be overwhelmed by grief and horror that this could happen in our own time. Gradually, however, we came to understand the central truth that those who carried out these acts of genocide were not, in the main, monsters or sadists or psychopaths. They were ordinary people – they loved their families, they played with their children, they patted their dogs. They had come to believe as a matter of fundamental creed that they had a right to live at the expense of others. The chastening thought for me was simply this: all of us have, at different times in our lives, both individually and collectively, have taken at least the first hesitant steps that lead to Auschwitz. If we ever benefit at the expense of others, whether in our corporate or personal lives, we prove ourselves to be children of Auschwitz.

These three unforgettable weeks taught us another lesson. It was fascinating to watch the differing reactions from the three nationalities, and to realise something of which many had been quite unconscious, namely that we were very much the product of our own communities and societies.

To the young Poles, Auschwitz was horrific but not particularly an unexpected phenomenon. Their history had led them to expect nothing more than attempted genocide. For long periods there had been no Polish nation. Russia and Germany together had constantly threatened their very existence, and Auschwitz seemed simply to be the next terrible step along a road with which their nation was painfully familiar.

For the young Germans there was an oppressive feeling of guilt and even denial. They could not of course deny that this actually happened. It stands to the honour of Germany that she has actually made it a punishable offence to deny the Holocaust as some with obvious political motives try to do. What our young Germans could deny, however, was the nationalism that had given rise to this.

Thus while the Poles were intensely nationalist, honouring the flag and wanting to remember every bit of their history with pride, the young Germans, on the other hand, wanted nothing to do with the songs, the emblems, the flags and even the memories of national identity. One night, during our social evening a girl from Coventry started to sing a little German folk song she had learned at school. The Germans froze and showed their horror and distaste. The singer was deeply hurt and baffled – all she had done was sing an innocent folk song. It was, however, a song that had been misused by the Hitler Youth. For the Germans, Hitler and the Nazis had spoiled for so many what was in itself good and pure.

Most interesting of all from my point of view was the reaction of the young people from England. For us the flag and the symbols of nationhood had been something neither to revere nor to decry. They are simply there, taken for granted like so much in our constitution. We were forced to realise – for many it was for the first time in their lives – that we too shared a national self-understanding and identity. I thought then of something which has often come to me since in the struggle for Scotland's freedom that the chief characteristic of English nationalism is its unconsciousness.

Those Coventry years were so rich with experience and

excitement that they could fill a book by themselves. Even before I came to Coventry Cathedral, the roots of its International Ministry were already deep. Naturally enough the reconciliation links had to begin with Germany. Many contacts were established with West Germany and young volunteers from the organisation *Aktion Suhnezeichen* (Action Atonement) were constantly at Coventry helping to run our international centre. Links with Communist East Germany, especially at the time of the Cold War were particularly difficult. But Provost Williams was convinced that Coventry's main project had to be in the city of Dresden, which had the same symbolic significance for Germans as Coventry had for Britons. The Provost made several visits to East Berlin to meet the Minister for Religious Affairs in the Communist government, who rejoiced the name of Zeigewasser. He was stonewalled and got nowhere at all until one day in conversation it came out quite accidentally that both of them had served in the Spanish Civil War. From that point, the doors were opened. Young volunteers from Coventry went, year after year, to Dresden to help rebuild a city centre hospital run by the Deaconesses of the German Protestant Church. Those who go to Dresden today can visit the hospital and see, prominently displayed on all three floors, the Coventry Cross of Nails and a plaque recording the work of reconciliation which rebuilt it.

In my study hangs a plain wooden cross. It was presented to me during a visit to Pastor Martin Niemoller, then well into his eighties. He had, of course, been one of the leaders of the so-called 'confessing church' which had opposed Hitler and spent many years in the concentration camps, his life probably only spared due to his distinguished military career. It was Niemoller who, standing before the first Synod of the German Church after the end of the war, spoke these unforgettable words:

"The Nazis first came for the Jews and I was not a Jew
so I did not speak up. Then they came for the
Communists and I was not a Communist so I did not

speak up. Then they came for the Socialists and I was not a Socialist so I did not speak up. Then they came for the Trade Unionists and I was not a Trade Unionist so I did not speak up. Then they came for the Catholics and I was a Protestant so I did not speak up. One day they came for me and, by that time, there was no one left to speak up for anyone. In order that this shall not happen again, injustice to anyone anywhere must be the concern of everyone everywhere."

Every time I look up from my desk and see that cross, I am reminded of those words.

Whilst Coventry's ministry of reconciliation began, inevitably, with Germany, it soon extended to healing the wounds in Coventry itself and to other situations, particularly that of Northern Ireland.

The Corrymeela Community, on the coast of Antrim, had a vision very close to that of Coventry. It was an attempt to bring together Protestant and Catholic in the divided Northern Irish society. Once Dresden was completed, the youth parties of Coventry went to Corrymeela and helped to build the Coventry House which still stands today. I cannot forget a young Protestant boy who pointed to a particular spot and told me that was where the Catholics murdered his people. When I asked when, he replied, with no hint of irony, "1689." Nor will I forget a young Catholic boy of twelve or thirteen who, in a Corrymeela conference started to speak with passion of how his people had been put out of their homes and sent into poverty and starvation to make way for settlers. Again when asked when this had occurred, he spoke of generations long gone and centuries long passed. The wounds of history are deep, painful and real.

The intense experience of Coventry's story leads me to believe that true repentance is not an easy path but demands four things.

1. We must *remember* together. There has to be between Jew and Arab, between Protestant and Catholic in Ireland, between

Scotland and England a reconciliation of memories, a willingness to understand where we have come from and to share each other's myths and heroes.

2. This has to lead to *repentance* together. So long as the finger of blame is always pointed at the other side and never shared there is no way forward. That is, of course, not to deny that in a situation where there has been oppression such as South Africa or indeed Israel repentance must begin with the oppressor and not the victim. It is however, a mark of the maturity of South Africa under Nelson Mandela, that a degree of genuine repentance on the part of the past apartheid oppressor, has been met by real understanding and even a willingness to confess their own shortcomings on the part of the oppressed.

3. There must be *restitution* – a willingness to put things right as far as things can possibly be done. In South Africa today, much can be forgiven, but things must also be put right. There must be justice as well as forgiveness. Part of that restitution in Scotland's case is the recognition of her right to her own decision-making process and therefore her own parliament.

4. Only after these three have been achieved can there be genuine *renewal* and therefore proper reconciliation.

In 1981, after eleven years at Coventry Cathedral, and seven years as director of its international ministry, the time was ripe for me to cease trying to be the messenger of the gods, to hang up my winged sandals and come back down to earth! I accepted an invitation to become General Secretary of the Scottish Churches Council based at Dunblane. I was to return to my native soil after a quarter of a century of having the world as my parish. Was it a valid preparation for that which lay ahead of me? The reader must be the judge.

CHAPTER 12

Scotland the What?

– learning about pollution

When I left India in 1970 my closest friend and colleague, the late Canon Biswas had told me bluntly "the best thing you can do for India is change Britain." Eleven years later, when I left Coventry Cathedral to return to my native Scotland, I remembered these words. By this time I had come to the conclusion that the best thing I could do to change Britain was to change Scotland!

I had been taken up the post of General Secretary of the Scottish Churches Council and Director of Scottish Churches House in Dunblane. The council was an ecumenical body, with nine major churches in membership, of which of course by far the largest was the Church of Scotland. Its great weakness was the absence of Scotland's other large church, the Roman Catholics – but this was corrected just before I left Dunblane in 1990 when the new ecumenical body Action of Churches Together in Scotland (ACTS) took over from the old council and was able to bridge the old gulf which had been almost as painful in Scotland as in Northern Ireland, between the Catholic and Protestant communities.

Apart from short holidays, I had not lived and worked in Scotland for nearly three decades. My return in 1981, after nearly thirty years of wandering the world, was to find a nation strangely ill at ease. In the referendum of 1979, a small majority for devolution was frustrated by the so-called 40% rule – the last minute amendment which insisted that a positive vote must be by at least 40% of the whole registered electorate. No one seemed to notice that by this rule, no Westminster government in living memory would have been legitimate! As it was, the result left nobody satisfied – and the retreat of the Conservative government from its commitment to devolution and from the explicit promise that a better scheme would be produced, frustrated any hope for swift action.

In previous chapters I have presented my life – or at least, glimpses of it – as a learning process, a progressive story understood fully only in retrospect, that prepared me with the insights and skills which I have been able to use to some effect in the Scottish Constitutional Convention. It is just as valid, however, to see another related pattern in retrospect. In each major sector of my life, in India and in Coventry, I had seen a clear and challenging task to be undertaken, believed it worthwhile, and left having achieved it. What was my task in Scotland to be?

Soon after my arrival I articulated it in this way: "To raise the profile of Scottish Churches Council and make it an effective instrument of the Kingdom of God in Scotland, and a means to unity both in the church and in the nation." For those unfamiliar with the language of the Christian faith, the concept Kingdom of God can be simply defined as where God's will is done on earth as it is in heaven. This means it is very much a social, political and economic concept and not just a religious one, since if we believe in God at all, His will clearly cannot be limited to what happens in church or in our private lives.

I found the Scottish Churches Council a body weak, ignored and marginalised. The churches paid lip service to an ecumenical organisation then took little notice of it. Early in my time I recall a conversation with the Reverend John McIndoe, at that time convenor of the influential Church and Nation Committee of the Church of Scotland. He told me that until I came on the scene, he hardly knew that the Scottish Churches Council existed. Certainly it had exerted no influence on his work and thinking.

Early in my time back in Scotland, I paid a visit to one of the great figures of the Scottish churches, the Reverend Archie Craig, then nearly ninety years old and living in retirement in Doune. His mind was as sharp as ever and I hope I was able to take to heart the memorable advice he gave me. "The danger of your job, laddie," he said, "is that of second rate omnicompetence." He was right. The temptation to try to do everything and therefore to do it badly was always present, but I determined that while the Scottish Churches Council must be a catalyst for the churches to do things together in every possible area, there were just a few priorities that we ourselves could follow.

Much of my time was, of course, occupied with Christian gatherings, synods and the like. I seemed constantly to be attending meetings of one kind or another, in all nine of the member churches! Frequently I recalled the question my infant daughter had once asked my wife during our days in India. "Why is it," she piped up, "that other people's daddies go to work and my daddy goes to meetings?" I have often wondered.

The second half of the eighties was taken up increasingly with the so-called 'inter-church process'. This was an attempt to bring the churches closer together and to bring the Roman Catholic church fully into the ecumenical family, which in the end succeeded and resulted in the creation of new – and we hope stronger – ecumenical bodies in all four nations of the United Kingdom.

I suppose even this experience was relevant to the constitutional debate, for our efforts resulted in a quasi-federal structure for the inter-church bodies in the UK. Not only did the Roman Catholic church both in Scotland and in England agree to be part of the new bodies, but for the first time the Scottish, Welsh and Irish councils were joined by the creation of an English equivalent, known as Churches Together in England, which left the new British body (the Council of Churches for Britain and Ireland) free to be truly 'British' and to concern itself with those things which covered at least two or more of the four nations involved.

Was this, I wonder, the churches' answer to the West Lothian question, or perhaps the West Iona question? Certainly in the political sphere, so long as no 'English' assembly, or regional assemblies in England exist but some form of legislatures in Northern Ireland, Scotland or Wales do exist, the West Lothian question remains an anomaly. The willingness of the Conservative government to allow a degree of home rule in Northern Ireland – and certainly to allow the people to decide what they want – means that the anomaly has already been accepted in principle.

In Scotland's case it is, in any event, a much smaller anomaly than the injustice in which we have lived for fifty years, highlighted certainly in the last eighteen. It is often said that people get the government they deserve. Unfortunately we in Scotland have repeatedly got the government England deserves!

Perhaps more important for the subject of this book however, was my political development at this time. The deep sense of the need to change an unjust society, which goes back to my school and university days, was given shape and precision by my living experiences in India and in Coventry's international work. India taught me about development – that the divisions between rich and poor nations, and between rich and poor within nations, were not accidents of fate but the direct results of a system of world development that spawned beneficiaries and victims. Coventry taught me about peace and reconciliation – that the divisions of history, race, colour, ideology, language and national identity – which should be the source of rich and welcome diversity in harmony – had become open wounds of division which could only be healed by a painful and costly process.

I therefore returned to Scotland with the firm belief that the two great 'wounds of history' which were global and universal in their effect, and from which no man, woman or child anywhere in the world could escape at the end of the twentieth century, were wounds which could effectively be terminal and destroy our world.

The first of these remains the north/south divide. We live in a single world system which has effectively created two worlds – in which extremes of affluence and grinding poverty coexist and in which the gap between rich and poor is steadily increasing year by year, fuelled by the enormous burden of debt repayment which effectively ensures that the net flow of wealth is still constantly from the poor to the rich. Incidentally this gap is increasingly seen also in the fourth world, that is in the growing army of poor, marginalised and dispossessed within our own affluent industrial societies. This may be modified by the safety net of the welfare state – but the net is in disrepair.

The second great wound that is both universal and inescapable is the ecological crisis. If the first wound above is horizontal, between people, groups and nations, the second is vertical, between humanity and the earth itself. The ecological crisis is more than simply care for the environment. It has been defined as "expanding economic activity beyond the capacity of the natural system to sustain it."

By the time I reached Scotland in 1981 I was convinced not only that these were the two great issues of our time but that they were closely and inextricably connected and interdependent. We are facing not a series of different and separate problems, but the symptoms of a single human crisis that threatens the future of us all and of all our children. The years in Scotland were to strengthen that conviction. Before arriving back in Scotland in a published address I gave at a conference in the United States during 1975, I argued that the gross product of the world had tripled in the previous twenty years and said, "in so doing, it put a whole range of strains on the natural system which were hardly even dreamed of a generation ago. We now face the rapid exhaustion of many scare resources, global waste and pollution, the extinction or endangering of many species of animal and bird, a world where a whole range of environmentally induced illnesses are rampant, and even possible and little understood climactic changes in the earth's atmosphere."

Though I was not alone in uttering these warnings, they were dismissed as the utopian mutterings of marginal cranks. It is only now in the nineties that sustainable development has become respectable – the language of government, of industrialists, and of all who wish to be up to date and trendy! Unfortunately, not everyone who uses the words understands the implications.

The most dramatic and compelling statement of the global dilemma came in my hearing from the lips of the man I regard as one of the few true statesmen of this generation. On February 16th 1987, I sat in the great hall of the Kremlin, as one of some six hundred delegates to an international forum, and listened to the words of Mikhail Gorbachev. It was a distinguished audience from all over the world and every area of human endeavour. The temptation to name drop is overwhelming – indeed from where I sat in the Kremlin I could see, not far from me, such varied characters as Gregory Peck, Yoko Ono, Graham Greene and Billy Graham. It was typical of the western media present that, in their anxiety to find some reference to immediate political events, they missed the enormous philosophical sweep and importance of what Gorbachev said.

For the first time in its history, he argued, humankind as a whole and not only individual representatives, has begun to feel that it is one entity, to see global relationships between man, society and nature, and to assess the consequences of our activities. The policy of deterrence, for example, considered in an historical context, does not reduce the risk of military conflict. In fact, it increases that risk. Gorbachev's main thesis was that existence of nuclear weapons combined with the other major threats to human life mean that "humankind has lost its immortality." In a world where three quarters of the countries are deep in debt, while a handful of states are omnipotent, can one live content? His conclusion is clear – he called for not just a nuclear free world, but a world of justice and of ecological care, "for the sake of the immortality of human civilisation."

It is, I believe, one of the prime tragedies of our time that the depths of Gorbachev's thinking and reasoning were never really heard in the West or indeed in his own country. Thus the tragedy is that his vision, understandably and perhaps even in the long run inevitably, destroyed his own society. The gradual change he hoped for proved impossible and this great man was succeeded by a self-seeking buffoon in Yeltsin. The even greater tragedy is that his challenge, which was to all nations and to both sides of the Cold War, was never heard or applied in the west and that we have by and large continued along that path to the end of human immortality.

Thus my years at Dunblane and at Scottish Churches Council were taken up, partly on ecumenicism, but partly in pursuing these great issues of peace, poverty and pollution. In 1990, the inter-church process, which we had been pursuing with such energy for several years, bore fruit. Scottish Churches Council was wound up and succeeded by the new inter-church ecumenical body ACTS. The chief difference in the new body was that for the first time the Roman Catholic church was a full partner – though sadly that led to the withdrawal of the Baptist Union of Scotland. There were, however, other more subtle differences – primarily that the new organisation was much more firmly under the direct control of the official churches. I felt I had accomplished my main aims in the Scottish Churches Council. It had been given a much higher profile, accepted throughout Scottish society, and had succeeded in creating an even more representative and stronger body to succeed.

It left me, however, with a personal decision to make. Since the new organisation was legally and officially in continuity with the old, I could have continued as General Secretary, as my counterparts in Wales and Ireland did. My decision that the time had come to move on was made on two grounds, one negative and one positive. The negative reason was the feeling that my freedom of action would have been considerably more curtailed in the new body with its stricter rules. Scottish Churches Council had given a degree of creative freedom which allowed me to take initiatives and even occasionally stick my neck out a bit! In the new body I would have had constantly to have looked over my shoulder to discover what all the church leaders would allow me to do. That was not my way. In any case, I was by this time convinced that my role in the Convention was crucial and that a continuity of leadership there was necessary if the painstaking efforts were to be crowned in the end with success.

There was another and more compelling positive reason for my decision. By 1990 I had become convinced that all the global problems that threatened to overwhelm human life in our time – the problems of the growing gap between rich and poor nations, the evermore fearsome weapons of mass destruction, the population explosion, and the problems caused by environmental pollution – were all symptoms of a society in a decline which was in danger of becoming terminal; that there was a single human disease which had to be identified and cured, if ours was not to be the last generation to enjoy any real quality of life, and possibly even the last generation, full stop.

I was convinced that the single great issue of the end of the twentieth century was whether we could find our way to new social, economic and political structures that would allow us to choose life instead of death for our children. This was accompanied by an equally clear conviction that the churches must put this at the very centre of their life and work.

I asked myself what seemed to me then, and still does, to be the central question of our time – Can we build in time the economic, political and social institutions which are capable of controlling technology for human goals, of reversing our ecological decline, and of giving justice and a minimum standard of human life to all the world's people?

My successor, as General Secretary of the new body ACTS in 1990, was the Reverend Maxwell Craig – an old friend and colleague with whom I had worked closely and happily over the years, especially during the period when he was the convenor of the Church and Nation Committee of the Church of Scotland. We had been members together both of the Constitutional Steering Committee that gave birth to the Convention, and of the earlier Standing Commission on the Scottish Economy which, with its breadth of membership, served as a model for the design of the Scottish Constitutional Convention.

For myself, I took a leap of faith – and with virtually no resources except the blessing of ACTS and a small financial grant, started up an organisation called KAIROS (Centre for a Sustainable Society). The subtitle is clear enough, but I am often asked what the name means. Let me at once scotch the rumour that it stands, as my daughter's sense of humour suggested when we started, for "Kenyon's Attempt to Interfere in the Running of Scotland." It is a Greek word which means time, but in the special sense of the moment of decision and change. In the Greek of the New Testament there are two words for time. *Chronos* means simply the passing of the hours. *Kairos* means that decisive moment of change – that moment in the affairs of humankind which in the words of Shakespeare "taking up the flood leads on to fortune." Thus Jesus weeps over Jerusalem before his crucifixion because "they did not recognise God's moment when it came." To call the new initiative KAIROS, was therefore to build it on the conviction that we must live as we approach the new millennium, through such a time.

Largely through the support of Strathclyde Regional Council and particularly its leader at that time, Councillor Charles Gray, my wife and I were able to move physically into a building in Norse Road in Glasgow, rented from the Council, which served both as our home and the offices of the new initiative. With the help of small grants from the churches, local authorities and others, we were able by the middle of 1991, to identify that the most important issue in the immediate future was the preparation for the Earth Summit (officially the United Nations Conference on

Environment and Development) due to be held in Rio in Brazil in mid-1992.

This was already being billed by its organisers as: "our best chance, perhaps our last chance, to save the earth." Certainly it echoed the convictions of KAIROS by bringing together the issues of economic development and poverty on the one hand, with those of the environment, pollution, global warming and biodiversity on the other. Since it is my hope – and indeed my dearest desire – that Scotland's parliament will make our nation one of the pioneers in working towards a genuine integrated strategy for sustainable development, I believe it is relevant to outline what, though KAIROS, I was able to achieve in this area. In July 1991 we called together in Glasgow City Chambers, a meeting to discuss the idea of a Scottish charter for the environment, the quality of life, and for a Scottish environmental forum.

The twenty six people present represented COSLA, local authorities, STUC, the churches, and a number of key voluntary agencies and agreed to set up the Scottish Environmental Forum. This was the beginning of a body which has now become the recognised umbrella Scottish organisation for sustainable development. KAIROS, based on our tiny office with a single secretary, agreed to coordinate this initiative and set up a small working group. By January 1992 we had published six leaflets called *Pledges for the Planet* which were widely circulated throughout Scotland – and more than 20,000 pledges were made, to change behaviour in areas like use of transport, recycling, purchasing and so on. Strathclyde Regional Council backed this up by conducting a youth programme which they actually called KAIROS – Partners in Power, which involved thousands of young people throughout the region and led to the production of a youth charter for environmental quality of life and resulted in six young people being selected actually to travel to Rio for the Earth Summit and for its related events.

By May 1992, through a widespread process of consultation the forum was able to adopt, at least as a draft for discussion, the

Scottish Charter for the Environment and Quality of Life, which was duly sent as our contribution to the Earth Summit in Rio, which met in June 1992. Was that impressive meeting, attended by heads of government from all over the world, including our own Prime Minister, a turning point or just another set of fine words? The jury on that question is still out. Certainly, Agenda 21, the final document of the Rio conference is lengthy, repetitive and full of qualifications – and certainly has not, five years later, led to the major changes it calls for. Nevertheless, it is a major step forward. For the first time in it, the leader of the world's nations recognise the interdependent nature of the issues we all face, and set out at least some radical first steps to solve them. Basically, it is a call for sustainable development, for major policy changes to save the earth. It envisages the progressive integration of economic, social and environmental issues in the pursuit of development that is economically efficient, socially equitable and responsible, and environmentally sound. KAIROS is now working for a sustainable society in Scotland.

CHAPTER 13

Now for the Hard Bit

The first meeting of the Scottish Constitutional Convention on March 30th 1989 elected Liberal Democrat MP David Steel and Labour's Harry Ewing as joint chairs – both of course now have Lord attached to them as a prefix to their names. I was also elected chair of the executive committee. I warned the representatives that a great deal of hard work lay ahead. As to the urgency of our task, I recalled to them an experience I had shortly before, when visiting a deprived inner-city area. I was about to leave a group of residents when one woman called after me, "this time do not betray us."

I am delighted to say that despite the difficulties we have faced we have not betrayed the Scottish public. I have to admit that since that inspiring day in March 1989, we have sometimes come perilously close to that betrayal. It has been a long road, we have kept right on to its end and in the end we have kept faith.

The euphoria of the day quickly subsided and the harsh reality of the work that lay ahead dawned on those who had participated, including the media observers who pointed out the work that had to be done and the agreements reached before the Convention could claim to have done anything.

It was natural that our political opponents would try to write us off. Malcolm Rifkind, then Secretary of State for Scotland is reported to have remarked with some confidence that if the Convention really succeeded in achieving agreement on a plan for Scotland's future he would jump off the roof of the Scottish Office. Despite our successes I have never asked Malcolm Rifkind to carry out his promise. I have to say that it has saddened me to see how Malcolm Rifkind has moved on this issue. Without being too unkind it appears that he has allowed himself to be guided by the prevailing noises coming initially from above him in the Conservative Party, namely Mrs Thatcher. After all, he did vote Yes in the 1979 Devolution Referendum, and he is on record as stating that he found federalism "intellectually appealing". His move on the Scottish constitutional issue mirrors the way he has also changed his views on Europe, in recent years seeming to wish to establish his Eurosceptic leanings.

But even on our own side Donald Dewar described the Convention as a "high risk strategy" pointing out that there were major differences of policy, and sometimes principle which could not be wished away. "These will," said Donald, "have to be explored perhaps in some cases finessed or sidelined." Donald has always been recognised as a careful, canny and highly responsible politician. But he spoke from the heart when he said:

"Throughout my political life there has been a need to recognise and harness the feeling of Scottish identity which has grown and strengthened over the years. I believe there is an opportunity here which Scotland expects us to grasp."

Malcolm Bruce, leader of the Scottish Liberal Democrats also warned of the difficulties which lay ahead but at the same time said, "to decry the venture as doomed to government rejection and failure was to underestimate the force of popular support." Members of the Scottish press also warned us of the hard road ahead. The *Scotsman* editorials on two successive days were headed 'Convention off to good start', and 'Now for the hard bit'. The editorial struck a note of realism:

> "These difficult times are not hard to predict. When the searchlight of public attention has been switched off and the discussion falls to detailed argument then it might be easy to lose sight of the expected destination."

The *Herald* too warned that the Convention, though "no improvised ill thought-out affair," would have the task to " keep up public and political pressure." Such hardheaded realism was quite correct, and welcome, but in the period immediately following the first Convention meeting, we received plenty of encouragement from different sectors of Scottish society.

Only a few weeks later the annual congress of the Scottish Trade Union Congress unanimously backed our efforts. An example of how the Convention had started to act as a catalyst in Scottish society came during the Congress when Malcolm Bruce MP, and leader of the Scottish Liberal Democrats was given a warm welcome. The STUC had long been seen as a firm stalwart of the Labour Party but the delegates applauded when Malcolm warned that proportional representation was central to the success of a future Scottish Parliament. These eight short years ago proportional representation was not an electoral concept popular with trade union activists accustomed to voting on the basis of first-past-the-post. Malcolm told the delegates it was crucial to ensure that a parliament in Scotland was genuinely representative of the country's geographical and political diversity. We simply could not sell a parliament that did not offer fair representation, he told them. "Even though we may have differing views as to the kind of government we want for Scotland," Malcolm concluded, "we can join forces to campaign for our own parliament."

While welcoming a new ally in the Liberal Democrats the

Congress went on to criticise the decision of the Scottish National Party not to participate. "They are not entitled," said Scottish President of the National Union of Mineworkers to applause, "to opt out of the fight and divide the nation on such an essential matter as home rule."

More support came from the General Assembly of the Church of Scotland when they met in May. The General Assembly gave massive moral and historical endorsement to both the *Claim of Right for Scotland* and the Scottish Constitutional Convention in a report presented by the Church and Nation Committee. The Committee provided a closely reasoned, historically and theologically based argument for the moral imperative of the Scottish understanding of sovereignty. The committee members spoke of a "crisis more real than apparent within the constitutional foundations of Scotland and the United Kingdom. The crisis is real in that it involves a clear conflict between totally opposing notions of sovereignty in the Scottish and English constitutional traditions."

They quoted Lord Hailsham's view that the British State has become "an elective dictatorship" and concluded "from a Scottish constitutional and theological perspective this English constitutional tradition of State absolutism has always been unacceptable in theory. It is now intolerable in practice."

To reinforce their argument the Church and Nation Committee quoted the late judge, Lord President Cooper of Culross who is regarded by many as the greatest Scots lawyer this century. In a 1953 judgement on John McCormick's attempt to drop the II from EIIR, he stated, "The principle of the unlimited sovereignty of parliament is a distinctively English principle which has no counterpart in Scottish constitutional law." This argument found favour with the Church and Nation Committee members who declared:

> "It is our conclusion that it is not possible to resolve
> the question of the democratic control of Scottish

> affairs and the setting up of a Scottish Assembly apart
> from a fundamental shift in our constitutional thinking
> away from the notion of the unlimited or absolute
> sovereignty of the British Parliament towards the
> historic and reformed constitutional principle of
> limited or relative sovereignty."

On this basis the committee recommended that the Church of Scotland should resolve to participate fully in the work of the Constitutional Convention on the grounds that "a Constitutional Convention with the authority of national support grows out of the Scottish constitutional tradition of popular sovereignty, understood in the medieval and reformation Scottish Christian traditions as existing under the divine sovereignty." The committee expressed the view that the Convention offered the best way forward towards realising the General Assembly's often expressed desire that the affairs of Scotland should be subject to the democratic control of a Scottish Assembly.

The General Assembly not only decided to receive this report but also went further to pass the following resolution by a large majority:

> "The General Assembly reaffirms the tradition of
> theological reflection on Constitutional matters
> outlined in the report and its view that the Scottish
> people should be accorded a greater say in the
> Government of Scotland through a democratically
> elected assembly within the United Kingdom; and
> instructs the Church and Nation Committee to
> continue this reflection in cooperation with the other
> bodies which are discussing the constitutional future
> of Scotland, including the proposals set out in *A
> Claim of Right for Scotland*."

It was largely because of the activities of the church representatives on the Convention that the Convention has begun with the radical *Claim of Right* statement rather than simply a political message.

During the debate at the General Assembly the Rev MacKay Nimmo of Dundee had illustrated Scotland's long tradition of limited sovereignty which came from the people when he recalled in a humorous fashion that in the Declaration of Arbroath of 1320 the Scots had told even the great Robert the Bruce – "Awright, you're the King, but if you dinnae dae what yer tellt yer on the buroo."

As I have said in an earlier chapter, the second Claim of Right in Scotland's history in 1842 was made by the General Assembly of the Church of Scotland itself when the gathering rejected the right of the Westminster Parliament to impose patronage on Scotland. The Claim led directly to what was known as the Great Disruption in which the Church of Scotland was split from top to bottom for some eighty years. Only finally in 1922 did Parliament take the remarkable and unprecedented step of recognising the Church of Scotland's freedom from Parliamentary control of its own affairs. Indeed one of the arguments of the General Assembly report was "if the Established National Church of Scotland has won recognition from the British State that State sovereignty does not extend to the Church's own affairs, may the concession to the notion of society where sovereignty and autonomy are distributed among several bodies not be extended to the United Kingdom itself, and to national affairs within its multinational state?"

This argument is of course greatly strengthened by the *de facto* sharing of power represented by the changing European Union and by the doctrine of subsidiarity which is such a fundamental tenet of most advanced European thinking. Subsidiarity is the philosophy which believes that decisions should be taken at the lowest level practical in society, encouraging governments to devolve power to the people. Scotland and her Church clearly stand shoulder to shoulder with most of Europe in rejecting the centralised and archaic doctrines that maintain the power of the British State, of the Crown in Parliament, without any secure basis of alternative power and without any checks or balances.

It was an irony not lost on many Scots that John Major as Prime Minister argued for subsidiarity to be applied to the European Parliament in Brussels, but he believed that such devolving of power by Brussels ended in London. In several speeches during the 1997 General Election campaign he made scathing references to the concept of a Europe of the Regions, a concept which is growing in strength throughout the rest of Europe but one which successive Conservative Governments since 1979 turned their back on.

Although I have written in this chapter about the support given by the General Assembly of the Church of Scotland it would be wrong to give the impression that they alone among the Churches supported the work of the Convention. Initially when I had begun to take an active part in the lead up to the formation of the Convention I had been General Secretary of the Scottish Churches Council. This was a body which represented nine Churches but did not include the Roman Catholic Church.

The Churches involved at that time were the Church of Scotland, Scottish Episcopal Church, Baptist Union, Scottish Congregational Union, United Free Church of Scotland, Society of Friends (Quakers), United Reformed Church, Methodist, and the Salvation Army. At the time I was approached to join the constitutional steering committee I told the members that it was my intention to be involved, and received their support. Twice a year I gave them a report of what first the steering committee was doing, and later the Convention, and they always backed me.

The Catholic Church was not involved in the Council of Churches at that time but originally Bishop Devine agreed to take part in the constitutional steering committee though he later withdrew because of pressure of other work. The Catholic Bishops in Scotland did not replace him. There may have been within the Catholic Church at that time a certain amount of wariness among the bishops about any move to devolve political power to Scotland.

Catholic education plays an important part in Catholic Church life, and of course is backed by the Catholic Education Bill (1919), an arrangement which the Catholic Church would not wish to see disturbed. However the Council of Churches was replaced in 1990 by Action of Churches Together in Scotland (ACTS) and the Roman Catholic Church joined this body. They also appointed Tim Duffy of the Scottish Justice and Peace Commission to be their representative on the Convention.

It is true to say that all the Scottish Christian churches have broadly supported the work of the Convention and have played an important role in the background in shaping what has finally come out.

Chapter 14

The Devil is in the Detail

Immediately after the first Convention meeting in March 1989, the executive committee met to get down to the serious business of drawing up a scheme which would meet with the wide approval of the Scottish people.

The main parties to the Convention were included on the Executive Committee including obviously both the Labour and Scottish Liberal Democrats, the Communist Party, later to become the Democratic Left, and the Scottish Green Party. Others around the table included COSLA (Convention of Scottish Local Authorities), STUC (Scottish Trades Union Congress), the Federation of Small Businesses, churches and the Campaign for a Scottish Assembly.

In May 1989, in the same week as the General Assembly of the Church of Scotland was meeting, the executive committee announced a two stage process aimed at carrying the debate to every corner of Scotland. In the first stage, which we launched immediately, we asked over one hundred and fifty key organisations to give their opinions on the way forward. The questions put to them were genuinely open. They were asked what kind of parliament they would like to see for Scotland. None of the options including the *status quo* on the one hand and total independence on the other were ruled out at this stage.

I was quoted in the *Scotsman* newspaper by the local government correspondent as calling for:

> "widespread and very carefully planned programme of public debate and consultation throughout the nation . . . we are not in a hurry to chose a single option. Our minds are far from closed and our ears are wide open to hear all opinions. Decisions will be made on the basis of the widest possible consultation and with the real conviction that the option chosen represents the thinking of the people of Scotland and not merely of a small group."

By the time the full Convention met again on July 7, 1989 in Inverness the executive had formed five working groups, and a coordinating committee to meet in between full executive meetings so that quick decisions which might need to be taken could be dealt with. The five working parties were: Constitutional Issues, Powers and functions of the Scottish Parliament; Finance/Treasury; Women's issues; and lastly a committee to deal with public participation and support.

Most importantly a sixth working group was formed on an *ad hoc* basis to look at the special role of the islands within Scotland's proposed new constitutional structures. By the time the Convention gathered together in Inverness the committees had done important preliminary work.

The Constitutional Working Party were able to report as a result of the consultation exercise they had carried out that although they were not in the position to rule out any option, they could report that there appeared to be a strong consensus among the responses received from organisations for a Scottish Parliament within the range of options covered by devolution/ home rule / federalism.

The first report back from the powers and functions working group created a great deal of interest in that not only had they identified a considerable list of functions which they would be proposing a Scottish Parliament should be responsible for, but they asked for guidance for some of the principles to which they should be adhering. These included confirmation that the Convention should not seek to produce a devolution scheme but a decentralising one, that is, a scheme genuinely transferring power, and secure against arbitrary intervention by the United Kingdom Government. This committee also proposed that in relation to all functions to be decentralised the parliament should have both legislative and executive functions.

In the area of finance the committee responsible was obviously struggling with difficult issues and taking expert advice but had yet to come to any firm conclusions. This was not surprising.

The group on women's issues had instituted their own consultation procedure by organising a conference on A Women's Claim of Right which was destined to have a major impact on the future working of the Convention and on the scheme that was eventually proposed. The members of the group raised fundamental questions – how would 50/50 gender equality work? how could it be achieved, ensuring equal numbers of men and women in Scotland's parliament? Such an outcome could work quite differently from Westminster and be much more answerable, accessible and open to the people. They also raised an issue which was to haunt the Convention for a long time to come – that of the electoral system to be used to ensure fair and effective government.

The fact that we appointed a working group on women's issues from the start, and that this continued to be a central part of our thinking right up to the unique proposals for achieving gender balance in Scotland's parliament, is a tribute to the creative contribution made throughout by a number of women. No one would argue that the Convention itself did not reflect the gender balance we planned for the parliament but despite this the women who were on the executive played a pivotal role. Apart from Rosemary McKenna, we also had round the table, Jean McFadden, the Glasgow Councillor. We also had Isobel Lindsay, a well-known academic who despite being a prominent member of the SNP stayed in the Convention as Convener of the Campaign for a Scottish Assembly after the SNP's departure. Isobel eventually announced following the 1992 General Election that she had joined the Labour Party. Others such as Maria Fyfe, Labour MP for Glasgow Maryhill and Yvonne Strachan from the trade unions and the Women's Forum stand out in my memory from the early days of our work together. Scotland's parliament will indeed be a lively and stimulating place if it includes such women as these.

The Convention had already identified specific issues that the working groups had to look at. These included the voting system for a Scottish parliament, where we realised that consensus would be extremely difficult to achieve; the implications of a Scottish parliament on the United Kingdom; the relationship of Scotland with Europe. Other areas which we asked the groups to consider included how a Scottish parliament would actually function and the effect on business and industry. The radical suggestion of a Bill of Rights for Scotland had also been raised.

We also tackled early on the fears which we realised our opponents would attempt to raise such as higher taxation or a loss of business confidence. We stated that these fears "seem unnecessary and unjustified and the finance group will develop the detailed case for this confidence." Events since then have proved we were correct to recognise that there were forces within Scotland who would attempt to play on such fears.

Prior to the April 1992 General Election the Conservative Party suggested that companies with head offices in Scotland would transfer these to England if a Scottish parliament was established, and Lord Weir, chairman of the Weir Group, and a long-declared opponent of any form of devolved government launched a Save Our Union campaign which placed adverts in several papers during the lead-up to the election. Sadly one major insurance company stirred fear among their staff by circulating a memo stating that the creation of a Scottish parliament could have implications on their job security.

After the 1992 General Election Michael Forsyth, the Conservative Government's Secretary of State for Scotland constantly misrepresented the proposed power of a Scottish parliament to be able to raise or lower the standard rate of tax by 3p as meaning that taxation in Scotland would inevitably rise, labelling this the Tartan Tax. At the same time government ministers encouraged companies to enter the debate obviously believing that if they did, they would come out against the Convention's proposals.

Some well-known Tory supporters in the CBI lobbied to force the CBI in Scotland to make a statement on the issue. It is a mark of how the Convention has won the argument when you consider that in 1996 when Lord Younger, chairman of the Royal Bank of Scotland, and a former Tory Secretary of State for Scotland made a speech against the Convention's proposals, the bank issued a statement stressing that Lord Younger was making a personal statement and that the bank had no position on the matter.

During the 1997 election campaign both Standard Life and Scottish Widows issued statements saying that they were neither for or against a Scottish parliament. I am sure that this shift in public position was the result of the efforts that the Convention members had made to meet bodies representing business and industry to explain our scheme.

However in the summer of 1989 all this was before us. The Convention was anxious to learn from the mistakes of the ill-fated Labour Scottish Assembly proposals of 1979. It was recognised that many Scots living outside of the Central Belt viewed these with some suspicion as they had no desire to merely swap rule from the southeast of England with rule from Edinburgh.

At the July meeting of the Convention, Councillor Edwin Eunson, convener of Orkney Islands Council, reminded us that the majority of voters from both Orkney and Shetland had voted against the devolution proposals in the 1979 referendum. However both councils had come to the view that they should be involved in the Convention and the executive committee had recognised these feelings by forming an islands working group which was led by John Goodlad of the Shetlands Movement. Both councils welcomed the formation of this working group which recognised that the Convention planned to consult opinion in the islands around Scotland's coastline.

Journalist Iain MacWhirter writing in the *Scottish Government Yearbook* of 1990 wondered, "The Convention is now almost half way through its yearlong deliberations. How far along the road is it now towards the 'new body for a new age?' The Convention has been working through a series of committees trying to resolve, in a very short time, issues which were the subject of full scale Royal Commissions in the 1960s and 1970s. There are serious problems and it is not yet clear how these can be resolved."

Among the serious problems MacWhirter identified was what he considered the most pressing issue – the method of election. He pointed out that the Liberal Democrats were "employing a little bit of brinkmanship," having stated that they would withdraw from the Convention if Labour did not concede proportional representation. Quite rightly MacWhirter pointed out the difficulty this created for Labour whose dominance of Scottish politics would be seriously challenged by any proportional system. Under a proportional representation voting system, he indicated, "Labour hegemony would be ended."

The psychological hurdles that Labour had to overcome when considering a form of PR can be illustrated by the fact that in 1987 Labour won 70 per cent of the Scottish seats with only 42 per cent of the popular vote. Understandably in these circumstances many trade unionists and party activists were therefore opposed to Labour throwing away the prospect of "ever again having an absolute majority in Scotland." MacWhirter was quite correct when he identified PR as a major potential source of trouble for the Convention, though the Scottish Secretary of the Labour Party,

Murray Elder, was on record as saying that serious study of PR was "an inevitable consequence of Labour's participation in the Convention."

The political journalist also identified other potential difficulties in the area of how a Scottish parliament would be funded. "It is a complex problem," he asserted, "requiring expertise in taxation, law, accountancy, local authority finance and fiscal theory." Donald Dewar encapsulated this problem as being "how to unblock the block grant."

The article also highlighted the apathy of the Scottish electorate and also how any scheme could in any event be implemented given the then Government's continuing intransigence. This latter problem has of course been resolved with the defeat of John Major's Conservative government in 1997 which also saw the Tories lose every seat in Scotland. Given that John Major made the "defence of the Union" one of the main planks of his election campaign there can be no doubt that the Scottish electorate supports the aim of establishing a Scottish parliament, and of course following the May 1997 election, we now have a government led by Tony Blair which is committed to establishing a parliament firmly along the lines agreed by the Convention.

However on the question of apathy it has to be accepted that even in the run-up to the 1997 general election the Scottish public still did not fully understand in detail what the Convention is all about. If there has been one single failure of the Convention, at least until recently, it has been to get across to the majority of the Scottish people the enormous new hope, confidence and change for the better, that Scotland's parliament would bring and the fact that it would effect the quality of life of every man, woman and child in our nation. MacWhirter thus identified the massive problems that lay ahead and the gulf that was still between the Convention members. He summed up an attitude prevalent at the time:

"Yet for all that, the Convention can congratulate itself for having had a radical impact on Scottish politics in a remarkably short time. The transformation of Labour's attitude is almost entirely the consequence of the Convention experience, which has helped Labour shake off the discredited doctrines of devolution . . . the party is now talking the language of 'entrenched powers' and 'constitutional guarantees'. The closely argued paragraphs of the *Claim of Right for Scotland* helped Labour discover its new Scottish policy for good or ill."

There is no doubt that during this demanding phase our opponents sat back and waited confidently for what they thought would be our inevitable failure and collapse. I made the solemn if somewhat dramatic vow that the Convention would fail over my dead body.

Work was proceeding, not only in the business meetings of the working groups but also in our continued public consultation procedures. Towards the end of 1990 we produced two further documents, the first, a leaflet, 300,000 copies of which were distributed, was headed *A Parliament for Scotland*. This invited a public debate on the subject and a request that people make their views known to us. This turned out not to be as successful as our first consultation effort among Scottish organisations, but it nevertheless did result in a substantial response which confirmed the majority desire for a Scottish Parliament with real and entrenched powers firmly within the United Kingdom. This option became the clear objective of the Convention from this point onwards.

Would that still have been the case if SNP on the one hand, and bodies such as the CBI on the other, had joined the Convention when they were invited to do so? This is clearly a question to which we will never know the answer, but the clear evidence of the most widespread piece of public consultation that has been undertaken in recent years, made it clear that the majority of Scottish organisations, and indeed the Scottish public, wanted to remain within the Union but to have democratic and permanent control over their own affairs. The consensus was clearly around this point of view.

The second document we produced at this time was a 103 page Consultation Document and Report to the Scottish People which outlined the findings of the various working groups and asked for opinions on them. The result of this consultation process was, that when the Convention met for the third time in January 1990 it had the benefit of thousands of responses from organisations and individuals throughout Scotland. This gave us the confidence that the main lines of thought developed by the working groups faithfully reflected the thinking of the majority of the Scottish electorate.

Each of the working groups owed much to the character of the person who chaired it and each threw up at least one issue that was a hard nut to crack. The constitutional group was chaired by Bob McCreadie, a young Liberal Democrat lawyer who had previously been a member of the Labour Party. His incisive intelligent and detailed thinking was matched only by his fiery temperament and his tendency to lose the rag with those who were not quick to grasp and agree with his points. I recall presiding over ding-dong battles between Murray Elder, general secretary of the Scottish Labour Party and Bob McCreadie, the chief negotiator for the Liberal Democrats. Where Bob was fiery and inclined to have a very short fuse before he exploded, Murray by contrast would make his case firmly, but with a quiet calmness. Both were in their own ways, absolutely sincere and skilled negotiators and it was, for me, a political education to have to hold the line between them. The early successes in achieving consensus on the central constitutional issues was certainly due to the chemistry we managed to generate together.

This group thought long and hard about the thorny question of entrenchment – that is, how could we ensure that Scotland's parliament and its powers were established in such a way that they could not be removed or altered by any future Westminster government except with the explicit consent of the people and parliament of Scotland. Given the *Claim of Right* and its declaration of the sovereignty of the Scottish people, it is not surprising that the issue of entrenchment was to be one over which the Convention would agonize in the years to come.

The working group on powers and functions of the Scottish Parliament was chaired by Rosemary McKenna, then Provost of Cumbernauld, and included the only card-carrying Conservative on the executive, John Jamieson, an independent councillor who was at that time Convener of Dumfries and Galloway Region.

In their interim report the working group on powers and functions described the two approaches they considered taking when looking at how the division should be made between a Scottish Parliament and Westminster. They stated:

> "there is more than one way of approaching the range of powers and functions which should reside with Scotland's Parliament. We have considered what is effectively the reverse approach – i.e. identifying a core of functions which are to be retained by Westminster, with the remainder of the functions either being clearly within the ambit of the Scottish Parliament or a matter for further discussion.
>
> "Whilst this may be an appropriate approach if there are parallel discussions in other parts of the United Kingdom, the conclusion has been reached that at the present time it is more practical to have the prospective powers of the Scottish Parliament identified positively."

In April 1990 I addressed the STUC annual congress and told the delegates:

> ". . . there is a consensus for a Scottish Parliament within the United Kingdom but with extensive and well-defined powers that cannot be removed by any future Westminster government. That much is already clear,

but there is a long way to go yet. Before a scheme can
be published, we hope later this year, there remain the
difficult questions of Scottish revenue-raising powers,
and perhaps most difficult of all, proportional representation. We must not allow the opportunity to slip out of
hands, not let party or other self interest destroy our
unity, at least until we have achieved our goal. Once we
have a Scottish parliament to speak for Scotland, we can,
and doubtless will get back to our old scrapping!"

At long last after what must have seemed a tortuous and difficult
process, the executive was ready by the autumn of 1990 to present
a package for discussion by the full Convention. It was agreed that
there should be a meeting to debate the package on September
27th, then to hold a more celebratory event on St Andrew's Day
November 30th, at which the completed scheme would be
presented formally to the people of Scotland.

In the lead up to the September meeting of the full
Convention meeting the *Scotsman* reported:

"It has been a long and tortuous route, one littered with
many political obstacles, but the Scottish Constitutional
Convention is now within sight of reaching the end of
the first crucial stage of its journey.

"Agreement is expected on detailed proposals which
will draw together and present as a single package the
various issues, like powers, financing and voting
arrangements, which have been the subject of debate
and not a little controversy during the eighteen months
since the Convention was first established."

The report went on:

"There has been compromise, some fudging of issues
and there are still some matters, notably on the role of

electoral reform and the role of Westminster
Parliament, that are yet to be finally resolved. But it
appears that the broad measure of agreement now
achieved will enable to Convention to unveil its final
plan at a celebratory event on St Andrew's Day."

At the September 1990 meeting in the Queens Hall, Edinburgh the Convention faced up to the probability that the first part of its remit would be completed by St Andrew's Day and that the time had come to move decisively on to the second part, securing the approval of the Scottish people. To that end, Harry Conroy, the former General Secretary of the National Union of Journalists had been appointed Campaign Director at the start of the month and given the task of promoting the Convention's proposals to the people in the period coming up to the 1992 General Election.

The broad package presented under the title *Towards Scotland's Parliament* to the Queens Hall meeting was for a legislature with power over major areas of life. These were defined as encompassing "sole or shared responsibility for all functions except those retained to the United Kingdom Parliament. The primary matters retained to the UK Parliament would be defence, foreign affairs, central economic and fiscal responsibilities and social security policy."

Looking back at this document the actual proposals were underdeveloped and covered only four pages of text. At the time we regarded it as definitive and indeed expected it to be implemented had the Tories not won the 1992 General Election. In the light of our later work, and especially compared against the present document *Scotland's Parliament, Scotland's Right*, there is no doubt that *Towards Scotland's Parliament* was very much like a first draft.

We were probably wiser than we knew in calling the first document *Towards Scotland's Parliament* for despite our hard work over twenty months, it revealed the strains and pressures we were under and can only be seen now as a stage on the way. Bitterly disappointed as we were at the failure in 1992 to achieve change, an incoming Labour government would have had an unenviable task in turning our proposals then into effective legislation. The extra five years we won by that failure, however depressing at the time, gave us the opportunity to produce something very much stronger and more viable.

The weaknesses in *Towards Scotland's Parliament* were of two kinds, both largely overcome since. They were problems, both of commission and omission, both in mistakes in what we did say, and in vast areas we left unsaid. With the benefit of hindsight we really did need six or seven years to do justice to our task. We have a better scheme because of it, so Scotland may be the gainer after all, even if we have had to wait rather longer for our Right.

The main weakness in our original proposals was the rather over-complex financial arrangements, whereby, apart from the marginal right to vary income tax, Scotland was to be financed by assigning all Income Tax and VAT collected in Scotland, and then topping this up by a further allocation based on the equalisation principle. This would in the end have had exactly the same effect as the scheme we now propose, that is, to give Scotland her assigned proportion of UK revenue, but coming "as of right" based on the principle of equalisation. It is important to state that this is a principle upheld by governments of all political colours, that Scotland's share is calculated on the basis of needs, calculated by an agreed formula, and not on a proportional per capita basis. Though the end effect would have been the same, the system we then proposed would have been cumbersome, bureaucratic and complex. What we later came to propose is recognised by expert opinion to be much simpler and workable and achieves the same goal of providing stable finances for Scotland.

There were also glaring and open omissions but we had come a long way, in agreeing that we could not accept the present first-past-the-post system even if we could only rather lamely promise to find a better one.

CHAPTER 15

Hope Springs Eternal

The Convention grew accustomed to being told by the media that the "hard bit" still lay ahead. This was the forecast of at least one national newspaper the day after the inaugural meeting of the Convention in 1989, and the same prognosis was made twenty months later when the Constitutional Convention met for the seventh time to present to the Scottish people the consensus document *Towards Scotland's Parliament*.

They were correct both times. We had indeed embarked on what was to be a very hard and stony road, and the amazing thing is not that we stumbled and quarrelled often along the way, but that somehow we managed to remain "pilgrims together". Along the way we may often have threatened to part company, but the ability to argue things through to a common mind, has become something of a habit. Having travelled so far over such difficult ground, I have no doubt that we will keep right on to the end of the road.

At the inaugural meeting I had rather naively predicted that we would take "perhaps a year" to reach our consensus. I was then, as so often, rather over-optimistic. In the end it took twenty months of widespread consultation, hard bargaining and detailed discussion to produce *Towards Scotland's Parliament* which can now be seen as effectively the first draft of our proposals. At the time we assumed that they would be the only draft, given the expectation of a change of government following the 1992 General Election.

During this period as we approached consensus on most issues, there was a gradual change in the attitude of our opponents. Those who had refused to be part of the Convention and had remained aloof and cynical had begun by ignoring us in the obvious expectation that we would simply go away, believing that our motley crew of strange fellow pilgrims would soon fall out, and certainly not reach any destination. As it became clear that this was not going to happen they stopped ignoring us and instead began to attack.

On the eve of our celebratory event in Glasgow's Royal Concert Hall the Scottish Green Party threw, if not a spanner, at least a small tack in the works when it suspended its membership of the Convention. The Greens had been part of the consensus which had worked to finalise the document, and although they walked out of the Convention they did not disown everything we had achieved. In a letter to Bruce Black, the Convention's secretary, they stated, "We have respected and encouraged the process of consensus by which the Convention has reached decisions, and in so doing have had to compromise on many issues."

The fall out came about because at the executive committee a few days prior to the St Andrew's Day meeting the Greens representative Philip O'Brien had pressed the Convention to commit itself to holding a multi-option referendum before moving to legislation for a Scottish parliament.

Since the question of a referendum has raised its head on many occasions and is now very much in the political arena, it is interesting to record the response of the executive. "In present circumstances," explained a letter to the Greens from the Convention secretary, "it is clear that the way to test public opinion is at the General Election, when parties endorsing the Convention's proposals will be making a manifesto commitment to secure the earliest possible implementation of the proposals. Whether a referendum is necessary after that – and what form it may take – will depend on the outcome of the General Election and the willingness of the Westminster Parliament to accept the clearly expressed mandate of the Scottish people."

The Green Party however, felt that this rejection of their proposal for a multi-option referendum was of such importance that they would have to withdraw. "We were honoured to sign the *Claim of Right*," the Greens replied, "which enshrined the right of the people of Scotland to decide their future. We could not now sign a document which failed to endorse that principle. We have been under considerable pressure from the Convention to sign on Friday but this we cannot do. We will now with regret suspend participation in the Convention." In 1995, the Greens were welcomed back into the Convention.

The SNP were also pursuing this line and we will see in later chapters, how this question of a pre-legislative referendum was to be raised again, both immediately after the Conservative victory in the General Election of 1992, and in the Labour Party's proposals in a unilateral policy decision in the summer of 1996

Within days of the Convention's meeting, however, a much more significant event was to occur in British politics. The wicked witch of the south was slain. Mrs Thatcher was defeated as leader of the Conservative Party and succeeded by what some might have called the human face of Toryism. Throughout Scotland there was an almost palpable distrust and dislike of Maggie but on that day when she failed to gain a majority in the first ballot by a measly two votes, I found myself singing to her, "Will you no come back again?" My lament for Maggie sprang from my fear then and I believe borne out by events, that those two Conservative MPs who refused to give her the majority she needed would condemn Scotland to five more years of division and despair. I remain convinced that had Mrs Thatcher continued in power, there would have been a change of government in the 1992 election and the Convention's first scheme would have been polished up and implemented.

It is worth reflecting briefly on Mrs Thatcher's role in Scottish politics. She was, I firmly believe, the unwilling and unwitting midwife of Scotland's new-found community of purpose. This was not only because of the strident tones of her provincial English nationalism, which obviously meant much to southern voters and to the tabloid press, especially after the Falkland's adventure.

However her style fell on Scottish ears with all the appeal of the wicked stepmother offering Snow White the poisoned apple. Her style certainly repelled most Scots. Witness the glee and instant recognition with which my remark "what happens when that other voice we all know so well says 'We say No, and We are the State?' at the Convention's inauguration was met when I answered my own question with 'We say Yes, and We are the People.' "

Scotland's rejection of her imperious style was based on a much more profound understanding of her political goals and ideology. She herself, I am told, was profoundly puzzled and distressed by the astonishing level of opposition and animosity she seemed to arouse in Scotland. She was unable to see that it sprang from a deeper source than simply her cultural style.

There were I think two fundamental reasons why she was midwife at the birth of something in Scotland which will grow and flourish. First we perceived that she was imposing on Scotland, not just policies broadly rejected and even detested – the Poll Tax being the single most painful and obvious example of many – but worse was the imposition of an alien ideology that rejected community and expressed itself as an attack on our distinctive systems of education and local government. This behaviour was seen in Scotland as a moral or ideological issue and not simply as a series of unpopular policies.

The second reason was even deeper – the grim centralisation of power, the determined attack on all alternative sources of real corporate power in local government and elsewhere. There was also the use of Royal prerogatives to extend ministerial control through quangos and in other ways. All this made us see with a clarity that we had never had before, that we could never again rely on the British state or live comfortably with its constitutional doctrines of the absolute authority of the crown in parliament.

Mrs Thatcher's personal crusade in which she scorned the consensus approach to politics and described her attitude as being driven by conviction politics taught us unmistakably and irreversibly that the theoretically unacceptable was now practically intolerable. We came to see that if Mrs Thatcher could so misuse the powers of her office, the crown prerogatives, the extent of patronage and the parliamentary system to cut down all real power elsewhere in the name of spurious individualism, then any future Prime Minister could do the same. We realised that our real enemy was not a particular government whatever its colour, but a constitutional system. We came to understand that our central needs, if we were to be governed justly and democratically, was not just to change the government but to change the rules.

Her failure to understand what makes Scotland tick was amply illustrated when she spoke to the General Assembly of the Church of Scotland outlining her basic moral philosophy. She revealed that she recognised nothing between the power of the state and the individual, and that she was not interested in the morality of distributing wealth. She believed in the "trickle down" theory, but not in the morality of wealth creation. Shortly before her unexpected downfall Arnold Kemp, then editor of the *Herald* wrote perceptively that "home rule sentiment does not arise from the perception that it will make us rich. It arises from deeper cultural feelings of loss and confusion. Elsewhere Mr Kemp told how his mother "used to say that it was better to live in a free country and a poor one."

For ten years the Scots had been able to find an explanation for this in the person of Thatcher who united Scotland to a degree unprecedented since the Stewarts thrust Episcopalians down our throats in the seventeenth century.

Professor Christopher Smout in his *History of the Scottish People* suggests that Mrs Thatcher has been "a scapegoat for the Scots" but this inability to understand that Scotland's Thatcher phobia was primarily cultural and not economic was unfortunately shared, if less stridently but equally fatally, by John Major and his ministers. You need look no further than the results in Scotland of the 1997 General Election, when the Conservatives were wiped out as a parliamentary party, for the proof of this statement.

It is remarkable to remember that when Mrs Thatcher was elected leader of the Conservative Party in 1975 she attended a rally in Edinburgh and pledged support for Scottish devolution with an elected assembly. She told the gathering of the party faithful: "we are absolutely in tune with the theme of devolution. The establishment of a Scottish Assembly must be a top priority to ensure that more decisions affecting Scotland are taken in Scotland by Scots." What a pity that in this at least the lady *was* for turning.

The Iron Lady's days in power had come to an end when the Convention met on St Andrew's Day, November 30th 1990 in the splendour of the newly opened Royal Concert Hall in Glasgow. The meeting began with a procession of more than fifty of the sixty-four civic heads of Scotland's local authorities, led by the Lord Provosts of our four great cities, Aberdeen, Dundee, Edinburgh and Glasgow, most of them weighed down by their chains and regalia.

The Convention's proposals were formally introduced by Harry Ewing and David Steel, the joint chairs of the Convention, and statements of endorsement were made by representatives of the six major groupings in the Convention – the Churches, the Labour Party, the Scottish Liberal Democrats, the Convention of Scottish Local Authorities, the Scottish Trades Union Congress and the Campaign for a Scottish Assembly.

John Smith, then Shadow Chancellor, on behalf of the Labour Party said that the proposals being made were "both more extensive in scope and stronger in substance than anything it had been possible to achieve in the Scotland Act which failed in 1979." Even more memorably he used for the first time a phrase that was often to be quoted especially after his untimely death. He spoke of the desire for constitutional change and a Scottish Parliament as being "the settled will of the people of Scotland."

The speeches were followed by readings and songs from prominent Scottish artists, among them William McIlvanney who read his allegorical tale *The Cowardly Lion* which slinks back into his cage afraid of the freedom on offer! It was an allegory from the past, but it came too close to the truth after the 1992 General Election result to be comfortable. Maybe the lion's courage has yet to be fully tested.

A Declaration was passed and signed by all present, reasserting the *Claim of Right* and the commitment to the remaining tasks of the Convention. The Declaration reads:

> We, gathered as the Scottish Constitutional Convention, being mindful of the Claim of Right asserted at the first meeting of the Convention on the Thirtieth Day of March Nineteen Hundred and Eighty Nine, do hereby present to the people of Scotland proposals for the establishment of Scotland's Parliament. In so doing we fulfil the first part of the Declaration adopted at that meeting in Edinburgh. We remain committed to seeking the best interests of the people of Scotland and believe our proposals achieve this.
>
> We further declare and pledge that our best endeavours and our energies will be directed at fulfilling the other elements of our declaration, namely securing the support of the people of Scotland for these proposals and ensuring implementation of the scheme as soon as may be possible.

In a month which had seen the fall of the house of Thatcher and the emergency of a new Prime Minister, I began my address to the

Convention by asserting that when the significance of all that happened that month was assessed, "the event of the greatest historical and constitutional significance, the event that will be most important for the new decade that we are about to enter, will be seen to be . . . what we are doing here together today. We have witnessed the death of an ideology. We are part of the rebirth of a nation."

I believe that, poised as we now are five years later on, in the last furlong to the establishment of a Scottish Parliament, my assertion has stood the test of time.

I then went on in my speech to announce the launching of a campaign to assure public approval of our proposals throughout Scotland. It had to be a campaign of education and awareness to show clearly that all the ills and hurts the Scottish people so resent – from Poll Tax to poverty trap, from the erosion of education to the threats to Ravenscraig – all were symptoms of how Scotland is governed. They are all constitutional questions. A Scottish parliament with the powers we proposed would have dealt with all these issues. Even our mistakes would have been our own! I ended with the words:

> "In 1707 when the Scottish parliament met for the last time in Edinburgh, Chancellor Seafield said it was 'ane end of ane auld sang'. What we do here today is only the start of a new song for Scotland and the United Kingdom, a song of remarkable harmony fully in tune with the music of the new Europe of the peoples.
> "With high hopes and with firm purpose we welcome today 'ane beginning of ane new sang'."

It was a high hope but it was longer than we thought before we heard its music clearly.

CHAPTER 16

High Hopes and Disappointment

The Conservatives had always attacked the Convention as being unrepresentative. This was rich coming from a party with a total of 10 MPs and MEPs and who had control of no local authorities. But after publication of the scheme two main lines of attack became clear and have remained remarkably consistent ever since. They can be described simply as the Tartan Tax fable and the Slippery Slope myth, i.e. the assertion that our scheme would inevitably mean higher taxes in Scotland, and that it would lead to Scotland becoming independent and the break up of the United Kingdom.

The first was an insult to our integrity and the second an insult to our intelligence. Our integrity was insulted by the obvious assumption that Scotland's parliament could not be trusted to act responsibly with even minimal fiscal powers, as opposed to a Westminster which has unlimited power and can presumably be totally trusted! The insult to our intelligence is the confusion of the unitary centralised state with the Union. Britain at present is the most centralised secretive super state in Western Europe. The sharing of power through regional and devolved government is the norm in Europe not the exception – and there is not a single case in which it has led to an increase in the demand for independence. The very opposite is true.

These however are arguments to which we will have to return since they remained the central case of a government which was unwilling to engage with us on the real central issues of culture, democracy and vision. However while these arguments were easy enough to counter at least at the rational level there remained very real weaknesses in our scheme.

The *Herald* editorial of December 1st 1990, headed 'Well-intentioned Woolliness', criticised the financial arrangements as set out in our scheme, as being "unnecessarily complicated". They argued, "it would be better if the parliament were to have a block grant, calculated according to the present formula, with the power marginally to vary either sales or income tax. The reason for assigning to the parliament marginal powers of taxation would be to reduce the likelihood of it behaving with fiscal irresponsibility". This charge of an over-complicated financial arrangement was one which the Convention was to tackle only some years later.

Though the scheme did represent substantial and real progress, there were still glaring omissions – areas in which we had not been able to seek agreement. Most of these were honestly indicated in the report itself. I can identify at least five major areas in which the gaps were substantial.

1. While there was a general commitment to the entrenchment of the powers of Scotland's parliament, the Scottish executive and the relationships with the UK and the European Community, "in order that these would be incapable of being unilaterally amended at a later date at the Westminster Parliament" no mechanism for ensuring such entrenchment was put forward. Given the fact that the Westminster Parliament operates by an unwritten constitution which gives it absolute authority and makes it impossible for any parliament theoretically to bind its successor this remained a fundamental difficulty. The Convention's commitment to the *Claim of Right* – i.e. the sovereignty of the people, made this intention to entrench absolutely crucial and

central, but no way was suggested.

2. The area of financial powers remained insufficiently clearly worked out and as the *Herald* suggested rather complex.

3. The electoral system was not yet agreed. The Convention had in fact agreed on six principles which ruled out the present first-past-the-post system which "does not produce a truly representative assembly," but did not specify what system would actually meet the criteria. The statement was in fact made that "having secured the firm commitment of all the major participants in the Convention to these principles including equality of representation of men and women, the Convention will seek to identify the precise electoral system which best meets these criteria." That was at best as statement of intent.

4. The working structures and patterns of the parliament, with a view to making it more genuinely participative, were still undecided. We merely made the statement "the Convention will undertake further work which will ensure open, accessible and democratically accountable government." Again this was merely a statement of intent.

5. Finally the scheme confessed, "this paper represents a summary and is not an exhaustive listing of the range of powers which should be held by Scotland's parliament. Other areas, an example being the implications for broadcasting, will require further consideration by the Convention or by Scotland's parliament itself."

Hidden in this statement is a debate which is still open and undecided, namely whether the powers of Scotland's parliament will be defined by inclusion or exclusion. The statement in the first draft scheme read, "Scotland's parliament would have a defined range of powers and responsibilities which would encompass sole or shared responsibility for all functions except those retained to the United Kingdom Parliament. The primary matters to be retained to the United Kingdom Parliament would be Defence, Foreign Affairs, Central Economic and Fiscal responsibilities." That debate whether the right thing to do was to define the powers retained to Westminster and leave everything else to Scotland's parliament, or to seek to spell out in great detail the range of responsibilities which would come to Scotland's parliament – that debate is yet to be settled but is of the greatest importance.

As we embarked on the eighteen month period up to the General Election of 1992, we were conscious of these important remaining areas in which we had either not been specific enough, or in some cases as yet unable to achieve consensus and agreement. However we were all agreed there had to be a major emphasis now on campaigning.

Some criticised us for spending so long on the details of the scheme. We had no choice, but the time had come to turn to the second goal of the Convention, to secure the understanding and approval of the people for our work. To this end, a grant from the Joseph Rowntree Reform Trust, obtained through the Campaign for a Scottish Assembly, enabled the Convention to appoint a Campaign Director for the period up to and beyond the forthcoming General Election. It should be said that in September when we made the appointment we had anticipated a short sharp campaign with a General Election being predicted for June 1991. The removal of Margaret Thatcher as Prime Minister changed this anticipated timescale.

Harry Conroy, a former General Secretary of the National Union of Journalists in the UK, and as a man of imagination and commitment well known throughout Scotland, having worked in Scotland with the *Scottish Daily Express* and *Daily Record* before going south, admirably filled the post. Harry was provided with a zero budget. He was asked to fashion the bricks of a campaign but given no straw whatever! With a remarkable patience and resilience, he acquired through the good offices of the print unions a campaign office in Glasgow and basic equipment and material. He then set about an effective and active campaign which astonishingly was self-financing. Two issues of an eight page tabloid were published, with 100,000 copies of each widely distributed. The production costs were met from advertising and sales income, largely through corporate bodies in Scotland. Similarly 100,000 copies of a leaflet

We Say Yes were published. The usual selection of We Say Yes pens, badges, key fobs, matchbooks and T-shirts were produced! A number of folk singers got together to make a tape of Songs for a Scottish Parliament, some old and some written for the purpose. I joined in the singing of these songs outside what is now the Parliament Building and also in Princes Street, Edinburgh with Ewan McVicar and the other songwriters.

The main thrust of the campaign was obviously to seek media publicity in order to reach the mass of the public. This was partly successful but was obviously affected by our usual shortage of resources, and by the fact that certain major world events very much dominated the political stage in this period, including the Gulf War and events in the Soviet Union. Despite these we managed to keep the Convention in the public eye, largely owing to Harry's constant and tireless efforts.

Meanwhile local authorities throughout Scotland were invited to pass resolutions along the lines of 'Aberdeen says Yes', and the great majority of both regional and district councils did so enthusiastically. Many councils laid on meetings or delegate conferences at which leading members of the Convention's executive were able to speak and carry the message to all parts of the nation from Shetland in the north to Dumfries and Galloway and the Borders in the south.

I can scarcely remember the details of that hectic year in 1991 but certainly built up an enduring respect and I hope friendship, for the other member of the 'gang of four' who stomped the country from north to south, east to west meeting with local authorities and speaking at various public meetings and conferences. The four were Donald Dewar then Shadow Secretary of State for Scotland for the Labour Party, Malcolm Bruce leader of the Scottish Liberal Democrats, Campbell Christie the General Secretary of the Scottish Trades Union Congress, and myself – usually accompanied also by Harry Conroy. I have blurred memories of travelling with them in cars, on buses and trains and of the regular pattern of speaking which we adopted. Donald Dewar would often say with a laugh that it was my job to raise the tone of the meeting and his to bring it back down to earth again!

I have always tended to share the general and growing distrust of politicians, but my respect for Donald's honesty, integrity and steadfastness of purpose grew steadily as we worked together in that busy year. He will make an honest and able Secretary of State for Scotland.

In 1991 a postcard campaign was launched inviting people simply to sign a postcard addressed to the Prime Minister, John Major with the legend "We Say Yes to a Scottish Parliament." In June Allan Stewart a Scottish Office Minister well-known for his opposition to a Scottish parliament told the Commons that the Government had received 246 pieces of correspondence on the constitutional issue with 222 opposing change. What he failed to tell Parliament was that the 222 opposing change were postcards copied from our positive message which had been distributed at the Conservative Party conference. The cover was blown when a rather naive Conservative member wrote to the press trumpeting the fact. On June 25th we were able significantly to trump this by handing in some 8,000 signed We Say Yes cards to the Scottish Office.

There were a number of what might be called media events such as the occasion in Edinburgh on November 21st when the Lord Provost and I signed a giant card together. At the Edinburgh Festival we conducted a debate on the effect of a Scottish parliament on culture and the arts, and an important seminar, attended by leading figures from the world of broadcasting, including Gus MacDonald of Scottish Television on the Scottish parliament's role and responsibility in that area. The Lord Provost of Edinburgh and I also released some 1,000 We Say Yes balloons!"

Was all this frantic activity helpful or not? Certainly the level of general support for constitutional change has remained remarkably steady in Scotland. Justifying John Smith's comment on "the settled will of the people," in virtually every opinion poll for years, something between 75% and 85% of the people have consistently supported a Scottish parliament of some sort, and equally consistently, with an occasional blip, two thirds have supported a parliament with real powers but within the United Kingdom. The problem has not been to generate that general support, but to get across to the people the real nature of the proposals now being made and how they would actually affect and benefit the lives of ordinary men and women in Scotland.

In April 1991 the Joseph Rowntree Trust in association with MORI conducted a major poll on 'The State of the Nation' which for the first time went beyond Scotland and examined British attitudes to change. In Scotland itself the response was predictable. 51% opted for a devolved scheme within the United Kingdom, 32% for independence and 16% for no change from the present system. Less predictably the comparable figures for the whole of the UK were 43% for devolution, 16% for independence and 30% for no change – with a much larger number, 11% as opposed to 1% of don't knows.

In a press release I pointed out that while support in Scotland for some form of Home Rule was five to one, in the UK as a whole it was two to one. These I said were "dramatic figures which lend support to two conclusions – that the Convention's scheme is gaining support in Scotland and – that the diminishing support for the *status quo* indicates that the time has come for constitutional change which reflects public opinion." It remains one of the failures of the Convention that we have not taken sufficient account of the need to persuade people in England and other parts of the United Kingdom, that our scheme is not for the benefit of Scotland alone, but for the creation of a more democratic and humane United Kingdom fit for a new century.

If there was a minor failure in the campaigning area it was our tendency to have an unrealistically high expectation. We often discussed privately – but tended to dismiss – the so called doomsday scenario which was posed by a journalist the day after we presented our scheme to the Scottish people. He wrote, "one central question however still faces supporters of a Scottish parliament – what do they do in the event of the so-called doomsday scenario – a Conservative Party opposed to any form of devolved power to Scotland being re-elected by English voters but overwhelmingly defeated in Scotland." He also then wrote, "Convention leaders yesterday refused to even consider such a prospect."

We confidently expected a change in Government by 1992. Failing that, with greater confidence we expected that the Conservative Party would pay the price of its opposition to democracy in Scotland and would be heavily penalised, if not wiped out, in the General Election. These expectations meant that the very modest increase which actually took place in Conservative votes and the gaining of a single seat allowed them to present the 1992 result as some kind victory. With 11 out of 72 seats in Scotland, they were able, having made no claims and having had few expectations, to speak about revival.

Thus despite our efforts and despite the fact that the great majority of the Scots had again voted overwhelmingly for change, we faced the doomsday scenario. A change of government would have created a Scottish parliament; a substantial loss in Scotland would have compelled the Government to rethink Scotland's demands and negotiate with the Convention – especially if it were virtually unable to staff the Scottish Office. We faced the worst result we could have anticipated – and the Convention almost foundered on that rock. If we managed at last to avoid the reefs and keep the ship afloat and eventually on course, it was with great difficulty.

In May 1992 I spoke to meeting of the Conference of the MSF Union at Bournemouth and said, "it was an expert in propaganda – Joseph Göbbels – who said that if you repeat a lie often enough, people will believe you. The opponents of Scottish democracy are taking a leaf out of his book, by repeating on every possible occasion the formula that our plans 'would inevitably make Scotland the highest taxed part of the UK' that is quite simply a lie! But so often repeated that we need a health warning against it. The propaganda exercise would be more believable if it were not repeated *ad nauseam* by a Government which has used the unlimited powers of Westminster to pour public money down the waste pipe of the Poll Tax. The simple fact is – Scotland will have marginally higher – or lower – income tax only if that is what the people want, from a government which is really theirs. Do we not trust them?"

Throughout 1991 and early 1992 the Convention followed a twin track approach. One was the campaign – and the second track the attempt to tackle some of the outstanding issues on which agreement had not been reached. In May we appointed two working groups to report before the General Election. One chaired by the Rev Norman Shanks, who was then the convenor of the Church and Nation Committee of the Church of Scotland, was on the electoral system to be used. The second chaired by Bob McCreadie, the Liberal Democrat Lawyer, was on Procedures and Preparation for a Scottish Parliament. This second group was asked to look at the kind of standing orders and ways of working that would make the parliament more truly answerable, accessible and open. Both groups met frequently through that autumn and winter and brought reports to a full meeting of the Convention in February 1992, two months before the General Election.

Meanwhile however, some work had been going on outside the Convention. The Convention's executive had decided not to undertake any further work on the details of entrenchment, but Jim Ross the former civil servant who had played such an important part in the drafting of the proposals that led to the forming of the Constitutional Convention, wrote to me expressing his intention to begin to try and draft a Bill. He wrote, "with or without an invitation I will toy with a draft Bill during the winter." He was exercised both about the importance of ensuring that the Labour Party was clearly committed, not just to devolution, but to the Convention's scheme. He was also concerned that the *Claim of Right*, which "expressly repudiated the notion that the fate of Scotland could any longer be wholly dependent on the results of

British elections" must be the ultimate consideration and starting point. By Autumn 1991 he had used his expertise to draft a possible Bill "to provide for the establishment of a Scottish parliament for the purpose of assuming the responsibilities of central government so far as they affect Scotland only, and to make consequential provision." Although his attempt was not officially sanctioned by the Convention, and indeed was looked upon with some suspicion by the Labour Party which regarded this particular task as its own responsibility, I have no doubt that Jim Ross's expertise will be of use to those who now have the task of translating the Convention's final scheme into legislative form. Even more important Jim Ross tackled head on the problem of entrenchment i.e. the problem of how to ensure that the Scotland Act giving us our own parliament, could not be repealed or radically altered without the consent of the Scottish parliament or people.

He proposed that this should be done by a separate and prior Bill which he described as "a Bill to create a Class of constitutional provisions and to provide for Parliament to bind itself and its successors as to the procedures by which such provisions may be promulgated, amended or repealed." This was a much shorter Act which at least attempted to do what many declared impossible i.e. to ask Parliament to bind its successors. The same problem was faced much later in the life of the Convention through the proposal of the Labour Party, approved by the Convention, to ask Parliament to make a solemn declaration prior to the passing of the Scottish Bill.

The Government's response to all this activity was for a long time simply to repeat the falsehoods about taxation and the break-up of the Union. Finally however on St Andrew's Day 1991, the then Secretary of State for Scotland, Ian Lang, suddenly called for a "wide-ranging debate on the future of the Union." On that St Andrew's Day we published quarter page adverts in the *Daily Record*, the *Herald* and *Scotsman* listing individuals and organisations who said Yes to a Scottish Parliament. The £6,000 cost was paid for by those attaching their names to the adverts.

The adverts also contained a little box asking for donations and more than £2,000 poured in from individuals, the first being a 50p piece popped through the letter box of our Campaign Office in York Street, Glasgow. Lang's intervention was no doubt in response not only to the Convention's success but to the repeated findings of polls that a substantial minority, sometimes a majority, of Conservative voters in Scotland actually favoured some form of constitutional change. I was reported as welcoming this "death bed conversion" but as asking in some exasperation "where has Ian Lang been? We have had a massive debate throughout Scotland. Where was he when we invited him to repeatedly to join the Convention in search of a consensus."

At this time the other task of reaching consensus, in areas as yet unagreed, continued through the two working groups on the electoral system and on the procedures and preparation for parliament. Between 1989 and 1990 there had been no fewer than seven meetings of the Convention culminating in the great celebration of St Andrew's Day 1990. Throughout 1991 the full Convention never met. This was largely because the detailed work of this period and the campaigning was clearly a task for the executive and for smaller groups. However by February 1992 with a General Election two months away the time had clearly come when the Convention had to meet again to receive and approve any advance on our work.

On the question of the electoral system, the group had a number of recommendations, some of which were accepted but others remained controversial. Working from the six principles already agreed which called for a degree of proportionality, a balance and equality of seats for men and women, the Convention accepted a report from the working group which "confirmed broad agreement on a number of key points which represent a substantial advance towards a new and fairer electoral system for Scotland." These points were:

1. Agreement on the need to move towards closer correspondence between seats and votes;

2. Acceptance of an additional member system (AMS) as a means of achieving this;

3. Acceptance of a statutory obligation on parties to put forward equal numbers of men and women candidates, and acceptance also that the AMS should be used to achieve gender equality if not achieved by the constituency elections.

Although approved by the executive and Convention the third point was to prove not only controversial but also a rock on which the Convention nearly foundered. The original wording had been "acceptance of a statutory or other obligation" to achieve gender balance. The executive had removed the words "or other" in the final report and, while reluctantly accepted at the time, this wording became a major source of friction and near disaster in the period after the 1992 election.

The working group however also reported that its more detailed recommendation was not acceptable to the executive committee. They said, "our recommendation was for a directly elected parliament using existing Westminster constituencies, with two members elected from each constituency and each party being obliged under an obligation to put up a man and a woman in each constituency. In addition, we proposed there should be between 36 and 50 additional members to bring the total number of seats won by each party more closely into line with the votes cast." This was a very precise and detailed proposal, but was one on which it was impossible to achieve consensus, mainly on the grounds that it was too prescriptive using statutory means to force gender equality. The actual report to the Convention said, "the executive committee discussed this fully but had reservations on two grounds; first that the scheme would not necessarily provide a sufficient degree of correspondence between votes gained and seats won; and second that the parliament would be larger in numbers (it would be between 180 and 194) than might be desirable." In the light of future decisions, this was an important starting point and marker. Thus, in effect, though some advance was made the question of the electoral system to be used to achieve the proportionality and gender balance which all desired was still left open and was still potentially a source of considerable disagreement, friction and even disaster, as many of our opponents and the media were quick to point out.

The other major matter which came to the Convention at its meeting in the Assembly Rooms in Edinburgh on Friday, February 28th 1992 was the report of the other working group on Procedures and Preparation for a Scottish Parliament. This group had been given the remit "to prepare for effective constitutional change and an open, accessible and accountable Scottish parliament" and did so by a very widespread process of consultation with individuals and organisations throughout Scotland. They accepted important principles which in their view would make Scotland's parliament very much more democratic than the Westminster system. These principles included:

1. Accountability – the decision making process including the activities of the parliament, ministers and the civil service must be subject to effective scrutiny and control;

2. Participation – parliament must ensure that ordinary citizens are able to participate directly in this process of government;

3. Subsidiarity – political decisions should be taken as closely as possible to the people who are affected by them.

The other two principles were those of balance and efficiency. The rest of the report was in the form of a recommendation to Scotland's parliament rather than a decision to be made directly by the Convention. We have always made a very clear distinction between the Convention's role to set out the constitutional principles and the details to be included in the founding legislation or the Scotland Act; it has never been the Convention's role to tell Scotland's parliament what to do with its powers. Nevertheless the area of procedures is so important that the Convention accepted the need to make strong recommendations in this area. This was because of the conviction expressed by the committee that "the

Westminster Parliament as presently structured fails to satisfy any of the general principles which guided us in our thinking. We have therefore rejected it as the model for a Scottish parliament." They went on that "the Scottish Parliament should be of its own kind . . . it should strive to make genuine participation and critical scrutiny of government policy making a reality." They recommended a President, which was later modified to a Speaker, a fixed parliamentary term probably four years rather than the Westminster system of allowing the Prime Minister to decide, and parliament to be opened formally by the Head of State at the beginning of each parliamentary term (the assumption is, of course, that the Queen remains Head of State). However, "instead of a Westminster style Queen's Speech, the Prime Minister should use the occasion to deliver a State of the Nation address at the beginning of each parliamentary year."

There was also a clear proposal that the parliamentary year should take account of school holidays and that there should be a sensible working day. Good facilities for all MSPs were thought to be important as were comprehensive "in-house facilities for the media and for members of the public to meet members of the Scottish parliament." Childcare and daycare facilities should be made available. As far as members were concerned, the recommendation was "it should not be possible for members of parliament to be simultaneously members of the UK and European Parliaments or local authority councillors." However an exception was proposed for people already serving out original terms. It was also proposed that the salaries of MPs "should be fixed by reference to an appropriate point on the salary scale applicable to civil servants."

In the light of subsequent concern about sleaze in government there was an important recommendation that "members should be prohibited from holding any office of profit under the Crown and be required to declare all financial and other relevant interests in a public register. They should be prohibited from receiving payment for representing the interests of any person or organisation in parliament." This was followed by a proposed code of conduct for members and a disciplinary procedure.

Perhaps the most important proposal of the committee was for parliamentary committees, which would effectively combine the functions of Westminster standing and select committees and shadow government departments. They would have both legislative and investigative functions. A list of such committees was in fact proposed in the report and all of these should have the power subject to adequate safeguards not only to scrutinise and to amend legislation proposed by ministers but also to initiate it themselves. ". . . . all important interest groups in Scotland would have direct and guaranteed access to the appropriate committees." This provision could be of the very greatest importance in developing a more participative style of government than the secretive and closed Westminster system.

There was also a proposal for women's committee because "the Convention has put great emphasis on the need to illuminate discrimination against women." Another important recommendation was that all public appointments should be a responsibility of parliament not ministers. This is of the greatest urgency in removing the enormous patronage which is at present exercised by the system we call the Crown in Parliament, but in effect puts power in the hands of Ministers and especially the Prime Minister. In our case "appointments should be the responsibility of a Public Appointments Committee chaired by the President (Speaker). Merit and gender balance should be the main criteria for appointments to public bodies. When making judicial appointments the Commission should act on the recommendation of the Lord Advocate, assuming that to be the title of the Scottish Minister of Justice and the Lord President of the Court of Session."

There is also an important proposal that the Prime or Chief Minister, and in fact all ministers should be confirmed in their positions by a simple majority of the full parliament. Here again, this limits the power of the patronage in an important way. Although all of these would be recommendations and would not, in themselves, form part of the legislation which sets up the parliament but rather would have to be decided by it when it first meets, the Convention has stressed the centrality of these matters if Scotland's parliament is to escape from the beginning from the temptation to be a pale imitation of the rejected Westminster model.

Many of the ideas put forward in the report of the working group were taken up and amplified and turned into a set of proposed standing orders by Professor Bernard Crick and David Miller working under the auspices of the John Wheatley Centre. Their important work entitled *Making Scotland's Parliament Work (standing orders for the Parliament of Scotland)* was published as a pamphlet. Their work deserves scrutiny and certainly means when Scotland's parliament first meets it will have before it guidelines for more democratic standing orders and procedures than would otherwise have been the case. There will be little danger of it falling by default or laziness into copying the senility of the Mother of Parliaments.

Derek Bateman writing in *Scotland on Sunday* passed the following judgement: "the Convention has confused its critics by proving to be more than a talking shop. For some on the inside it has become a crucible into which bold ideas on government and democracy have flowed. It has provided a unique forum in which the government of a small country has been redrawn and the example of Westminster discarded."

"The working group," he went on, "reveals a parliament dramatically different from the Westminster model. From the beginning it builds in a decision-making role for all political parties. The scheme shows how far the Convention is prepared to go in throwing out the concept of a Westminster government in favour of a power-sharing parliament."

The Convention, having accepted these two further reports, began to move confidently towards an expected victory in the General Election of April 1992. As the weeks passed however, it became ever clearer that the result was no foregone conclusion but looked very likely to be close. One important change did take place however. The emphasis put by the Prime Minister and others on the devolution question meant that the London-based media suddenly woke up to the fact that something was happening in Scotland. There had only been one important previous occasion when they had suddenly trekked north, which was when one rogue poll, significantly just after the closure of Ravenscraig, had showed for the first time a majority for independence as opposed to constitutional devolution which had somehow set the haggis among the doves. England suddenly rediscovered Scotland.

However, in March 1992, we witnessed an amazing procession of government ministers coming to tell the Scots how well-off we are and how important the debate is. I asked the question in an article addressed to England, "where have they been all this time? For the government who ignored the debate so long in the belief and hope that it would just go away, suddenly now to call for a debate is rather like ringing the dinner gong when everyone else has already reached the after-dinner mints."

I challenged the Government to "come out openly and say that, whatever its own opinion about the future of Scotland, it will agree to accept the democratic will of the people. There is a fundamental immorality in their position. They argue that the only choice Scotland can have is between the *status quo* and total independence and if the majority of Scots want complete separation they must have it. But, if as seems probable, most Scots want a Scottish parliament within the Union why can they not have that? The danger of this position is not just that it is undemocratic but that it is most likely to lead to the break-up of the United Kingdom!"

I ended the article with an appeal to our neighbours in the rest of the United Kingdom? I asked them to understand what we are saying and that our challenge is to the way we are all governed. As a bonus I said we in Scotland would be eternally grateful if they do not impose on us another Tory Government. To our dismay they did. The appeals to greed and to fear apparently worked again.

CHAPTER 17

How Long, Oh Lord, How Long?

The year from April 1992 to April 1993 was undoubtedly the Convention's lowest and most dangerous year. We might call it to borrow a phrase our *Annus Horribilis*. For in the twelve months after the disappointment of the General Election of April 1992, the Convention came close to paralysis and disintegration.

In that at least we were not alone. On April 10th 1992 Scotland was a nation in shock. An almost tangible pall of gloom, depression, self doubt and guilt seemed to descend on much of the nation.

William McIlvanney writing in *Scotland on Sunday* called it "ebony Friday, to differentiate its gloom from lesser blackness." He spoke of a nation "wandering bereft of its own country. That Friday I passed through George Square in Glasgow. Watching the people, I reflected we could have renamed it hangover square such was the obvious mood of the people. Gone was the cheeky ebullience, the whats-gaun-on-here then curiosity. Most of us wore gloom like some uniform from Orwell's *1984*."

Developing his theme of the national hangover McIlvanney wrote, "all the symptoms were there: the nervous debility, the gloom no medication will shift, the self-contempt, the disbelief at how spectacularly stupid you can be, the conviction that you are never going to get it right, the desire to find someone who will tell you that it wasn't really as bad as you think."

For the Constitutional Convention it was the start of a year in which we had to move forward from despair. But to what? The choice seemed to be disintegration or renewal. Our opponents spoke gleefully of the Convention as "a dead duck" but could we prove it to be a phoenix?

The one thing that was clear however was that business as usual was impossible. There had to be a genuine effort to rethink and renew. The initial gloom and paralysis quickly gave way to periods of spontaneous and rather disorganised reactions. A few days after the election result Scotland United was established at a rally attended by several thousand people in Glasgow's George Square.

William McIlvanney in the article already quoted went on to write that he was back in George Square again after the election three days after. "It seemed a suitable time lag for a resurrection." He was attending the rally organised by Scotland United, a group formed across party boundaries by artists and MPs and people who refused to accept supinely the government which had been inflicted on a majority of Scots who didn't vote for it.

He wrote of its astonishing success which he found moving. His clear conclusion was that "as a people we have been condemned to an intolerable situation. We must not learn to tolerate it. I think it was the relevance of British Party politics to Scotland that died on April 9th 1992. It is the system that is dead. It can no longer function meaningfully in Scotland."

It is my own view that after the understandable period of confusion, despair and self-doubt the election result confirmed again, if any confirmation were needed, that Scots cannot live for much longer with a system which denies them any meaningful form of democratic control over their own affairs.

But during those days of darkness in April 1992 we knew

that William McIlvanney was right when he wrote,

> "It will be a long haul and the outcome can't be
> certain. But at least the fight is on, the fight for a
> Scottish parliament outside the cynical machinations
> of Westminster. It is I believe the fight most worth
> fighting in Scottish politics today. I hope you join it.
> Pick your side. To say nothing is to say no change.
> There isn't much room for neutrality here."

These words, and the conviction behind them, echo my own profound belief that the issue is moral and not just political.

Alongside Scotland United a whole series of other organisations sprang up. Common Cause, formed at a well-attended meeting at Carberry Tower, the Church of Scotland conference centre, was a gathering of the great and the good from Scottish society committed to the common cause of democracy for our nation.

The weekend after the election a group of people under the name Democracy for Scotland began a vigil outside the proposed parliament building in Edinburgh just opposite the symbol of Scotland's undemocratic administration, St Andrew's House. That vigil which was gradually to become established with its own hut, posters and signs, has to the credit of all who have taken part in it been maintained on a 24-hour-a-day basis 365 days a year over the years since then. It was a constant reminder to the minority who governed us that whatever the state continues to say, the people still consistently and constantly say Yes to Scotland's parliament. The vigil has resolved to remain there until Scotland's parliament is secure – almost exactly the promise I have made over and over again about the Convention itself. Our job and theirs is done only when Scotland's nationhood, and therefore her right to decide her own future, is finally recognised.

A number of other groups also sprang up, some national, some local – and eventually the Scottish Trades Union Congress

(STUC) through Campbell Christie, brought the separate groups together in a Coalition for Scottish Democracy which was fully supported by, but distinct from, the Constitutional Convention. The Coalition has proved to be a most creative and useful instrument and eventually led to the establishment of the Scottish Civic Assembly, of which more later.

The emotional impact of those days led to a call from some quarters for a degree of civil disobedience. This was perhaps inevitably rather exaggerated by the media and made to appear something like a call to arms.

Indeed, even a month before the election, giving the keynote address at the annual conference of COSLA (the Convention of Scottish Local Authorities) I had anticipated at least the possibility the return of a government that would deny Scotland her democracy and had called on local authorities to spearhead resistance and to be ready "to live a little dangerously," a phrase borrowed from Donald Dewar's comments during the early days of the Convention.

Questioned by the press I said perhaps unwisely that I would rule nothing out except violence, but refused to be more specific than that. Shortly after the election, I shared a platform at the STUC's annual Congress, with Councillor Charles Gray, the leader of Strathclyde Region who was at the time described in the press as "Scotland's most powerful local government politician".

Charles Gray had been a staunch and enthusiastic member of the Convention's executive, a president of COSLA, and he became a firm friend in this period. Both he and I stressed in our address the vital need for unity. I warned the leaders and members of every political party that if at that time of opportunity and danger, they did not stand united, the people of Scotland would not easily forgive them or forget. Charles Gray was even blunter. He said, "our objectives for our country and our self-respect is a damn sight more important than piddling party politics." He did however go on to issue a careful and measured but nevertheless clear call for the use of "legal civil disobedience" as a last resort. He said, "there may come a time, if the government remains totally intransigent to the wishes of the Scottish people, when we may have to step across the line and live dangerously."

This was unfortunately widely misunderstood as some kind of call to immediate action. What in fact he said, which remains incidentally my own conviction at this time, is there would be a breaking point for Scotland and that it could not be far off.

He added, "I don't believe that the Scottish will remain passive to the end of the century if repressive policies continue. The Scots are traditionally slow to anger. But everyone has a breaking point." In that warning he was right.

The Convention's response to the defeat of 1992 was developed gradually. The executive met on 17th April, a week after the election and agreed a four point action plan.

1. To create the greatest possible unity within the Scottish people and to call on all political parties not active in the Convention to enter into an open conversation on tactics and objectives for the next period.

2. The achievement of a multi-option referendum as the goal – stressing the need for the government to recognise the will of the people.

3. We agreed on an immediate approach to the Prime Minister in a fairly conciliatory tone, welcoming the appointment of a minister in the Scottish Office with special responsibility for constitutional issues, requesting that he enter into dialogue with the Scottish people on these matters and meet with the Convention and calling on the government to organise the multi option referendum already referred to "the questions in which should be the subject of consultation in Scotland."

4. The fourth element was simply the resolve to study more detailed proposals for the future organisation

and activities of the Convention at future meetings.

On Saturday April 18th these decisions were widely reported in the Scottish press as was my judgement "that we are again in the situation where the democratic will of the Scottish people is likely, if we are not very careful and very strong, to be ignored and be thwarted."

In general there was support for the call for a multi-option referendum, under the circumstances, and certainly an almost universal call for greater unity. The *Scotsman* editorial went so far to say, "thanks to the Scottish Constitutional Convention a wee bit of the fog that descended on Scotland's political landscape on April 10th has lifted." The paper supported our referendum call and urged the Prime Minister to "accept the Convention's request for a meeting. Face to face he could explain to its executive what he is doing to reduce Scotland's democratic deficit."

On April 22nd I wrote to the Prime Minister in the conciliatory tones suggested above. His reply, significantly two months later, was to reiterate his commitment:

> "to the undertaking I gave before the election – that the government would take stock of the constitutional question in Scotland in the light if the outcome. At the election the overwhelming majority of the Scottish electorate voted for a continuation of the Union. I am currently considering how the government of Scotland might be improved within a strengthened United Kingdom."

On this basis he met our request for an early meeting with a polite brush off – "at present I think a period of calm and considered reflection is necessary to review all available options."

Eventually a meeting with Lord Fraser of Carmyllie, the minister given responsibility, was arranged but it was clear that there was absolutely no intention on the government's part to move towards anything other than cosmetic changes that left the basically undemocratic situation unchanged.

On April 28th while speaking to a meeting of civil service trade-unionists, I used the opportunity to put forward a set of proposals for a way forward, which was purely my personal view but which was widely reported the following day. Calling "all groups and parties to sit together with the Convention to agree on the basis of unity, the aim of unity, and the strategy for unity", I proffered a six point programme.

1. A shadow Scottish parliament to meet quarterly in Edinburgh to consist of all Scottish MPs and MEPs and perhaps also elected representatives of regional and island councils.
2. A Civic Forum representing Scotland's civil society created by the Convention in consultation with other organisations such as Common Cause, Democracy for Scotland and Scotland United.
3. An annual State of the Nation day at which the shadow Scottish Parliament, the Civic Forum and other bodies would report to the people.
4. A new appeal to Europe and the international community. I said "we have an unanswerable case in international law as well as morality."
5. We should extend sincere cooperation to any government initiatives and proposals, while ensuring that the Scottish people were not sold short by purely cosmetic changes.
6. We had to agree on a strategy for an effective campaign.

Though I received very substantial backing for these ideas by letter and by telephone from a large number of people, the political parties in the Convention were considerably less enthusiastic.

In practice the executive of the Convention firmly rejected

the idea of any shadow Scottish parliament, but encouraged further work to be done on the other ideas I had put forward especially those of a Civic Assembly and Civic Summit. Since the Convention's role and mandate was very clearly the direct area of constitutional change, and as this gave us a distinctive purpose which was different from though complementary to that of the many other bodies that had sprung up, the idea of a Civic Assembly was in practice passed over to the Coalition for Scottish Democracy, and did in fact later come to fruition.

By June 1992 it was clear that there were many even among supporters and members of the Constitutional Convention, who felt that its work was done and that it should quietly fold its tents and creep away. The *Herald* reported on 10th June that "many in political circles in Scotland fear the Convention has foundered after weekend decisions by the SNP finally to reject calls to join it and by the Liberal Democrats to place constitutional issues on the back burner." Leading members of the Scottish Liberal Democrats had voiced feelings following the election result that they had suffered as a result of their close linkage with the Labour Party in the Convention and that they had to put some distance between themselves and Labour.

In addition there were a number of Labour MPs who were openly questioning whether the Convention had any remaining purpose. Some had seen it purely as a means toward a General Election victory and no more, fearing that the continuation of its power might limit the Labour Party's freedom of action and ability to make unilateral decisions when in office. That fear no doubt remains and is fully justified!

My own faith that the Convention had to be reborn, never wavered. I said on June 10th, "we simply cannot go on as before. We must find a new purpose in the new period. It is unlikely that the Convention will disappear because nobody is going to turn their back on the hard work over the past two years. However having produced a scheme for a Scottish parliament, we cannot go on for the next five years refining it."

At a fringe meeting at the Labour Party's Blackpool conference that summer, I aired my conviction that the Convention had to be reborn, broadening and deepening its scope and "developing a civic forum for a nation." I said that if the Convention were to go back on its achievements of uniting so many Scottish institutions it would betray not only the people of Scotland but the hopes of the UK for better and more democratic government.

There was undoubtedly at this stage a genuine danger of disintegration. Not only was there hesitation among some of the more suspicious Labour MPs, but a number of the Liberal Democrat MPs who were re-elected in April, had only done so with very reduced majorities, and in some cases came near to losing their seats. This was particularly true in the case of Russell Johnston, and Malcolm Bruce who as leader of the Scottish Liberal Democrats had been an integral part of the Convention's thinking and planning.

Throughout the spring and summer of that year however a number of political events unfolded which were to eventually ensure the Convention's renewal.

In July, John Smith was elected leader of the Labour Party. He had often spoken to me of his strong support for the Convention and made a point of attending every meeting he could. His handwritten note of thanks to me for my congratulations and good wishes, repeated that commitment. In the wake of his election, two longstanding and conscientious members of the Convention were replaced, fortunately by others whose enthusiasm was as great.

Donald Dewar moved on to the Shadow Social Security portfolio, and was replaced by Tom Clarke as Shadow Secretary of State for Scotland. Another of the chief architects of the Convention's scheme had been Murray Elder as General Secretary of the Labour Party in Scotland. He moved to London to be, in effect, John Smith's right hand man, but was from our point of view very fortunately replaced by Jack McConnell, who as a young councillor in Stirling District had been an unwavering supporter of the Convention through thick and thin. In his earlier days as a Labour activist, Jack had been a leading member of Scottish Labour Activists, a fringe group in the Labour Party committed to forming a Scottish parliament.

There was change in the Liberal Democrat camp too. Andy Myles replaced Ron Waddell as General Secretary of the Scottish Party, and proved to be a skilled, firm, but friendly negotiator. Jim Wallace became leader of the party replacing Malcolm Bruce who had given so much time and energy to the Convention, but who had I think developed reservations about being so close to other political parties as a result of his electoral experience. Jim Wallace however was to prove, especially in later negotiation with George Robertson, that he combined political realism with a genuine vision of Scotland's future.

Meanwhile I was deeply involved with an event which might have seemed irrelevant to Scotland, but which I believe will prove to be crucial for the future understanding of our nation and its culture and purpose. Far off in Rio, the EARTH Summit took place (more officially, UNCED, the United National Conference on Environment and Development). As chair of the Scottish Environmental Forum I was deeply committed to the preparation for Rio and later to the follow-up in the attempt to apply the radical proposals of "Agenda 21" to the strategy for and creation of a sustainable society in our nation.

That is a story which belongs more properly to the chapters of this book in which I describe my personal life and experiences, but it begins from this point to intertwine with the story of the Convention, and certainly with our hopes for a Scottish parliament which would create a renewed and more realistic nation.

In the second half of 1992 the United Kingdom assumed the presidency of the European Community and worked towards a European Summit which was held in Edinburgh in December.

It was therefore unsurprising that the Convention, still in the throes of its search for a redefinition of its role, turned in the second half of the year to a concern for Europe. Scotland had always been closer to the European vision, certainly than the more nationalist elements in England, and our local authorities and others had often clearly seen the European Community as at least a partial safeguard against the worst excesses of Westminster's control.

Prior to the summit I spoke at an international conference in Edinburgh, and made points which I honestly believe, especially in light of more recent developments and with the benefit of hindsight of course, to have been prophetic. In the year in which we celebrated the 500th anniversary of the voyage of Christopher Columbus, Europe I maintained had a chance to repent and to make up for "the trail of blood and tears spread across the globe in these five centuries." I said that Scotland had a distinctive contribution to make to the new Europe within a new world order which is Just, Participative and Sustainable.

I warned that the great danger of the current crisis in the European Community was that the debate would "get bogged down in details of economic links, currency schemes and power struggles." I plead for a sense of overall purpose or vision of Europe's global role which could be lost in the economic debate. Europe must be united by something greater than simply economic self-interest. We needed a greater degree of European unity not just for the sake of ourselves and our children but for the state of a sustainable world. I stated then and still believe that Europe should be the steward of Agenda 21, "the minimum necessary to turn the tide of environmental pollution and economic decay."

The ninth full meeting of the Constitutional Convention took place in Strathclyde Regional Council in Glasgow on St Andrew's Day Monday 30th November 1992. There were two debates – the first was on the State of the Nation and passed a declaration of principle which was clearly sensitive to the forthcoming European meeting. It read:

> A Scottish Parliament, elected by a fair system, will
> renew our vision, restore our sense of purpose and

work for a better Britain and a new Europe. Europe is increasingly committing itself to the sharing of constitutional power. We are witnessing a movement towards more participative government, closer to the citizen.

We reaffirm the principle of subsidiarity, as a democracy 'in which decisions are taken as closely as possible to the citizen'.

On the threshold of the European Summit in Edinburgh, Scotland has a vital interest in ensuring that the European Community reinforces its commitment to subsidiarity and democracy. Subsidiarity asserts the demand for democracy at all levels in Europe, in national state Parliaments, in the legislatures of appropriate regions and nations such as Catalonia, Bavaria or Scotland, and in the chambers of local government.

Only through the establishment of a Scottish Parliament will Scotland be properly placed to take advantage of and fully contribute to the evolving European structures.

The second debate was specifically on Subsidiarity and Europe and it ended with the unanimous endorsement of a second declaration of principle addressed directly to the European heads of government. Again its importance justifies its quoting full.

In the preamble to the Maastricht Treaty all 12 Community countries confirmed their resolve 'to continue the process of creating an ever closer union among the peoples of Europe, in which decisions are taken as closely as possible to the citizen in accordance with the principles of subsidiarity'.

We urge that in your consideration of subsidiarity you reaffirm the principle of subsidiarity and not just its procedural application to relations between the Community and its member states. We believe that:

1. Subsidiarity is the exercise of democratic decision making power as close to people as possible.

2 Subsidiarity demands democracy at all levels of government. The dispersal of constitutional power means that democratic control must be exercised simultaneously by the people at different levels – in a strong European Parliament, in the parliaments of the member states, in the legislatures of appropriate nations or regions and in local government.

We note the commitment you made at the Birmingham summit to the importance of the Committee of the Regions, on which the nation of Scotland will be represented. We urge that this commitment be extended to ensuring that those who represent a 'Region' in this Committee are democratically accountable to the people of that 'Region', rather than answerable to the government of the member state concerned.

We urge you to recognise that Scotland has a vital interest in ensuring that the European Community does not retreat from a wholehearted commitment to the principles of subsidiarity and democracy.

In this context we draw your attention to the constitutional demands of the Scottish nation within the new Europe and reassert our claim of right to self-determination.

Two days later the joint Chairs of the Convention, the Rt Hon Sir David Steel MP and Lord Ewing of Kirkford and I jointly signed a letter to the Presidents or Heads of States of all the members of the European Community. The letter welcomed them to Scotland, sent them the declaration of principle above, and pointed out that Scotland is "an ancient nation with its own legal system and distinctive institutions but, despite the repeatedly expressed will of our people, has no democratic legislature."

In welcoming them we put two urgent requests. First to be sensitive to the authentic voices of the Scottish people. We sent them separately a bound copy of the two historic documents; the *Claim of Right for Scotland* and our earlier report *Towards Scotland's Parliament*.

Second and perhaps even more important we asked them to ensure that the discussion on subsidiarity "is not limited to the procedural application of this to relations between the community and its member states, but that you firmly reassert the basic principal of subsidiarity as contained in the preamble to Maastricht and as redefined by the Commission on 27th October, namely that subsidiarity means government as close to the citizen as possible; means the genuine sharing of power at different levels; and means democratic control at all levels. Only if this is done will we be true to our vision of European unity."

This message was reinforced in two important ways. First on the actual eve of the summit in Edinburgh the joint chairs of the Convention handed over to Kenneth Munro the European Commission representative in Scotland, a copy of our documents which he received on behalf of Jacques Delores, president of the Commission and promised to pass on.

At that presentation I said, "We want our guests from the other Community countries to be in no doubt that they are meeting in a country which needs and demands its own parliament. We know what the Scottish people feel, and what they want by way of constitutional change, and it is important to get this message over. Scotland has a right to self-determination and control over its own affairs, a right which would not have to be argued for in other European countries."

An even more dramatic reinforcement came when on December 12th 1992 in one of the largest demonstrations in our recent history, some 30,000 people marched through the streets of Edinburgh to a rally in the Meadows, which was addressed by the leaders of all opposition parties and others. Organised by the Coalition for Scottish Democracy, that rally adopted a "democracy declaration of Scotland" which simply stressed the majority of Scots now demand the recall of our own parliament as a modern and democratic body empowering all our citizens.

It reiterated the point about the true meaning of subsidiarity and said "let it be brought to your attention that subsidiarity – decision making at the level closest to the people concerned – is being denied to the people of Scotland by the British State. It limits subsidiarity to relations between London and Brussels and seeks to remain the most centralised state in the European Community."

The importance of this declaration and indeed of all our work, is that it puts the emphasis firmly where it properly belongs, on the question of democracy. The opponents of the Convention have constantly tried to shift it off this strong ground onto ground of their own choosing – usually that of a rather narrow argument about taxation. The Convention has at times been too passive in allowing this to happen. Our ground is clear and firm – it is the cultural and political demand of the Scottish people for the right to decide their own future, quite simply to democracy and justice.

It would be wrong to say that in the 1992 St Andrew's Day meeting, the Convention had already found its clear pattern for the future but we were near to that turning point.

As I presented the executive's report to that meeting, I said, "in the gloom that followed an election in which the people's will for change was denied yet again it was small wonder that many lost heart – that we saw, not really outrage and defiance, but rather a depressing mixture of resignation and disillusionment with politics itself. If democracy is repeatedly and constantly denied we should not be surprised when the democratic system itself is debased and devalued."

I argued however that there was evidence that things were changing rapidly. On the one hand we were deeper in economic recession and social decay. For increasing numbers of our young people that year had been just the latest in a decade of despair and lost opportunities. On the other hand we sensed the stirrings of a sea-change. The false god of the market had proved at last to have feet of clay. Not only does it fail to deliver social justice or environmental protection – it cannot even deliver economic prosperity or plain common sense! But then Scotland had never really been taken in. A nation which had stood for so long unbowed before the handbag, was hardly likely to kneel under the assault of rolled up charters – however many there may be!"

At this stage I obviously felt confident enough that the Convention would not disappear but was on the road to a redefinition and a renewal of its role. I was able to say with confidence "those among our fairweather friends who tell us that the Convention's work is done, simply prove that they never really understood what we were all about in the first place."

I ended my report to the meeting by quoting the words spoken to me by the Prime Minister of Spain's autonomous Basque region who said, "you have a Constitutional Convention of remarkable breadth and depth, which many others look to as a model. If you throw that away, not only will you not get your Scottish Parliament – you will not deserve to!"

Tom Clarke, the new Shadow Secretary of State for Scotland and therefore the Labour Party's chief presence in the Convention, had neither the presence nor the oratorical skills of Donald Dewar, or for that matter his successor George Robertson. He was constantly under attack from the media and was widely criticised as not having the stature or the style for the job. I found him a man of integrity and although quiet he was extremely conscientious.

Tom Clarke made a speech early in 1993 in which he thoughtfully analysed the changes in Scottish politics that had taken place since the election. He said with great honesty that he believed the Labour Party was the only party capable of reflecting and achieving the aspirations of the Scottish people and there was a very real trust built up between the people of Scotland and the Labour Party. Though arguably this statement could be more accurately applied to Labour's dominance of the more populated central belt, Tom Clarke went on to say "the size of our vote in Scotland reflected the covenant of trust we establish with the people of Scotland. To deny that would be dishonest but it would be even more dishonest to deny that, by our own failure to win at a British level that covenant of trust has been severely strained."

The new Secretary of State for Scotland went on to underline that the covenant of trust must include Labour's continuing commitment to a Scottish Parliament and said, "here the Constitutional Convention has a continuing significance and importance. The Convention must be the forum by which political parties in Scotland continue to demonstrate – by their participation and their campaigning – that there is a better way for Scotland to be governed."

Importantly Tom Clarke pointed out however that work still needed to be undertaken on the best form of legislature for Scotland, building on but improving on the work already done. He also stressed the need to advance the campaigning work of the Convention, to ensure that the Scottish people understand how a Scottish parliament will actually benefit them

Reiterating this firm commitment to our work he said "the Convention has proved a constructive forum for the Labour Party to work alongside others on the issue of a Scottish parliament, especially the Liberal Democrats. We are enthusiastic about extending the membership of the Convention – that is why the invitation to the SNP remains open and we are particularly keen to see individual subscribing membership and the affiliation of national organisations interested in home rule for Scotland."

After discussions, the turning point came in April 1993 when the executive reached the point where it could confidently map the way forward. It agreed unambiguously that "the Convention must continue in being" and the executive also mapped out two important steps forward.

First we agreed to establish a Constitutional Commission, chaired by a distinguished Scot, which would work with agreed terms of reference and report back in due course to the executive committee. This was the Convention's way of trying to find a way through the differences which still remained and which had made the consensus, however remarkable in its scope, incomplete in some key areas.

The Constitutional Commission was to work quite independently of the Scottish Constitutional Convention in its membership and operation though set up by us, and had terms of reference which were clear, even if difficult to implement. The Commission was asked to consider and make recommendations on:

a. Proposals for elections to and representations in a Scottish Parliament (including electoral systems and gender balance provisions) and

b. The constitutional implications at United Kingdom level and for local government of the establishment, and Scottish representation in the Westminster Parliament."

This mandate prevented the Commission from reopening any question already settled in the Convention, but allowed it to undertake the thorny and difficult tasks which the Convention had at that point been unable to tackle on these crucial areas. It took several months to appoint the Commission and get it off the ground. The very decision to appoint it was a watershed for the Convention, and having overcome the problem of its remit we began to move clearly in the direction of the completion of our work.

The other major decision was to embark on a programme of Preparing for Change – series of discussions and briefing meetings with representatives of key sections of Scottish society to look at the actual implications of the Convention's proposals for the future of Scotland in key areas; and at the same time the production and publication of campaigning and educational materials to put our scheme across to the people.

The attempt to redefine the Convention's work on the one hand, while building a wider tactical unity on the other for the single demand of Scottish democracy, was only partly successful. The Convention did succeed by April 1993 in finding the proper way forward. However the tactical unity which would clearly would have had to involve the Scottish National Party. Several olive branches were held out to the SNP but even limited unity proved impossible to achieve. The SNP seemed to remain convinced that its understandable commitment to the goal of total independence, ruled out any real possibility of their working closely with others on the broader platform of the demand for Scottish democracy itself.

From the Convention's point of view however, after the trauma of the 1992 election result, we were at last on our way. Our critics who had at every stage, told us repeatedly that it would not work, and that we would not achieve any new consensus, parroted their old cynicism. Would a Commission succeed where the Convention had failed? Would this not be yet another exercise in postponing the evil day when the Convention revealed its feet of clay? It took us a further two years to find the answers but our faith was justified.

CHAPTER 18

If You Can Keep Your Head . . .

–we turn the corner

The two and a half years from the recovery of nerve in April 1993 to the final completion of our consensus and its presentation to the people of Scotland in November 1995, brought the Convention into the centre of Scottish politics. Most of the groups that had been founded in the heat and self disgust of the 1992 General Election aftermath had, by 1993 either disappeared or, in many cases, sunk back into only occasional activity. The one most obvious exception was, of course, the Democracy for Scotland Group who maintain their impressive and demanding vigil outside the parliament building at Calton Hill.

The group recorded each day that they have maintained their vigil on a board for all passers-by to see. They resolved to remain until their a Scottish Parliament is established. On the day of the 1997 General Election their board recorded their presence for 1847 days through cold, heat, rain, shine, light and dark. I honour them.

I had never doubted that the Constitutional Convention remained the only rock on which the solid foundations for

Scotland's Parliament could be laid. Through the spring and summer of 1993, the executive of the Convention was preoccupied with the task of tending the embers of the proposed Constitutional Commission and ensuring that it had good leadership.

As a small but interesting aside to this task, I travelled to London in May to speak at a conference on 'The Monarchy Debate' at the Queen Elizabeth II Conference Centre. I shared with my audience Scottish Constitutional history and particularly the warning of the Declaration of Arbroath that the monarch ruled only subject to the assent on the community of the realm. I also pointed out, I hope mildly and without undue polemic, that just as James VI of Scotland became James I of the United Kingdom, "the respected monarch whose name graces this conference centre may be Queen Elizabeth II of England but she is the first of her name to reign over the UK."

The main point I made however, which was received with surprising approval by many of the delegates present, was that Scotland questioned not the monarchy *per se*, but the Constitution which had created the Crown prerogatives, giving us an elective dictatorship and effectively depriving us of any checks and balances to power, and of any single source of secure constitutional power at any level. I informed my audience that there were few republicans in Scotland. I pointed out that even the SNP sought only to end the Union of Parliaments not the Union of Crowns and that all evidence pointed consistently to the Scottish wish to remain within and indeed strengthen the Union.

My concluding assertion would be anathema to the growing band of Eurosceptics in the then Tory government. I said,

> "subsidiarity may be the buzz word of today but it
> expresses a reality that Scotland understands much more
> clearly than the present Government. It is the British
> (really English) Constitution that fosters this paranoia
> about the loss of sovereignty to some imaginary
> monstrous European superstate. To most of Europe,

federalism is a way to ensure that power is shared and dispersed. To our government it means centralisation and loss. To most of Europe, and to Scotland, power is more like love than wealth. To share it is to increase the total sum! The genuine dispersal of constitutional power actually empowers people, provided it is accompanied by democratic institutions at all levels.

"I look forward to the day, not far distant, when three flags fly, with equal honour, over the parliament of Scotland in Edinburgh, the Saltire of Scotland, the Union flag and the blue and gold stars of Europe. When that day comes, we will all be closer to the kind of society we all want. One which is economically just, politically participative and ecologically sustainable."

Meanwhile the central task of appointing the Commission continued slowly and painfully. A number of those approached to chair the Commission declined, in every case not because of any lack of support or enthusiasm for our proposals but because they realised the difficulty and time-consuming nature of the job they would be undertaking. In the end Joyce McMillan, a widely respected writer and journalist, and John Pollock, the retired General Secretary of the Educational Institute of Scotland (EIS), agreed to be co-chairs. None of the Commissioners were members of the Constitutional Convention itself, thus maintaining the Commissions independence.

As chair of the Convention's executive it was agreed that I should sit in on meetings of the Commission, mainly in order to answer any questions they might have about the Convention's scheme and its implications. I took no part, however, in the decisions made by the Commission and had no voting rights. The Convention's secretary, Bruce Black, provided the secretarial services for the commission until his retirement, in April 1994, when Liz Manson, also of COSLA took over this task.

The Commission met for the first time on 6th October 1993

and met twelve times over the following year. It received a massive amount of written and oral submissions from a wide range of institutions and individuals.

The Commission had hardly begun working when the Convention was suddenly shaken by an unexpected earthquake that came close to causing its collapse. Since the Commission's mandate instructed it to start from the agreed position of the Convention, the secretary prepared, for the Commission's use, a number of key relevant extracts from the Convention's existing proposals for a Scottish parliament. Some of those were, of course, from the original proposal *Towards Scotland's Parliament* but others reflected later decisions made in February 1992, on the basis of proposals from the two working groups on electoral arrangements, procedures and preparation.

On the electoral system the notes repeated the six major principles and the further decisions made by the executive, to use an additional member system as a means to achieving balance and included a phrase which we all thought the executive and full Convention had discussed and approved in February 1992, namely "Acceptance of a statutory obligation on parties to put forward equal numbers of men and women candidates." This caused an explosion.

The Scottish Liberal Democrats, realising most probably that such a mandate to the Commission would confine it to a statutory solution for the 50/50 problem and that removal of the bracketed words "statutory (or other) obligation" was from their point of view a fatal mistake, made it known, first privately to the Labour Party and to other members of the Convention, that they could not accept this phrase. It was agreed in private conversations that this problem would be brought to and discussed at the executive of the Convention on Friday, 5th November, 1993.

The whole debate may seem to many rather esoteric, but it hinged on the belief of some, mainly in the Labour Party and STUC, that the discrimination against women's participation was such that only some form of statutory provision would enable anything like gender balance. On the other hand the Liberal Democrats and some other groups held the equally strong conviction that there should not be this kind of interference by law.

The Liberal Democrats believed strongly that gender balance could not be enshrined in legislation and had made this point strongly at many executive meetings. They stressed time and time again that this was a position supported by their female membership. They believed gender balance had to be left ultimately to the parties and particularly to the electorate to decide.

The original proposal of the working group was to achieve this was by having two members from each constituency, one male one female, both chosen by the entire electorate. This did not achieve consensus in the Convention for the reasons stated above and therefore, the form of words which was eventually passed in February 1992 envisaged a statutory obligation not through the electoral system, but on the parties in their choice of candidate.

This was seen already as a considerable concession to those who wanted the electorate to have the final decision but, on further reflection the Liberal Democrats felt this must be changed. Unfortunately, before there could be further private discussions for this to come directly to the Executive, the party chairman of the Liberal Democrats, Sandra Grieve, who was frankly found by many of us to be somewhat abrasive in her approach, went directly to the media with a threat to pull out of the Convention. The *Scotsman's* political editor reported this in a 'who said what in row over voting system' article writing, "If the dispute is not resolved at a meeting of the Convention's executive this Friday, a Liberal Democrat pull-out would fatally undermine the already fragile existence of the Convention and bring to an end the last vestige of cross-party working on Home Rule." We were suddenly and for most of us surprisingly in the midst of a crisis.

The dispute was not, in the first instance, about the wisdom of the phrase, but about whether or not the Convention had actually approved it in February 1992. Sandra Grieve said that she had been told by Bruce Black that the statutory obligation for gender equality had been agreed by the Convention before the last election. She however, disagreed maintaining "that the then Liberal Democrat and Labour leaders had agreed that the matter would be left to one side". She then said that the party's executive had decided that unless the reference to statutory obligation was removed from the remit of the Commission then the Liberal Democrats would quit the Convention.

Inevitably a teaspoon full of a bad news and conflict gets more publicity than a gallon of consensus! The press had a field day. Like the *Scotsman*, the *Herald* reported that "the Scottish Constitutional Convention could finally be killed off this week if the Scottish Liberal Democrats carry out a threat to withdraw."

Sandra Grieve's action in taking this to the press caused considerable anger within the Convention. Jack McConnell for the Labour Party said "for them to make a public statement in advance of the executive that falsely distorts the truth is a fairly shabby way to act." Mrs Grieve retorted that "as far as we can see there is no point to the Convention continuing if it is not committed to a fair electoral system. We regard that as a non-negotiable aspect."

Bruce Black though an efficient and highly competent secretary of the Convention had a well justified reputation for not suffering fools gladly. His letter of November 1st to Sandra Grieve, which he circulated not to the press but to the executive committee of the Convention, breathed fire and brimstone. He wrote to her that "to the uncommitted observer these regular threats to leave the Convention have the look of a wish hoping to be fulfilled. Presumably, as soon as someone takes you up on your threat, you would then be able to leave blaming others."

His letter then turned to the substantive question and he asserted "there is no doubt that the paragraph which concerns you was agreed in these terms although the version of which the executive committee had before it referred to 'acceptance of a statutory or other obligation'. But the words 'or other' were deleted by the executive committee."

The letter, though personal and sent without previous consultation, does reflect his real frustration and anger at what had been the last of a series of such threats to leave the Convention. He was particularly annoyed at the public debate and wrote, "I explained all of this by letter and by telephone. You indicated that you would write to me to set out the position as you saw it and the issue would then be discussed at the executive committee on 5th November. However in what was no doubt intended to be a pre-emptive strike we see the whole matter laid out before us in today's newspapers. What a way to conduct business!"

Sandra Grieve immediately responded denying any personal wish to leave the Convention and making the point that "this is not about who said what eighteen months ago. This about the position taken by the current (Liberal Democrat) executive and office bearers and would be their position regardless of what was agreed eighteen months ago." She then claimed that she was approached by the press and gave them the facts.

Having seen both of these letters that same day, I felt that this was a matter important enough and sufficiently dangerous for the Convention's future for me to intervene. I therefore wrote to Jim Wallace, the Liberal Democrat leader at the House of Commons with a copy to Sir David Steel in which I made clear my own astonishment and sadness at the news in two major Scottish papers that the Liberal Democrats were threatening to leave the Convention. I said "this kind of public statement, made before any discussion of any kind had taken place in the executive, or even in the smaller coordinating group, seems to me not only highly irresponsible and contrary to the spirit of our agreement to work by consensus, but calculated to make agreements more difficult to achieve by hardening attitudes on what should be a relatively secondary matter." I then reiterated my understanding, shared by virtually everyone who was actually there, that the earlier decision had been taken with the Liberal Democrat representatives accepting after much discussion that "while they could not accept any statutory obligation to make gender balance absolute, they could live with a statutory obligation on the parties with respect to candidates." I made it clear that Sandra Grieve was simply factually mistaken if she claimed that this was not agreed.

This was at the time a private letter and not made public but now, I think it important that the Convention's story is told in full and that the nature of our difficulties in achieving consensus should be made clear.

It remains my personal view that Jim Wallace, whom I have always found to be open, positive and genuinely seeking accommodation and progress rather than party advantage, probably had little to do with the way in which Mrs Grieve had spoken to the press.

The substantive issue remained. At the executive meeting on 5th November we were able to reach the kind of creative compromise which has been the mark of the Convention's success. We agreed quite simply that the Commission would be free to look at all forms of achieving the desirable 50/50 gender balance and not simply statutory forms. We effectively restored the words 'or other'. This was done on the clear understanding, endorsed by all parties, that this was the only change made in the consensus we had arrived at prior to the General Election and that all of our other common decisions stood firm.

The press, which had reported the problem, fairly reported the solution. The *Scotsman* reported that "a potentially damaging split was averted yesterday". They quoted the leaders of the Labour and Liberal Democrat parties and myself as claiming together that "peace has broken out over this issue".

To do him full justice, Jim Wallace joined George Robertson to deny publicly and decisively that there had ever been any prospect of the Convention reaching "breaking point" over this issue. They claimed in fact that "we have come out more united than divided."

I confirmed to the press that "while we had reaffirmed all other policies, it was recognised that there is no longer unanimity on the clause relating to the statutory provision." This of course did not represent any kind of final decision but at least left the Commission free to discuss any means it wished to look at achieving the desired result of a truly balanced and representative parliament.

George Robertson reiterated that there have been and will be many disagreements but said "while there are disagreements we are not going to let it wreck what we have already achieved." I commented with my tongue in cheek that any rows seemed to be seen by some commentators as the end of the Convention "the funeral oration of the Convention has already been pronounced at least five times!"

The *Herald's* report of this 'Storm in a Loving Cup' was very kind to me. They said, "it is a tribute to the dogged patience of Canon Kenyon Wright, Chairman of the executive that the Convention is still carrying on despite frequent media speculation that it had either run out of steam or could no longer keep its constituent parts together." The *Scotsman's* editorial was somewhat scornful of the Convention's "less than inspirational" record since the election and urged us to find convincing answers to the remaining questions rather than dreaming up difficult questions for ourselves! I hope we took their friendly criticism to heart.

It was when the full Convention met for the tenth time in the Signet Library, Edinburgh on 26th November 1993, that I was able to report that after some squalls we were firmly on course. I asked where the Convention now stood? And answered, "we have reaffirmed the unique and distinctive purpose of the Convention we have demonstrated despite the wishful thinking of our critics, that the reports of our death have been persistently and pathetically exaggerated. We are alive and well, and I say to you today that this Convention will die happy, only on the day when Scotland's democratic parliament is born."

During the days before our meeting, the South African Constitutional Convention had been able to move decisively toward the creation of a democratic and nonracial constitution for their country after apartheid. Many features of their constitutional provisions had obvious lessons for us, including their recognition of the need for shared power. The Convention passed at that meeting a message of friendship which was sent to the leaders of the South African Constitutional Convention, at that time State President FW De Klerk and ANC President Nelson Mandela. That message I believe is important enough to quote in full. It read:

> As your country takes a decisive step forward towards a democratic constitution, we send you our warmest congratulations on your astonishing achievement, and our hopes that the difficulties ahead will continue to be overcome.
>
> Your work in the South African Constitutional Convention is both an inspiration and a practical lesson for the Scottish Constitutional Convention.
>
> The constitutional grievance of the Scottish nation can never be compared with the oppression suffered by the majority population in South Africa, as none of us have suffered imprisonment or death. If justice and democracy can win in South Africa then those of us elsewhere trying to enhance democracy, should never lose heart.
>
> Like you, we have a legitimate claim to represent the majority of our people.
>
> Like you, our hard won consensus still excludes some sections of our society.
>
> Like you, we seek to move from a situation which is manifestly undemocratic, towards a Parliament genuinely answerable to our people.
>
> Like you, we have developed proposals which move away from our adversarial political system, towards one in which all major political forces can be fairly represented by a better electoral system, and indeed work together in government.
>
> Like you, we recognise the need for true subsidiarity – i.e. for power to be exercised at lower levels.

Like you, we are committed to a Constitutional Bill of Rights to protect our people from abuse of government.

Above all, like you, we are committed not just to change, but to government which will manifestly be better, more open, answerable and participative.

Scotland's Parliament will remain firmly within a reformed United Kingdom. Nevertheless, we look forward to the day when we can greet the leaders of the new South Africa in the Parliament of Scotland, and acknowledge publicly our debt to you.

A reply was received from the South African Embassy in London enclosing a detailed account of the transitional constitution and copies of the addresses given by both the State President and Nelson Mandela. At the opening of the special session of parliament in South Africa on 22nd November 1993, State President De Klerk made a point which could not fail to be of enormous interest to us in Scotland. He asked a question, "what is the essential difference between this new constitution and the South African constitutional dispensation as it has been so far?" His answer was this:

"South Africa's constitutional history was born and bred in the British tradition, the tradition of the sovereignty of parliament. In layman's language this means parliament is supreme. It can make any law regardless of whether it is just or unjust, regardless of whether it discriminates on the base of race, sex or creed: regardless of whether or not it flies in the face of universally accepted values: regardless of whether it is right or wrong.

"The new agreed constitution turns South Africa once and for all into a Rechtstaat, i.e. a state in which the rule of law is sovereign. In layman's terms that means that every law passed in future by parliament as well as every

decision in the cabinet has to meet with requirements of
a value system of prescribed norms and principles. No
law may be in conflict with the constitution or the Bill
of Fundamental Rights . . . this transformation from
parliamentary sovereignty to the sovereignty of the law
is far reaching. It changes the essence and character of
our State. It places an effective limitation on the abuse
of power by any majority. It replaces power as the
determining factor with values which define justice as
the decisive test.

"Henceforth, no government will be able to do just as
it pleases merely because it has a majority.

"One day, when the history of this era is written, this
incisive change in our system will stand out as the most
significant constitutional innovation of them all. We
have to stop believing that political power is everything.
In the future, it will be limited."

To those words all intelligent Scots can only say a hearty and heart
felt Amen.

The difficulties we have come through, real though they were,
cannot be compared to the pain, suffering and agony which gave
birth to the new South Africa. However, they clearly have much
to teach us and the principles are the same.

As we approached the end of 1993, I prepared a message for
the New Year. I began with the statement "it has not been a good
year for Scotland. We seem listless and stagnant. Battered by
injustice we are powerless to resist, many have lost confidence in
democracy and the political process itself. We sense an erosion of
common moral values but feel impatient. We desperately need a
renewal of vision."

The one part of my message that got more fully into the
public domain was the comparison I made between the hope of
peace for Ireland and Scotland. The government's pledge, explicitly
made "to uphold the democratic wish of a greater number of the

people of Northern Ireland" was contrasted with their denial of that same wish in Scotland. This seemed to convey a dangerous message, that bullets ultimately count more than ballots! I warned of the trouble we were storing up "if we even appear to be saying that guns and fear can achieve what has been denied to the constant democratic will of the people of Scotland. We must not be surprised if democracy itself is devalued."

My gloom was somewhat lifted on 30th December 1993 by the exciting news that Scotland's highest court, the Court of Session, had ruled for the Convention on a very important matter. Grampian Region had made a modest financial contribution to the work of the Convention and were taken to task by the Controller of Audit who decided that the Council's payments were contrary to law. This had been upheld by the Commission for Local Authority Accounts in Scotland who decided that they were contrary to Scottish Local Government legislation.

The Council took this to the Court of Session in Edinburgh claiming that matters of public importance had been raised over the interpretation of the law. To our delight, Scotland's senior judge, the Lord President of the Council, Lord Hope, accompanied by Lord Weir and Lord Prosser gave a written judgement which said, "the question whether there should be a directly elected legislative assembly or parliament in Scotland has been the subject of political debate in the country for many years." The justices proclaimed,

> "we do not see how the creation of a directly elected
> assembly or parliament for Scotland can be said to
> have nothing whatever to do with the interests of the
> Council's area or its inhabitants.

The judges therefore concluded that payments made by the region were within the council's power. Since the Scottish Constitutional Convention had been open from the start to all political parties and groupings and had invited their participation, their Lordships agreed "it does not appear . . . it was the intention . . . to embark upon party political controversy or publish material designed to affect public support for one political party as against another."

The consequences of this judgement for the Convention were, of course, huge and incalculable. They effectively opened the door for Scotland's local authorities, the vast majority of which were and remain members of the Convention, to contribute financially to our work, provided it was clear that these contributions were not for campaigning purposes but for the general administration and development of the Convention. That decision enormously increased the ability of the Convention to be effective in the following two years, and ensured that the work of the Constitutional Commission was properly funded and supported. In practice we wrote early in 1994 to all local authorities in Scotland and a majority of them contributed financially to the Convention in many cases for two separate financial years. Given the enormous and apparently limitless resources constantly available to the opponents of change, this simple decision by Scotland's highest legal authority, enabled the Convention at least to make a reasonable response.

Early in 1994, the City of Edinburgh District Council, acting on a resolution which had been proposed by Cllr Donald Gorrie of the Liberal Democrats, wrote to the Secretary of State for Scotland seeking reassurance that the Scottish Office would not sell off the former Royal High School building, and that a joint committee be set up to "consider appropriate uses for the building until the Scottish Parliament issue is finally resolved". This, of course, referred to the building which had, since 1979, been lying in wait for the Scottish Parliament with its chamber carefully prepared.

The Secretary of State's reply ended with the claim "that the issue of a Scottish Parliament was resolved at the last election."

Fortunately there was, in the original agreement, a reference to the fact that Edinburgh District would have first refusal if the building was ever to be sold off. In March 1994, the District

Council acquired the premises. I wrote a letter of appreciation to Cllr. Lesley Hinds, the Council leader in which I said, "your Council's action to save the former Royal High School as the home of Scotland's coming parliament is courageous and farsighted. The people of Scotland will have cause to thank you for saving a building which has come to symbolise our aspiration to have democratic control over our own affairs." Apart from anything else this decision meant that at least some future meetings of the Convention, and of related bodies such as the Civic Assembly, could actually be held in the building which was renamed the Scottish Parliament House.

The sudden death of John Smith in May 1994, plunged all of us into genuine grief. He had come across to all our people, not just those of us who were privileged to know him, as a man of integrity and honesty, for whom politics was genuinely a search for justice and truth and not a self-serving occupation. He had been a pillar of support for the Convention and our work and his commitment to a Scottish Parliament as "unfinished business" and "the settled will of the Scottish people" will not be forgotten. The closing words of his last note to me were "I have no doubt that we will get an opportunity before too long to discuss the way ahead for Scotland." To my undying regret we never did. But I believe I know what he would have said.

Meanwhile, the Constitutional Commission was painstakingly and earnestly pressing on with its work. Early in the year John Pollock had resigned from the chairmanship and membership of the Commission. Bruce Black, already noted for having a short fuse, had written to John Pollock criticising some remarks he made about the nature of the minutes. John's response was to resign and I was unable to persuade him to withdraw that decision. This left Joyce McMillan, fortunately a most capable chairperson, in charge of the Commission. It moved forward steadily and was ready by October 1994, a year after the beginning of its work, to bring a full report to the Constitutional Convention as a whole.

The fact that the Commission had had some difficulty

reaching conclusions was reported with some satisfaction by those parts of the press unfriendly to us. Joanne Robertson in the *Sunday Times* reported in July 1994 that "the lack of progress by the Special Commission set up to tackle difficult issues such as the electoral system has alarmed campaigners."

At the same time, much was made of the new Labour leader Tony Blair's failure to understand precisely what was happening in Scotland. In an article in July that year, Tony Blair maintained that "the exact details" of the devolution package would be drawn up by George Robertson and his team. He stated, "the Parliament will have clearly defined economic powers, empowered to legislate on Scottish domestic affairs. The exact details are being worked out by a team headed by George Robertson and the people of Scotland can be in no doubt that they will be realistic, meaningful and get the backing of the overwhelming majority of Scots."

The newspapers such as the *Sunday Times* and the *Scottish Daily Express*, whose headline read 'Labour Chaos on Home Rule', were quick to point out that Tony Blair appeared to be unaware that Labour was committed to basing its policies on the work of the Scottish Constitutional Convention. Predictably it was Conservative and SNP leaders who made this point most strongly. Alec Salmond for example said that the impression had been given that Labour was accepting a plan for the parliament drawn up by the Scottish Constitutional Convention and "it may well have come as a surprise to George Robertson to discover that his new leader expects him to start afresh."

Apart from this predictable mischief-making and gloomy prediction that the Commission would not be able to achieve its task, there was, in the Convention at least, some genuine concern that Tony Blair must be helped to understand more fully the role the Convention played and how closely the fortunes of the Labour Party in Scotland were not inextricably bound with our work.

CHAPTER 19

'Further Steps'

– the Constitutional Commission reports

By October 1994 yet another of the minor miracles that had paved the Convention's path was achieved when, despite the recurrent predictions of the press that this or that particular issue would prove fatal or would at least substantially delay matters, the Constitutional Commission presented its report .

Established in October 1993, the Commission had been given a year to complete the unenviable task of recommending a consensus view in those few but crucial remaining areas in which the Convention itself had not been able to achieve a common mind. It is to the credit of the Commission and especially its chair, Joyce McMillan, that they managed to keep to the timetable. The Commission presented its report at a press conference in Edinburgh on Tuesday 25th October 1994. Under the title *Further Steps – Towards a Scheme for Scotland's Parliament*, the Commission report covered three main points. They had looked at the questions of elections to and representation in a Scottish parliament. Recognising that they were restricted by their mandate which was to begin from the position already adopted by the Constitutional Convention, they proposed a form of the Additional Member System, whereby each elector would have two votes, one for a constituency MP based on the present 72 constituencies, and a second vote for a party or group list within the boundaries of the Euro constituency. They proposed five additional members for each such Euro constituency, which would produce a total of 40 additional members creating a parliament of 112.

The report in the *Herald* asserted that "the battle, to be resolved at a public meeting of the Scottish Constitutional Convention in December, hinges on whether these additional members be used proportionately or 'correctly', which would deny Labour a majority." The report then went on to quote George Robertson as wanting to 'look carefully' at the division of seats and that this question of whether the additional members should 'themselves be allocated proportionally, or be used simply as a corrective to the 72 first-past-the-post members'.

To forecast a battle on this seemed strange since the Commission's report was very carefully prepared and worded to avoid any ambiguity on this precise question. It reads:

"Five additional MSPs will be allocated to each Euro constituency so as to make the total representation of that area – including the individual constituency MSPs – correspond as closely as possible, within constraint of numbers, to the preferences expressed in the party/ group section of the poll

It was clearly the intention of the Commission that the additional members should be appointed on a corrective basis. This means, for example, that if in a given Euro constituency such as say, Glasgow, the Labour Party were to win all nine of the parliamentary seats by the present first-past-the-post method, and if there were as the commission had proposed, five additional members, then the total number of fourteen (the nine plus the five) would be made as closely proportional as possible to the votes cast on the party lists. In practice, this would mean that the Labour Party in such a situation, would be unlikely to gain any of the additional member seats, since they would all be needed to provide a degree of proportionality in the total representation of that area. We can only hope that this is not too complex. It certainly seems to work in Germany and in other situations throughout the world.

Michael Forsyth mischievously and totally inaccurately, maintained in one of his speeches that a substantial number of the members of Scotland's parliament would be appointed by the parties and not elected. This is totally untrue. Of course parties will continue to choose the candidates as they do now – both for the first-past-the-post seats and for the party lists, but the electorate makes the decisions. No party appoints anybody to the Scottish parliament, although obviously if a party under its present or any future system chooses a candidate for a seat which is regarded as 'safe' then it certainly eases his or her path to parliament.

The second major area in which the Commission reported was on the thorny question of gender balance and ethnic minority representation. In this area the Commission obviously was grateful for the removal of the initial restraint, which would have committed it to a 'statutory method' of achieving gender balance, at least by a legal obligation on the parties. The fact that the words 'or other' were placed after the word statutory allowed the Commission to do what it in fact did, namely to reject any "imposition on political parties of a statutory requirement that they field equal numbers of men and women candidates."

The Commission reported that it had given serious consideration to an idea which had previously been put forward by a working group of the Convention, namely that the most straightforward way of ensuring equal representation of men and women would be a 'double ballot' system in the constituency section, by which each voter, in constituencies doubled up, would vote for a male and a female constituency member. Every voter, male and female, would vote for both lists but each double constituency would therefore end up with a man and a woman MSP. This, however, was rejected since some saw insuperable objections of principle to such a system in that it would be a manipulation of the electoral process.

In the end the Commission's recommendation was comparatively weak in this area. It proposed what it called 'a target system' by which each political party in the election would be invited – initially by the Constitutional Convention, later by the parliament itself – to commit itself to a target of, say, 40%+ representation of women and fair representation of ethnic minorities, within five years of the setting up of a Scottish parliament.

All the press and other reports recognised that this was likely to be one of the hardest nuts to crack. This was a fairly safe prediction which proved to be accurate. The reality was that the Commission had simply thrown this one back into the lap of the Convention itself.

The third major area was that of the 'constitutional implications'. Here, the thorny old West Lothian question was decisively rejected by the Commission. They recognised it as "an anomaly" but rejected as unrealistic the idea that Scottish MPs might opt out of voting on English and Welsh domestic issues at Westminster. Their conclusion was that this was an anomaly that had to be lived with, at least for a time, on the grounds that "the setting up of a Scottish parliament within the UK is likely to take place as the first step in a dynamic process of constitutional change and decentralisation in the UK," which would be likely to lead eventually to a general reassessment of the powers and composition of Westminster.

Their second argument was that the powers remaining with Westminster were of crucial importance for Scotland, and they therefore recommended quite clearly that "the Convention should not propose an immediate reduction in Scottish representation at Westminster. But should promote the opening of a general debate on patterns of Westminster representation during a period of decentralisation, which might lead to agreed legislation on the issue at a later date."

On the role of the Secretary of State, the Commission recognised an important function in the transition to the full functioning of the Scottish parliament, but the long term future of the post as being much more uncertain, since all of its effective powers would be transferred to the Scottish parliament. The actual decision on whether a minister retains that title within the UK Cabinet or government is of course a matter for the UK Prime Minister.

The Commission had also been asked to look at the difficult issue of how to achieve the Convention's declared aim of entrenching the power of Scotland's parliament so that it could not be unilaterally altered or abolished at a later date by Westminster. The Commission accepted what all of us reluctantly know, that under the present unwritten British constitution "it is impossible to achieve full legal entrenchment of any institution," since the doctrine of absolute Parliamentary sovereignty, while totally unacceptable to the Scottish constitutional tradition, specifically gives Parliament unlimited powers to repeal or to amend its own legislation, and lays down that no Parliament can bind any of its successors. The Commission, however, put strongly the view that in practical terms "moral and political entrenchment of a parliament and its powers is at least as significant as full legal entrenchment in ensuring its survival." Both in some of the Acts which freed our former colonies, and in much of the European Union legislation, absolute parliamentary sovereignty is already qualified by decisions which are either totally or virtually impossible to change.

On this basis the recommendation of the Commission is that the Act should include clauses clearly stating the intention to entrench, and that there should be strong links developed as rapidly as possible between a Scottish parliament and the structures of the European Union.

Under this broad heading the Commission also looked at

the position of local government in Scotland and recommended that the Act setting up Scotland's parliament should include a clause committing the Scottish parliament to strong and effective local government, another committing it to the principle of subsidiarity as enshrined in the quote in the European Charter of Local Self Government, and a clause giving a general power of competence to local authorities along the lines suggested by the Charter. The Commission's recommendations solved some, but far from all, of our problems.

When the eleventh full meeting of the Convention took place in the old Royal High School, now the Scottish Parliament House, in Edinburgh on Friday December 2nd 1994, to receive and discuss the report of the Constitutional Commission, it was clear that there were still major areas in which opinions differed widely – notably on how gender balance was to be achieved, on the actual number in Scotland's parliament, and other details of the electoral system. George Robertson, the Shadow Scottish Secretary, welcomed the report very warmly but recognised that it was now up to the Convention to deliberate and for its various component parts to come to a conclusion on what the Commission had said. He made the claim, despite some continuing differences, that "in the interests of the people of Scotland, we have carved out a consensus, a remarkable and popular consensus at that, on the design of the Scottish parliament which will bring power and decision making closer to the people." For the Liberal Democrats, Jim Wallace also echoed that welcome and looked forward to an agreement on a system of proportional representation, which "fairly rewards votes with seats." He pointed out that this was necessary not just for fairness, but in order to create a parliament "less confrontational and more deliberative. One which is more open and encourages popular participation."

In my own speech to that Convention meeting, on the subject of *Towards Scotland's Democracy – The Next Steps*, I quoted a letter I had recently received, quoting the Brahan Seer, who many centuries ago wrote in one of his prophecies: "When men in horseless carriages go under the sea to France, Then shall Scotia arise anew, free from all oppression."

Thank God, I said, that the Channel Tunnel seems to be working at last! More seriously, I defined the unfinished agenda of the Convention as being "to complete, communicate and commend" our scheme. The job of completing the scheme, I said, will not be easy. But I called on everyone in the Convention to remain committed to the consensus already achieved and to show the same good faith – the readiness to listen without threats or party posturing, that had carried us so far and that I still believed could complete our consensus.

Privately at this stage I accepted and indeed discussed with some others in the Convention the possibility that we might reach the stage where some areas could not be settled and we would simply have to agree to differ. Even if that had been the case, a 95% agreement would have been the result of a series of remarkable minor miracles in itself – but as someone in the press told me at the time, "95% success is not news, 5% failure is." Inevitably, the media would have pounced on any areas in which we failed to achieve total agreement – so we had to do our utmost. It was perhaps the greatest of the minor miracles on the road to Scotland's parliament, that we did in fact succeed in achieving consensus on all remaining questions within the next year – but not without pain and struggle.

At that meeting, we also announced the beginning of our programme, Preparing for Change, which was a deliberate attempt to stimulate serious discussion on what Scotland's parliament could actually do with its powers, to make a real difference in key areas such as health, education, housing, local government, the environment and others. To promote and develop this programme, I was also able to announce the appointment of Mrs Esther Roberton formerly chief executive of the Scottish Community Education Council as Programme Coordinator of the Convention from the beginning of 1995.

Just as the New Year was about to begin, the Prime Minister

handed us a moral victory on a plate. In an interview on the BBC's *Today* programme, he indulged in an intemperate outburst, attacking Scotland's ambitions for our own parliament. With near hysterical and ludicrous hyperbole, he described this as "the most dangerous proposition ever put before the British people." No wonder that James Naughtie, who conducted the interview, said "the Prime Minister has offered to lead the argument and that should be welcomed by those who want change more than by those who don't. Major has given Scotland a New Year present."

My own response, which was widely reported at the time, was to write a New Year letter to friends and fellow citizens south of the border. In it I pointed out that the proposals which Major attacked as so dangerous, which he called the Labour Party's hastily devised plans, are in fact the result of years of deliberation in a Constitutional Convention which manifestly represents the majority of the people of Scotland. Above all, I argued that the greatest threat to the union does not lie in a Scottish parliament. It lies in the mistaken attempt to keep Britain the most centralised superstate in Europe, in which democracy is increasingly denied to the people of Scotland, and in which the people increasingly feel resentful because of that. There was a major battle to be won to persuade people across the UK that this is not some bee in a Balmoral, but a crucial concern to people throughout the whole of Britain.

A few days later, on the 10th January 1995, the *Scotsman* editorial, headed 'Quite Right Mr Lang' began rather archly by promising 600 words in agreement with the Secretary of State, as a rather traumatic shock. Admitting that they have often disagreed with Ian Lang on Scotland's future since his views have "usually struck us as dogged, dogmatic and wrong-headed", they proceeded to agree with a pamphlet coauthored by Ian Lang twenty years before. They extracted some delicious quotes from the document such as: "there are in Scotland reservoirs of capital, of talent, of experience and of adventure. With present policies and attitudes these are being lost to Scotland." Even more delightfully: "the proposed new Scottish assembly can be the catalyst – it must be demonstrably the case that in those fields of activity in which the new assembly has authority in Scotland, the Scottish Conservatives exercise complete autonomy in the formulation of policy."

Even more hilariously, the *Scotsman* itself made a judgement which condemned its own more recent attempts to play up the West Lothian question. It described that question as "a quibble, a minor anomaly beside the democratic shortfall which the *status quo* inflicts." Well spoken, *Scotsman!*

The editorial's final quotes from the Lang pamphlet are just as wonderful: "Too often we have appeared to speak to people rather than for people – there is a better way of running things." Well spoken, Ian Lang – the words were written of course in 1975, if they were true then, events since have exponentially increased their veracity.

Following the wipeout of their seats at the 1997 General Election the Conservative Party appears to be having an internal debate as the prepare to change their stance on the constitution recognising that the people of Scotland have overwhelmingly rejected their views on the *status quo*. This is to be welcomed but it saddens me that so many within the Conservative Party in Scotland allowed Thatcher to bully them into changing their support for a Scottish parliament.

In a television programme following the 1997 General Election I heard some prominent members of the Conservative Party call for a more radical parliament than proposed by the Convention while others wanted a watered down version. I am afraid it is too late for a debate of this nature. The Conservative Party rejected several invitations to join the Convention which has debated this subject for eight years. We even asked John Major to discuss our proposals with us, but perhaps due to the arrogance of power these approaches were rejected out of hand. Certainly Parliament will now debate the establishment of a Scottish parliament but the sad reality is that there will be no Scottish Conservative MPs in the Chamber to give their views.

By the start of 1995 it was already clear that the Convention must seek before the end of that year to present to the people of Scotland, as complete and definitive a set of proposals as possible. Now that we had the Commission's report before us, the hard task of securing agreement on the remaining issues and of preparing a full document which would build on our past work but presented in fresh ways, was clearly before us. There is no doubt that chairing the Convention over these long years had made me a political realist. I was only too aware of the kind of horse-trading and hard bargaining that formed the stuff of realistic politics. At the same time, however, I had strangely acquired a kind of sublime confidence.

So often I had witnessed not just hard work and hard bargaining, but the phenomenon I have described as a series of minor miracles along the way. I had become strangely confident that we were not now going to fail. There is a sense in which each minor miracle made the next easier – for we had by now reached a stage where no group or party was willing to run the risk of being seen as the wreckers, of being tainted with the charge of destroying the Convention or denying the consensus reached. This meant that, after all the hard bargaining and trading had been done, the pressure actually to achieve consensus, and to give and take, was ever greater. However, my confidence in minor miracles was to be severely tested in the following few months.

CHAPTER 20

Clearing the Highest Hurdles

The Constitutional Commission report had been extremely helpful but as we entered 1995 we still had major issues to resolve. Although we had reached agreement on 95 per cent of the matters before us, I realised that time was running out.

Our tactic had been at each stage of our long journey to achieve the widest possible consensus which produced what I have already frequently called a series of minor miracles. This however left to one side for future discussion, any issue on which consensus seemed particularly hard to achieve. This allowed our opponents, and often sections of the media, to accuse us of dodging the really hard questions. I am convinced this was the right way to proceed. After all, each success made the next issue that much easier to solve, if only by constantly reminding us of the sharply increasing tariff for failure.

We had three major hurdles ahead of us, any one of which could have proved insurmountable, and on which we might have ended up simply having to agree to differ. In simple terms the hurdles were Entrenchment, Gender Balance and the Electoral System.

At the start of the year on January 1st, I paid a personal visit to Andalusia and to Don Manuel Chaves Gonzalez, President of Andalusia in his office in the Baroque Santelmo Palace in Seville. Given that Spain offered the closest parallel to the potential British situation, I asked him about the two major issues which our opponents constantly used against us. I asked him about the 'tortilla tax' and the 'West Barcelona question', i.e. did the powers of the various autonomous regions to levy their own taxes within certain limits, make difficulties for business and industry or for the economy. I also asked the President if the fact that the various regions had differing powers, affect their rights to vote on all matters that came up in the central parliament of Spain.

On both these questions his reaction was bafflement. He could not understand how these were issues at all. His amusement when I described how Scotland was at present governed by ministers appointed from Westminster, and the ease with which he accepted the sharing of power, were both refreshing. His answer in particular to the question, under which circumstances the Andalusian parliament might exercise its power to tax, after eight years of autonomy during which they had not exercised this right, was illuminating. He said, "that is simple. If and when the people of Andalusia show us that is what they want."

I could not resist the temptation, when I wrote my account of this fascinating visit, to end with my own version of the song from *My Fair Lady*: "The reign in Spain makes Forsyth's fables plain!"

Following my return from Andalusia I attended in March the inaugural meeting of the Scottish Civic Assembly which brought together a wide range of civic bodies from all parts of the country. If a Scottish parliament does operate in a manner which is a more participative form of democracy, much more open and accessible to the people, then the existence of such a civic assembly would take on a new importance and significance. The first meeting discussed the whole area of employment and training and made a number of proposals for the emergence of an industrial strategy for Scotland. During March and April the Labour Party and the Liberal Democrats held their spring conferences and the STUC its annual congress. All three gave major attention to the outstanding questions and formulated their various responses to the Commission's report and recommendations.

Both the STUC and the Labour Party were highly critical of the Commission's recommendations in the area of gender balance. The STUC was "deeply concerned at the failure to grasp the opportunity of recommending a mechanism which would ensure, for the first time in any democratic parliament in the world, equal representation of men and women." They reiterated their view that gender equality should be enshrined in statute but went on to recognise that in the absence of agreement within the Convention they were willing to support a compromise position which had been put forward by the women's coordination group, which included the STUC Women's Committee, the Women's Forum Scotland and a movement called Engender.

The Liberal Democrats in a report to their conference entitled *Quarter Final Steps* repeated their total unwillingness to accept any statutory imposition of a 50/50 solution and reminded the Labour Party that "this mirrored Labour's outright rejection of the Single Transferable Vote in any form." This was of course a way of reminding the Labour Party that the Lib Dems had been prepared to give way on their favoured form of proportional representation and had been willing to accept the compromise of a system of an AMS (Additional Member System) which was not as completely proportional as the other. In effect they were saying "we have given way on this issue of importance to us – please be ready to give way on the question of any statutory or legal imposition of gender equality, which is equally important to us."

Gradually a possible consensus and compromise on this issue began to emerge. The Labour Party conference had received a report on the informal discussions that had been going on between Labour and Liberal Democrat women and others. They approved the proposal that there be an electoral contract or a formal agreement between the Scottish Labour Party and Scottish Liberal Democrats "to accept the principle that there should be an equal number of men and women members in the first Scottish parliament." The contract would commit both parties, and challenge other parties to do the same, to select and field equal numbers of male and female candidates, fairly distributed in winnable seats. It is a considerable tribute to the leading women in the parties and other organisations, who took this thorny question into their own hands and fashioned a way forward that was acceptable to us all.

Thus it was that after considerable further discussion on the detail, a formal electoral agreement was signed in Inverness on Thursday, November 23rd 1995, one week before the Convention's definitive document was presented to the Scottish people on St Andrew's Day. This electoral agreement, said,

> "The Scottish Labour Party and the Scottish Liberal Democrats formally agree to accept the principle that there should be an equal number of men and women as members of the first Scottish parliament. In order to achieve this aim, the parties agree and commit themselves to: Select and field an equal number of male and female candidates for election, taking into account both the constituency and Additional Member List candidates; Ensure that these candidates are equally distributed with a view to the winnability of seats; Use an Additional Member System (AMS) for elections; Ensure that the size of the Scottish parliament is large enough to facilitate effective democratic representative government."

This was formally signed, in my presence, by Rhona Brankin, chair of the Scottish Labour Party and George Robertson, Shadow Scottish Secretary and by Marilyne MacLaren, the convenor and Jim Wallace, the leader of the Scottish Liberal Democrats. It was,

I am sure, a moment of quiet satisfaction for the two women leaders who had played such an important part in hammering out this important agreement, which also poses a challenge to the other parties in Scotland. It is worth noting that the agreement specifically refers to "the first Scottish parliament." This is partly because of the belief that it is important to get it right from the start, and partly because any future electoral arrangements will be the responsibility of the parliament itself. The original signed agreement was handed over to me on St Andrew's Day, 1995, for safe keeping by the Convention. Part of the Convention's continuing task of ensuring the implementation of our proposals will certainly include the monitoring of the adherence of the parties to this crucial agreement when the time comes.

The issue of the electoral system and particularly the outstanding issue of the size of the Scottish parliament also had to be dealt with. This was to prove perhaps the most difficult of all the questions we had faced and the one that, even at the very last fence before the finishing post, threatened to bring us crashing down. The problem was that the spring conferences had taken firm positions that were mutually contradictory. The Labour Party predictably had happily accepted the Commission's proposal that the parliament should be a small one of just 112 members. The Liberal Democrats, equally predictably, had carefully examined the likely implications of such a system and had decided that it would not make the parliament sufficiently proportional. They therefore voted firmly for an equal number of additional members to those initially elected by first-past-the-post, i.e. an average of nine for each Euro constituency, which would make a total number in the Scottish parliament of 145 (this allows for the decision, which the Convention approved without any problem, that Orkney and Shetland because of their distinctive nature, had a clear case for a seat each, rather than a shared seat in the Scottish parliament).

This made the total number of first-past-the-post seats 73 rather than 72 and thus the total number proposed by the Liberal Democrats 145.

The STUC congress had gone even further. They had taken the view that we should not be afraid of our larger parliament, if it helped to ensure that the electoral system worked effectively. They argued for a parliament consisting of two members, one man and one woman, from each of the 72 Westminster constituencies, with a further 70 members drawn from the party lists, which would have given a parliament of 214 members, which they believed to be entirely in line with legislative parliaments in similarly sized countries in Europe. They also believed this larger number was necessary to ensure there were sufficient members to sit on the various committees etc. and to ensure that the executive and the Scottish civil servants were subject to full scrutiny and accountability.

We thus had three firmly held views backed up by democratic conferences, which were mutually contradictory – 112 from Labour, 145 from the Lib Dems, and 214 from the STUC. Initially the executive had proposed that there should be a full meeting of the Convention as early as the June 9th 1995 to receive our definitive proposals. Our continuing disagreements made this date impossible – we postponed it to September 26th, but this too proved over-optimistic – and in practice we used both dates for further executive meetings to hammer out our agreement. No group or party was willing to incur the charge of 'wrecker' by being the one to stop the negotiations and we therefore resolved, as much in faith as in real hope, that we simply had to fix a final date by which we would either achieve agreement or openly declare that we could not.

We therefore agreed that the full Convention would meet on Friday October 20th, to receive and discuss our definitive and final proposals. There would then be time for these to be properly revised and presented in a proper printed format to a more formal and celebratory meeting of the full Convention on St Andrew's Day November 30th, 1995.

Once again I have to confess that when we fixed these dates I was still most unsure that we would be able to come to full agreement. Indeed, I privately warned members of the executive that we might have to engage in a kind of damage limitation exercise – that we might be forced into the position of recognising that there were some areas in which we simply could not agree, and they would therefore have to be left to the parties to implement in whatever way the power struggle dictated. It would have been a barely acceptable compromise and it would certainly have greatly diminished the stature of the Convention's achievement.

At the beginning of September we were still no nearer to agreement. Despite intensive conversations with all the main people concerned, fixed positions were still being taken. In that situation I confessed that I encouraged the party leaders to take bold action to end the deadlock and shift the log jam. On September 7th, George Robertson, Shadow Scottish Secretary and leader of the Scottish Labour Party, and Jim Wallace, leader of the Scottish Liberal Democrats, issued a joint declaration that they had decided on a parliament of 129 members, 73 to be elected by the present system, and a further 56 (7 from each of the 8 Euro constituencies) to be elected from lists drawn up by the parties.

Writing in the *Herald* the next day, Ken Smith forecast that this bold move to seize the initiative after years of wrangling carried considerable political risk, as many party members would argue that their views were being ignored and that the lengthy consultation period was no more than a sham. My own view was clear enough, and I expressed it privately to the executive. Throughout my life I have been a believer in occasional times when there must be 'responsible disobedience', i.e. when leadership demands that we ignore the niceties and cut through the obstacles. This was just such a situation. While I recognised that the two leaders had acted in a way that bypassed our normal democratic structures, I was both glad and grateful that they had done so.

The reaction to the behind closed doors deal was mixed. Despite the fact that the new arrangement made the likelihood of a Labour majority in the new Scottish parliament even less likely, the Labour executive on September 9th, voted by 20/6 to accept these proposals. The Liberal Democrats were considerably less enthusiastic. Donald Gorrie, then Lib Dem group leader on Lothian and Edinburgh Councils and a leading member of the Convention executive, said "it was a bad mistake to agree to this figure at this time and without consultation." Sir David Steel, however, was forthright. "It is time we stopped dancing on the head of a pin, quibbling over numbers," he said "and progress the political momentum to secure the restoration of our parliament." My impression is that despite the anger of those who had been closely involved in the discussions at the way the decision was made, there was throughout much of the country a sigh of relief that we had moved on. While not entirely happy, the Liberal Democrats, no doubt in the interests both of party and wider unity, sanctioned the agreement.

More dogged and persistent in their opposition, however, were the STUC and particularly its General Secretary, Campbell Christie. The STUC had argued for a much larger parliament of over 200 seats and refused to support the deal on the grounds that it did not sufficiently address the issue of equal representation of men and women, or reflect Scotland's diversity. The *Herald's* editorial of October 6th, 1995, under the heading 'STUC Stumbling Block' was very critical of what they called "the doggedness of Mr Campbell Christie and other members of the STUC." Certainly at this stage I had to agree with their conclusion that "by arguing for an unyielding parliament and by bringing the process to a halt so near to completion, he is risking the enterprise for which he has worked so hard." With hindsight, I believe Campbell Christie and his colleagues were making a clever tactical objection, designed to ensure that the party leaders would understand that they could not always get it all their own way, and stitch things up in the assumption that the lesser parties and groups would be dragged along on the day. The Unions I believe also wanted to ensure that the issue of gender balance would be given careful thought along with the need for proper proportionality.

In the event, agreement seemed to break out yet again. The

STUC, having effectively made their point, stated that they were now convinced that, albeit reluctantly, the number now proposed would sufficiently meet their objections for them to withdraw their opposition.

Looking back, I have contradictory feelings. On the one hand I am glad the party leaders cut the Gordian knot in an issue which seemed otherwise insoluble and was in any event in danger of boring the people of Scotland. On the other hand, I am also glad that the STUC made the point they did strongly, as a warning to the party leaders that such unilateral action should not become a habit!

I have dealt with the question of entrenchment more fully in another chapter. Suffice to say here that this was overcome once again in a *real politik* manner as the Labour Party prepared for the approaching General Election and had to consider closely how they could fulfil their promise to deliver a Scottish parliament based firmly along the lines agreed by the Convention. The solution regarding entrenchment calls for Parliament to pass a Declaration committing Westminster not to attempt to abolish a Scottish parliament without the consent of the Scottish people either in a General Election or referendum. The Convention accepted this suggestion.

The year had also seen the local authority political map of Scotland being radically redrawn, and the first elections were held in April although the new unitary councils were not to take control until twelve months later in April 1996. In these elections Labour took control of new fewer than twenty of the twenty-nine new councils. Despite the fact that there had been widespread suspicion that the boundaries of the new councils had been carefully drawn to safeguard pockets of Conservative support, the Tories failed to retain even a single council. Scotland in effect became in local government, what it already was in European parliamentary terms, a Tory free zone, and as I write this has just become the same in the Westminster Parliament.

It is hard to prove that this development has a direct

connection with the constitutional debate but clearly many Conservatives believe that their decline coincides with their rejection of change. Shortly after the local elections, one of the small band of eighty-two Tory councillors in Scotland, Brian Meek, who described himself as "the last of the few" wrote an open letter to the Prime Minister in the *Herald*. He began with the story of when he was canvassing before the election of how a man rushed off to get his camera saying to him, "I just want to have a picture of a Tory councillor so I can tell the children what they looked like." Meek wrote that the man was not joking but more important in his letter Meek told the Prime Minister, "that a Scottish parliament is inevitable, that the Tories can make a big impact in such a body and that our party will have to come to terms with it."

Brian Meek warned the Prime Minister in what has turned out to be prophetic: "You can go on ignoring that fact, but you do so at great risk to the union. Listen not to the sycophants, read the election results." Meek was of course correct.

It is one of the unfortunate facts of Scottish politics that on every visit to Scotland John Major made as Prime Minister came either to lecture us on how wrong we were. He claimed when he took over the reins of power from Margaret Thatcher that he would be a listening Prime Minister. If he did listen it was to those who told him only what he wanted to hear. On his first visit to Edinburgh he had a breakfast with leading members of the Tory Party and business leaders who supported the Party. This summed up Major's listening powers – he only heard what he wanted to hear.

CHAPTER 21

The Final Doubts

– 'can we trust the politicians?'

It would be foolish not to recognise that over the past few years, there has been some erosion of the trust on which the Constitutional Convention was founded. Though the Labour Party has loudly and repeatedly denied that there has been any change whatever in its commitment to the Convention and to our joint scheme, other partners – and obviously large sections of Scottish opinion, even in the Labour Party – have had the gut feeling that, under Tony Blair's leadership, the commitment was not as firm and total as had been the case with John Smith.

Time will tell whether the doubts being expressed are true, or whether Tony Blair will prove his doubters wrong. The feeling surfaced most strongly when in 1996 the Labour Party announced its referendum proposals and again at several stages during the General Election campaign in 1997. As early as the end of July 1995 the Scottish press was warning Tony Blair against retreat on devolution and talking of him watering down his commitment. These accusations came as a result of the Labour Party's natural attempt, as it got closer to the reality of government, to work out how best actually to fulfil the Convention's commitment to entrench Scotland's parliament.

Labour came up with the proposal that this commitment would be better, not in the Act itself, largely because this would then open it to endless amendment and discussion in the parliamentary process – but rather that it should be achieved by the passing of a special 'Declaration of the Parliament of the United Kingdom' to be made before the legislation itself was debated. This declaration, to the effect that Scotland's parliament, once established, could not be abolished or radically altered without the consent of the Scottish people, tested through General Election or referendum, was in fact, and in the political reality, a way of strengthening the intention to entrench. It was a means of giving the parliament as much formal and legal sanction as the British unwritten constitutional system would allow, while recognising that the primary entrenchment would be in the hearts and minds of the people. It is, after all, recognised virtually by all, that once established Scotland's parliament could not realistically be abolished.

Though at this point totally unfair, the suspicion of hesitancy and a tendency to draw back from full commitments, was to grow over the period. The suspicion popped up a few weeks later, still during August 1995, and no doubt still part of the silly season for news, in the suggestion on the front page of the *Scotsman* that the arrangements for funding Scotland's parliament were now in terminal disarray. This was predictably put even more stridently by the *Daily Express* and Michael Forsyth yet again jumped on the bandwagon to charge that Labour was "beating a retreat" on its whole devolution commitment. Alf Young Economics Editor of the *Herald* wrote that all of this "owes more to the gapingly empty news agendas which inevitably accompany a sunbaked summer!"

In point of fact, what Labour proposed and convinced all the other partners in the Convention was that the original idea was unwieldy and unworkable – that the Scottish parliament should directly receive Income Tax and possibly VAT collected in Scotland, with the Treasury making up the Scotland's proper proportion from other taxation collected centrally. Instead Labour proposed that the proper solution was for Scotland to receive, no longer a block grant at the discretion of Westminster, but 'assigned revenue' i.e. a clear and assigned proportion of UK revenue, based on the present principle of equalisation. This is the principle that Scotland does not receive simply a per capita funding proportion based simply upon her population, but rather on the special needs, geography and character of the country.

This proposed solution made administrative sense, while not in any way changing the amount of funding that would come to Scotland's parliament – and it also of course left the commitment to have a power to vary Income Tax within limits, unchanged.

Inevitably, Tory media either misunderstood or misinter-preted this as some major change. It was nothing of the kind. Thus it was that finally and breathlessly, within days of the Convention meeting at which our final scheme would have to be presented on October 20th, we succeeded in jumping the last fence. We were able to present to the Convention as a whole and through them to the Scottish people, a scheme for a Scottish parliament which was more detailed and realistic than any previous attempt, and on which we were all agreed on every major issue. The consensus was complete.

The only remaining debate was the title to give to our final draft which was intended to be put before the Convention so that it could then be printed and presented in a celebratory way to another meeting of the Convention on St Andrew's Day. We finally agreed on the title *Scotland's Parliament: Scotland's Right*, subtitled A Report to the People of Scotland by the Scottish Constitutional Convention.

At last, on Tuesday October 17th 1995, we were able, with the deepest feelings of quiet satisfaction and even a little understandable jubilation to announce in a press conference that we had achieved a historic agreement. Speaking on that day, George

Robertson, the then Shadow Scottish Secretary, was able to say "against all the odds, the Convention has been able to reach agreement in the key areas which remained outstanding." The Scottish Liberal Democrat leader Jim Wallace proclaimed that "we have a scheme which has support from the broadest cross-section of Scots ever assembled. It represents a historic achievement, not just for the Convention, but for the new style of politics that the Convention represents." The next day, the *Scotsman's* banner headline proclaimed a "historic day in battle for home rule."

A few days later the scheme *Scotland's Parliament: Scotland's Right* was vigorously debated in a full meeting of the Convention in the setting of Scotland's Parliament House – the chamber which for nearly twenty years has lain silent and unoccupied, waiting for Scotland's parliament to come. When, on St Andrew's Day, the final revised document, well printed and presented, was received with acclamation and celebration in the Assembly Halls of the Church of Scotland, we all thought that the worst of our problems were over. After eight years we should have known better! Our optimism was indeed "a triumph of hope over expectation." The need to clarify beyond doubt the Labour Party's support for the Convention and to overcome the widespread suspicion that in some way the Labour Party was in danger of drawing back from its wholehearted commitment to the *Claim of Right* and to the Convention were to be themes of recurring and growing importance from this point onwards.

CHAPTER 22

Scotland's Parliament; Scotland's Right

– the consensus completed

Our success in overcoming the major hurdles which had faced us galvanised our opponents into action. St Andrew's Day, November 30th 1995 was the day set for us to put our final blueprint for a Scottish parliament before the people of Scotland. No doubt provoked by the thought of the media coverage this was likely to attract, Alex Salmond, leader of the Scottish National Party, announced that on St Andrew's Day they would outline their own proposals, and Michael Forsyth, Secretary of State for Scotland, whetted the political pundits' appetite by announcing that he would reveal dramatic and far-reaching new proposals for the better government of Scotland, also on St Andrew's Day.

At least it was clear that the Convention was setting the agenda. Forsyth's announcement had raised expectations. Iain MacWhirter wrote in the *Scotsman* that "Michael Forsyth must know that if he doesn't deliver something spectacular, he will be the object of ridicule and contempt." Forsyth had got off to a bad start. It had obviously slipped his mind that as the government's proposals were about the form of the Scottish Grand Committee he was compelled to inform the Commons on Wednesday, November 29th, rather than using the platform of Scotland on St Andrew's Day to make his announcement. The "far-reaching proposals" turned out to be a series of rather half-baked ideas for a beefed-up Grand Committee which would tour Scotland, but which would in practice have no more powers of real decision making than it ever had.

Apart from the predictable response from his own Party, and from this sycophantic elements among the media, such as the *Daily Express*, there was almost universal derision for these proposals. Writing in the *Herald* under the headline 'Where's the Beef?' Robbie Dinwoodie wrote, "the rabbit failed to appear from the Scottish Secretary's hat yesterday, prompting scorn from his constitutional critics, surprised by the lack of the unexpected."

The result was that of the three presentations that vied for attention in the media on St Andrew's Day itself, Michael Forsyth's – though it gained considerable coverage – was almost universally recognised to be by far the weakest. The *Herald* editorial said "Surely there must be more, Mr Forsyth?" and asked, "Can this be it?"

My own judgement was widely quoted and remains firm. I said, "The very fact that Michael Forsyth is talking about the constitution at all is a tribute to the work of the Convention. We have set the agenda – everything else is a reaction and nothing at all would have been offered without us. Imitation is the most sincere form of tribute, if not flattery. What was offered today was a pretty poor imitation. The acid test is whether it proposes giving real power to the people of Scotland, and by that test his ideas fail."

Alex Salmond of the SNP used the day to unveil their document spelling out the shape of an independent parliament for Scotland, entitled *Citizens, not Subjects*. The title was interesting, for it actually echoes words I had already written in my tailpiece to the Convention's major document *Scotland's Parliament: Scotland's Right*. My exact words were:

"We have come of age. We are adults not children. We are citizens, not subjects. We are partners, not customers. We are the heirs of a nation that has always prized freedom above all else. We deserve something better than the secretive, centralised self-serving superstate that the UK has become."

The Convention's event was recognised by most of the Scottish press to be by far the most significant and realistic. We had reached full consensus on virtually all the major issues which had divided us, and which our opponents had predicted over and over again would mean our failure and collapse. No wonder they reacted so vigorously to our success.

The solemn setting of the great General Assembly Hall of the Church of Scotland was full to capacity – with members of the Convention and the Scottish public. It was the first time we had met there since that inaugural meeting away back in March 1989 when the *Claim of Right* had been signed and the Convention embarked on its pilgrimage. It was fitting that we ended at least the first stage of that long journey in the same historic setting.

Some who had been our companions on the road were no longer with us. We felt their presence in spirit, especially John Smith whose consistent enthusiasm and vision had sealed the Labour Party's commitment. The actual details of the proposals we all adopted that day, have been set out elsewhere in this book, because they will form the basis of the legislation for Scotland's parliament. In the Assembly Hall, the members of the Convention again lined up this time to sign their names to the document, thus committing themselves firmly to its implementation. The people of Scotland will judge them by whether they keep that promise.

There were parts of the day that were certainly vividly memorable. We were welcomed by the Reverend Andrew McLellan, convenor of the Church and Nation Committee of the Church of Scotland, who reminded us of the Kirk's consistent support for home rule for Scotland and described it as "the best kind of nationalism that knows how to love our own nation more without loving other nations less." Jane McKay, speaking for the STUC, recalled the words of the first woman chair of the Congress, who long ago said, "Yesterday's vision will become tomorrow's reality." Both she and Isobel Lindsay, who spoke for the Campaign for a Scottish Parliament, of the increased role women had played in the Convention and in our proposals as "the most revolutionary thing that has happened in Scottish and British politics since women got the vote." They stated their belief that the decisive change brought about by ensuring that there were equal numbers of men and women would create a unique and new form of democracy. This was possible because we were starting from a clean sheet: "The simple fact that you are starting off with no incumbency factor, no bums already on seats, means equality becomes not just theoretically desirable but practically possible," said Isobel Lindsay.

Marilyne MacLaren, chair of the Scottish Liberal Democrats, told us that the gender equality provisions would ensure that the Scottish parliament would be different: "There's a desperate desire for this parliament to be different from the present system and we know if we don't have a lot of women in there it'll slide back into that old boys' club. And we only have this one chance to do it."

There is no doubt that for many people this item of gender equality is very important and symbolises the better form of politics that the Convention has come to represent. The writer Tom Nairn called this "an emblem of the kind of country and the style of nationalism people really want."

A moving moment came when the women handed over to me as chair of the executive for safekeeping, the electoral contract which had been signed by the chairpersons of the two parties, both of them women, and the party leaders in Scotland. This document which is now held by the Convention in trust, guarantees that the parties in the Convention at least, will field equal numbers of men and women in winnable seats. In receiving it, I said that it was certainly the most important thing for the future of Scotland. This was not simply a matter of numbers. I believe that bringing more women into parliament will have important consequences for the style of government, which should become less adversarial, more based on genuine issues and more consensual.

There was, however, one part of the day which many would have preferred not to have happened, or at least they would prefer to forget. The Reverend Robert Waters, then general secretary of the Congregational Church of Scotland, had been chosen to speak for the church representatives on the Convention, and chose a rather unfortunate extended metaphor. He began with the words, "I married a prostitute," and went on with a prolonged allegory on the relationship between England and Scotland in a way which only gradually dawned on many of his audience. In the words of Peter McMahon, writing in the *Scotsman*, "To the acute embarrassment of the Convention leaders and the private anger of many of the MPs present, he went on to say that the marriage between Scotland and England had gone sour because of one partner's lust for money."

Bob Waters has been a friend for many years and I have always admired his insight and understanding. I do not doubt his honesty, but he was unwise in his choice of comparison! He further alienated much of the audience by going on to state his view that one day Scotland would probably become independent and said of what the papers called his prostitute jibe that, "It is the only way I can describe what it feels like to be a Scot in 1995, one nation tied to another nation. There are ties of history, circumstance and mutual interest but revolted by a foreign monetarist culture which has turned out God in favour of money."

Any person reading his speech carefully would understand that the jibe of prostitute was in fact directed at the monetarist ideology of Thatcherism rather than at England as a nation, but it was too open to misunderstanding to be wise. In fact I was compelled in my closing address much later in the day, to depart from my prepared text, and to say, "We are not against the English, the Welsh, the Irish or anybody else, but respect all nations." The spontaneous and prolonged applause with which this sentence was greeted showed that everyone had certainly understood what I was saying.

Not everyone was annoyed – at least not for the same reasons. Lesley Riddoch of the *Scotsman* wrote, "Personally, I was offended on behalf of all prostitutes, and amused on behalf of all who liked to see at least one spanner in the works."

Both George Robertson, speaking for the Labour Party, and Jim Wallace for the Liberal Democrats gave ringing declarations of support for the Convention's work. Jim Wallace said, "Today is a day of celebration, but it is not the end of our journey. It is an opportunity to commit ourselves again to the great campaign which will only end when Scotland's parliament has been delivered.

George Robertson spoke of the Convention's work as evidence of a new era in the politics of Scotland: "Not just words or ringing phrases, not just hopes and optimism. Instead, we present with dignity and integrity a detailed plan worked out with pain and argument, time and travail, often mind-bending attention to detail, and built solidly and effectively on consensus and common sense. For the good of the country, for the good of the people, we are here today to give Scotland back her dignity."

George Robertson was certainly correct. Everything in this book bears witness to, and reveals, the long process which was necessary for us to reach this point. It fell to me again to sum up the day's proceedings. I described the day as Scotland's decisive day, or D-Day, but the victory is not yet won. "There may be battles ahead but we sense that a decisive turning point has been reached, that the victory is no longer in doubt."

I must admit when I used these words I did not think there would be quite so many battles ahead as there were in fact to be! In addition, I repeated the promise I had made so often through the years, that the Convention must remain in existence, until the Scottish parliament is securely established. In the light of events since that day, that promise is even more important. The Convention must be the guardian of the scheme on behalf of the people of Scotland.

At the end of my speech, I had a moment of combined pleasure and embarrassment when I was given a long and spontaneous standing ovation, that was reported in glowing terms in the press as a tribute to my dogged perseverance and leadership for so many years. It was unexpected and certainly unsought – but it was a moment of recognition that moved me greatly. It confirmed my growing confidence that our long journey was reaching its goal at last.

In assessing the day's events, the press was almost universally supportive. The *Herald's* leader, headlined, 'Scotland – the way ahead is clear', said, "There has been a hardening of opinion over the years in Scotland in favour of constitutional change. If such change is needed, and it is, the most acceptable means of achieving it lies in the work of the Scottish Constitutional Convention." The *Scotsman*, still free from the *eminence grise* of Andrew Neil who has brought about such unsubtle changes in its position, also said, "the only immediate workable improvement to emerge from yesterday's flurry of patriotic activity – is the blueprint for a Scottish parliament painstakingly drawn up over the last six years by the Constitutional Convention. Stunning excitement may not be numbered among its virtue: but it is sober, thorough and eminently capable of delivering that significant step away from unrepresentative rule longed for at every level of Scottish society."

Secretary of State, Michael Forsyth's reaction to our proposals was best depicted in the *Herald's* cartoon on December 1st. It was entitled 'The Wee Fly Poster' and showed Michael below a moonlit sky, putting up a huge poster which simply said in large letters, Tartan Tax Tartan Tax. He has been repeating this mantra on every possible occasion over his last two years in office, failing to recognise what the *Scotsman* pointed out to him on December 9th 1995, that "this restricted feeble diet will eventually scunner the waters. At the moment Labour is winning the argument. It is concentrating on ways to improve the governance of Scotland while Mr Forsyth creates a tax myth to frighten the voters. But they realise it is he who is frightened."

I take heart from the fact that by my rough calculation, the Conservative Party in Scotland lost at least one vote for every time Michael Forsyth repeated this vacuous slogan. Of course, I have no proof that there is any direct connection between the two, but I cannot help being glad that he has said it so often and that he mistimed it so badly. My first reaction had always been to give a rational answer – the obvious answer that it is simply insulting the people of Scotland to imply that we cannot trust our own parliament to act responsibly with very limited powers – but in the end I have come to the conclusion that it was in fact as well simply to leave it to the sense of humour of the Scottish people.

On that St Andrew's Day, as I was later told by friends in the press, Mr Forsyth on at least three occasions spoke of me personally as a former leader of CND in Scotland. Even if it had been true, it would seem to be rather irrelevant to the subject of constitutional change – but of course it was not true. I have never denied and would never deny, that I oppose nuclear weapons and shared the views of Lord Mountbatten that they did not increase our security but made things more dangerous. That remains my view, but I have never been a member of CND, still less its leader. I say this not because it would have been any shame to have been a member, but because it simply shows how even on minor matters Mr Forsyth or his spin doctors got their history wrong.

The jibe was, of course, taken up by his admirers. It was repeated in the press in the next few days by Bill Greig in the *Express*, and by no less a character than the colourful Alan Clark in *Scotland on Sunday*. It was also repeated later at a public debate with me, by Sir Michael Hirst. At least on this latter occasion I was able to put him right – but I have not troubled to react to the others. After all, as some friends pointed out to me, Forsyth's regular personal attacks on me must be a kind of tribute. If he repeatedly said this kind of thing about me, I must have been doing something right!

This may perhaps be an appropriate point to reflect briefly on the fate and future of the Tories in Scotland. As recently as the mid-1950s, they had half of Scotland's MPs and at least on one occasion, more than half of the popular vote – the only party ever to achieve that remarkable result. There is thus no historic truth in the claim that Scotland is somehow inevitably more left-wing or congenitally socialist. Since then, the decline, though occasionally temporarily halted, has been steady and in inexorable. Why?

There is no doubt that during the Thatcher period particularly, the Conservative Party was identified with an ideological kind of English nationalism which Scotland found not only theoretically unacceptable, but in practice outrageous. This was compounded by the retreat of the Tories from their firm commitment to devolution in the sixties, and their gradual opposition to any form of real democratic accountability in Scotland. It was a long way indeed from Heath's Declaration of Perth with its recognition of Scotland's right to self-determination, to John Major's ridiculous assertion that devolution was "the most dangerous proposition ever put before the British people."

I am on record as having said on many occasions, that I believe the Conservative Party's fortunes will revive only when there is a Scottish parliament. Certainly and paradoxically, the electoral system proposed by the Convention will favour most of all the Conservative Party and the SNP. It is they who will benefit most from the Additional Member System, since it is they who at the moment suffer most in Scotland from the inbuilt disadvantage of the first-past-the-post system.

Quite apart from that immediate electoral advantage which would give them, even with their present vote, a substantial presence in Scotland's parliament, it is in my view likely that their fortunes would revive. One of the obvious answers to Michael Forsyth's constant repetition of the Tartan Tax jibe is to point out that the Conservative Party in its policy statements and manifestos for Scottish parliament could promise, if it so wished, even to reduce taxation – though it would of course have to go on to say what services would be cut to achieve that.

Thus as the end of 1995 approached the members of the Constitutional Convention had a sense of quiet achievement and believed that we were certainly on course towards Scotland's parliament. Although a General Election was then still more than a year away, we probably felt that the path ahead of us was fairly smooth and that our task was simply to make our proposals more widely known in Scotland and beyond.

The days of the minor miracles seemed over – but the fates decreed otherwise. In practice, 1996 was to be perhaps the most difficult year we had ever known, as the Labour Party was perceived by some, both inside and outside the Convention, to be trying to pull back from its wholehearted commitment. Whether that accusation can be justified, we shall look at later, but it certainly meant for me personally, that 1996 was probably to be the most demanding year of all. Even at this late stage, the Convention might have fallen apart.

As we entered 1996, however, our task seemed clear enough. We had defined two tasks for the next period which were broadly, first education, information and awareness building, and secondly preparing for change. There was considerable criticism that while the Convention had done so much to prepare a scheme, it had somehow lacked energy in getting that out to the people.

In January, a *Scotsman* editorial said that "throughout their efforts, the Conventioneers appear to have done very little to campaign for their cause. Perhaps they have not had the resources. Perhaps too the cross-party and community approach that was so important to their progress, took its toll: keeping that particular show on the road required so much energy that there was little left with which to sell the whole enterprise."

Sadly, there was some truth in this – but our cause went deeper. For some reason there seemed to be a strange reluctance in the parties to get out and campaign against Michael Forsyth's clever but mendacious Tartan Tax campaign. In a paper I presented to the executive in January, I asked all members of the Convention and especially the parties to ensure that the truth is told as effectively and persistently as is wise, to discredit this unworthy campaign at the human and emotional level as well as by argument, and above all to ensure that we raise the debate above this petty point scoring level and get across the enormous challenge and excitement of Scotland's parliament and what it can do for all of us.

I have always believed that the Convention's trump card was ultimately a moral one – to keep the agenda away from the low road of fear and greed and on to the actual hope and confidence for Scotland's future. Through the early months of 1996 we dragged our feet. In retrospect, this was probably because the Labour Party in particular was engaged in an important but time-consuming internal discussion on how it could find the best tactics to ensure that it could carry the legislation for Scotland's parliament through Westminster. As power, or at least the possibility of power, drew closer, inevitably their minds were concentrated more on that question. It did, however, I believe, detract from the effectiveness of their campaigning. I myself did my best with constant speeches and press releases, but the media tend to pay less attention to anyone who is not directly engaged in the Parliamentary political process!

The other major programme on which Esther Roberton, our coordinator, was mainly engaged was what we called Preparing for Change. This was simply an attempt to spell out in much greater detail, what Scotland's parliament could actually mean in terms of changing the lives of people in specific areas. We had identified five areas as priority. They were education, local government, business and industry, health, and the environment (or sustainable development).

On February 25th, the day after one of Scotland's largest and most impressive marches in Glasgow, against school cuts, the editorial of *Scotland on Sunday* said, "Yesterday's march against school cuts drew a big crowd because people care passionately about education. The politicians leading the campaign for constitutional reform should learn the lesson. Too many of their discussions have been about constitutional mechanics, not enough about how a parliament would enable Scotland to nurture the things it holds in regard, for example education. It is up to them to put passion back into the constitutional debate.

This was an opinion with which I heartily agreed and which we sought throughout 1996 to do. A series of important consultations were held involving a wide range of opinion in Scotland. The first in February 1996 was a conference in Crieff on A Scottish Parliament – friend or foe to local government? In my introductory remarks, I said that the Convention's conclusion was that the Scottish parliament must operate by the principle of subsidiarity and maintain a strong and effective system of local government. In rejecting both the words foe and friend as an adequate description of the relationship, I asserted that the word partner was better. Scotland's parliament would in a new sense become the partner of local government in the development of Scotland. The report of that conference, which was organised by the Scottish Local Government Information Unit, will be a valuable tool in future as Scotland's parliament seeks to work with local government in practical ways. The one thing that is crystal clear is that contrary to the claims of our opponents, Scotland's parliament will not draw power away from local government, but will guarantee and protect its powers.

Later in the year, similar meetings or conferences were held on the themes of education, of housing and of health. The reports of all three are available and again give us the raw material and policy options for Scotland's parliament.

Without going into detail, what they all show clearly is that Scotland's parliament could use the powers we plan for it, to make a real and substantial impact and difference in each of these areas. Perhaps however it is worth placing on record here that none of these conferences received a great deal of attention in the media although we were engaged in what our critics in the media was advising us to do – tackle the practical problems a Scottish parliament would face. Constitutional questions are likely to remain for many people, rather esoteric and academic – and frankly, uninteresting – unless we can show, as these reports do, that it will actually and radically change our lives. The Preparing for Change programme has already demonstrated clearly in these areas and in others, that Scotland's parliament will make a difference to the quality of our lives.

In the area of business and industry, rather than a single conference, a whole series of consultations have been held with and through such bodies as the Scottish Council Development in Industry, the Chambers of Commerce and others. Here again these were not so much an attempt to persuade business leaders of the rights or wrongs of devolution, but to discuss with them how the powers could actually be used to create a more prosperous nation. There is no doubt that the attitude of business and industry had substantially changed. While there still remain, of course, many who fear any kind of change and are wedded to the *status quo*, an increasing number of leaders in the business and industrial world are now prepared either quietly to support constitutional change or at least to acknowledge that it would make very little immediate difference to the success of their enterprises one way or the other. Some have been influenced by the experience of their counterparts in such areas as Catalonia or Bavaria, where business clearly feels despite earlier reservations, that it has been greatly assisted by more open government closer to home.

The remaining area of Preparing for Change, that of the environment (or sustainable development) was taken up by a commission appointed by the John Wheatley Centre in Edinburgh, the report of which proposes a radical and effective programme which the Scottish parliament could institute, to make Scotland a clean and green economy.

All these and other proposals for the actual legislative options of Scotland's parliament and what the consequences of these would be, are of crucial importance, but are too detailed and complicated to be given here. My hope is that, as soon as is practicable, further work can be done on various policy options for Scotland's parliament, so that these could be published by the Convention in a way that will be an exciting testimony to the difference our parliament could make. It is no part of our task, of course, to tell a democratically elected body what to do – but we can prepare the way for it by involving the maximum number of people in Scotland, in thinking through the possibilities, spelling out the options and assessing the consequences of different courses. That exercise alone will be part of the more participative kind of government which we hope and expect an Edinburgh parliament will represent.

It was also in February 1996 that the referendum issue began to reappear. As I have said elsewhere, there were several occasions in the Convention's life when this was considered, but it had eventually been put aside as something on which the Convention had no direct view. The assumption was that legislation could proceed after an appropriate General Election result. The referendum issue, however, was over the coming months to become something of a monster.

The first sign appeared in February when the rather mischievous Tam Dalyell suddenly called for Tony Blair to hold a referendum before implementing legislation for a Scottish parliament. George Robertson responded – and I know that he was sincere in his response – that "we have no proposals for a referendum because we want to legislate early and quickly for this outstanding commitment, and that is the clear party policy." George maintained that a General Election victory would be sufficient mandate for devolution. Jim Wallace of the Liberal Democrats agreed with this view but did not totally rule out such a test; he said, "I'd never say never. If a case can be made that this would help to establish a Scottish parliament, fair enough. But in the past this tactic has been designed to frustrate that process."

At this stage, although I did not doubt Labour's commitment in any way, the public discussion was already beginning to raise questions and I wrote to George Robertson asking for a meeting with him and Tony Blair together, which I felt would be valuable to clear the air and reinforce the clear commitment to Scotland's parliament and to the timetable for its implementation. At the time that meeting could be arranged, however, we were into the long hot summer, and Labour's out-of-the-blue referendum proposals had caused a minor earthquake.

However, just before the earthquake struck, the constitution unit, set up as an independent enquiry into the implementation of constitutional reform and based at University College London, published its major report *Scotland's Parliament – Fundamentals for a New Scotland Act*. This is a substantial and comprehensive report, which took the Convention's work as its starting point, and goes thoroughly into how this could be translated into actual legislation and implemented. The clear judgement of the constitution unit is that the Convention scheme is basically workable and realistic, but their analysis of the difficulties of earlier attempts at devolution, make them very aware of how difficult and complex this can be, and how much opportunity there is for parliamentary mischief and delay along the way. The report is therefore extremely valuable since it points to how this can best be avoided, and how the government can both prepare and pass the Scotland Act, in time to keep its promise to legislate within a year.

The most significant of their many valuable proposals is that the Act should list only the powers retained at Westminster rather than those devolved. They saw as a great mistake the attempt of the 1978 Act to define with great precision the legislative competencies of the devolved assembly and in fact they traced how this attempt to go through every government department to define exactly what would be devolved, was in fact fatal to the passing of the Act. This strong recommendation must be taken very seriously. The Convention's own proposals in *Scotland's Parliament; Scotland's Right* are ambiguous on this point. On the one hand, they do say that Scotland's parliament "will have a defined range of powers and responsibilities" and go on in an appendix to list many of these. On the other hand, these are explicitly said to be illustrative rather than inclusive or exhaustive, and we also say that the powers of Scotland's parliament will encompass "sole or shared responsibility for all functions except those retained to the UK parliament."

I have always believed that our formulation, whether deliberately or by accident, leaves open the crucial question of how this definition should be done. My own view is that both for the practical tactical reasons already mentioned, that is the ease of getting the legislation through in time, and for an even more important reason of principle, namely the commitment to the doctrine of subsidiarity, Scotland's parliament should be given, in effect if not explicitly, a power of general competence. By defining precisely what powers are reserved to Westminster, the implication clearly is that the Scottish parliament has powers in all other areas, unless there has been specific negotiation in a particular case.

As to the financial arrangements for Scotland's parliament the constitution unit's judgement on those proposed by the convention were that they formed "a sensible basis on which to establish parliament, but do not propose stability in the longer term." They therefore proposed that the Bill should accept our proposals but should aim to "promote greater stability by specifying mechanisms for keeping the funding formula under review and making adjustments when necessary." This is clearly a sensible proposal. However, it is worth noting that the constitution unit is very strongly in favour of the proposed power of Scotland's parliament to vary income tax by up to three pence in the pound one way or the other. They clearly judge that "the proposed variation of three pence in the pound would have no significant macro economic effects for the UK as a whole," but they also judge that "autonomous revenue raising powers are essential to achieve a sense of fiscal responsibility and accountability to the Scottish electorate."

When the constitution unit presented its report in Scotland, leading economist Professor Gavin McCrone was asked to justify this view. He did so by pointing out that even if this power were never used, it must be there to safeguard Scotland. He gave the hypothetical instance of a future Westminster government which had so cut back on all public expenditure that Scotland's "assigned revenue" (even if it came to Scotland "as of right" and even if the proportion remained unchanged by the equalisation principle) was substantially and severely diminished in its actual amount, a Scottish parliament might need to use its limited taxation powers to save such services as health and education in Scotland. It was a hypothetical case but made his point. Forsyth's tartan tax jibe – and especially the false implication of election posters that this limited power would inevitably be used and would therefore increase taxes, clearly confuses a power and a policy. Each party is free to have its own policy on taxation and the Labour Party has indeed made it clear that its policy would be not to increase tax in the first parliament. The power, however, remains.

The other area of great interest on which the constitution unit pronounced clearly was in the question of how to achieve significant entrenchment, that is, how to safeguard the legislation against abolishment or major alteration by any future Westminster government. They approve of the Convention's proposal for a Westminster Declaration, which will at least "introduce a political hurdle to repeal or significant amendment of the devolution legislation."

They then discussed the question of a referendum. In the light of the Labour Party's change of policy which was just about to break when the unit reported, their conclusion is worth quoting in full:

> "The choice whether to hold a referendum on the question of Scottish devolution will be a political one. Strong and explicit popular endorsement of the principle of establishing a Scottish parliament might add to the political inhibitors in the way of repeal or emasculation of the devolution legislation. If obtained in advance, a positive referendum result might also smooth the passage of the legislation through Parliament. But in those circumstances the

237

> referendum itself would require a short Bill. No
> referendum result could be binding on the
> government; nor on the Scottish people, who would
> reserve the right to pass judgement on the parliament
> in the light of experience once it had come into
> operation."

The unit later published findings of its commission on the conduct of referendums which should be helpful now that the Scottish referendum is going ahead.

It may have been partly the constitution unit's thinking which led the Labour Party to change its policy on a referendum. The Constitutional Convention had not directly pronounced on this one way or another and the actual tactics by which the political parties would ensure the speedy and efficient passage of the legislation was a matter for them and not for us. The Labour Party, having thought long and hard about how it could keep the difficult promise to legislate within a year, came to the conclusion, partly no doubt inspired by the constitution unit's findings, that a pre-legislative referendum would make very much easier the passage of the legislation through both Houses of Parliament and would make direct opposition, or the development of wrecking amendments, that much more difficult.

With the publication of the constitution unit's detailed report, we might have been forgiven for thinking that the Constitutional Convention's path ahead was now smooth and straightforward, apart from the major hurdle of a General Election. We could not have been more wrong. Unexpectedly and without warning, the greatest storm we had faced even in seven stormy years was about to break. It was a storm that could have so easily blown us apart.

Chapter 23

Hurricane Referendum Strikes!

The first cloud on the horizon appeared at the end of May 1996. Several London-based newspapers reported in what appeared to be a kite-flying exercise that the Labour leadership was about to go back on the plans for tax-varying powers for the Scottish parliament.

A *Guardian* editorial even went so far as to commend Tony Blair for his wisdom in this, but said, "It is not very flattering for Labour, apparently so strong in Scottish politics, to shift its ground on an issue so close to its heart." Writing in the *Scotsman* on June 2nd, Iain MacWhirter maintained, "Speak to anyone in the metropolitan political press corps just now and you will be told that Labour has effectively shelved its 'popular' tax-raising powers in Scotland." Three days later the *Scotsman's* editorial told us "over the last few weeks, the longstanding suspicion that the Labour leader, Tony Blair, was growing distinctly cool over the tax-levying element of the proposals appeared to be confirmed by apparently well-sourced leaks to several London-based newspapers. It is profoundly disappointing that it has taken Mr Wallace, Mr Robertson and the Convention's executive chairman, Canon

Kenyon Wright, so long to recognise that they were being outflanked. Mr Wright's call yesterday for a campaign to sell devolution to the Scottish people is therefore welcomed, if a little tardy. At least it is a start."

It is indeed true that the day before I had issued a strong appeal to all members of the Convention to stop their bickering over this issue, to accept the Labour Party's clear and unambiguous statement that there was no retreat from its commitment to the Convention's scheme in its entirety, including the comparatively marginal tax-levying powers, and that the important task was to stop being frightened by 'Forsyth's Fable' of the tartan tax and begin to sell devolution positively and with vision to the people of Scotland. Where the *Scotsman* was wrong was in the assertion that I had somehow suddenly done this for the first time. For months, indeed for years, I had been calling for us to ignore or even scorn the Tartan Tax jibe, which obviously had had so little effect on the people of Scotland, and to concentrate on a positive presentation of the enormous difference that a Home Rule parliament would make to the lives of ordinary people.

Jim Wallace, the leader of the Liberal Democrats in Scotland, welcomed George Robertson's reassurance on this issue but accused the Labour Party in London of being "petrified by the mere mention of the word tax." Meanwhile, the Tory Government's friends tried to keep the issue alive. Allan Massie, staring out at us from the pages of the *Scotsman* with that look of owlish disgruntlement which he seems perpetually to wear, told us that "Michael Forsyth's campaign against the tartan tax has got Labour worried."

In the same article on June 5th, it is worth mentioning in passing, he raised another issue which is now coming into prominence. He wrote, "if Labour wins the next election with a majority that is big enough to make at least two terms of office probable, then the urgency of creating a parliament which will guard Scotland against an unrepresentative Tory government naturally diminishes. Might it not, Labour unionists will be saying, be wiser to coast for a bit? After all, what could a Scottish parliament do for Scotland if a securely based Labour government couldn't?" The answer to his last question is of course clear enough – only a Scottish parliament could secure Scotland's right to control her own affairs democratically, for good. It is precisely because of this kind of speculation, that the Labour Party's firm unambiguous and clear commitment to legislate rapidly for the Convention's scheme is so crucially important for Scotland and must not be allowed to be watered down or delayed.

The suggestion that the Convention was once again about to break up soon faded into the background, at least for a few weeks. But it was to return with renewed strength. There was a brief lull before Hurricane Referendum hit us in midsummer 1996!

On June 24th, the executive committee met in Edinburgh in an atmosphere of some confidence that the worst was over. We were assured of continuity in an efficient secretariat. Douglas Sinclair, the general secretary of the Convention of Scottish Local Authorities (COSLA) was the official secretary of the Convention, but the work had in practice been carried out by one of his assistants. Since the departure of Bruce Black, Liz Manson had filled this position with enthusiasm, efficiency and good humour. She was now succeeded by Andy O'Neill who has served us well in the difficult days since. At that meeting I presented a report on the future strategy, maintaining that the Convention had now entered a new phase of life, concentrating on our second and third aims, namely, to secure the approval of the Scottish people for our proposals and to secure their implementation. On this basis I proposed a clear strategy to counter the myths and misinformation put out by our opponents, but also and more important to rise above these to a fuller discussion of the vision of what Scotland's parliament could actually do for the nation. The minutes of that meeting record that their was a lengthy discussion and that George Robertson MP emphasised the need for a major counteroffensive in term of a PR campaign to be launched. A number of detailed proposals for such a major counteroffensive in the summer were agreed. Indeed, just after the meeting, a press release was issued with the headline 'Convention plans long hot summer for Major.'

Before we could even begin to make things hot for Major, however, things rapidly reached red heat for us! The day after the executive committee George Robertson rang me with the rather cryptic message that neither I nor the Convention need be alarmed about the news which was about to break. On Wednesday June 26th, the Labour Party announced a change of policy. If returned to power, it would hold a referendum of the Scottish people, on the basis of a white paper rapidly prepared and based on the Convention's scheme. The referendum would ask two questions – a straight yes or no to the proposals in the white paper; and a straight yes or no to whether that parliament should have tax-varying powers.

The reaction was immediate and explosive. The press next day carried headlines such as 'Tartan Tax Referendum U-turn Splits Labour'. The Scottish *Sun* with its usual hyperbole called this an "Insult to Every Scot who Trusted Labour" and said "Labour's climb-down on devolution is one of the most cynical acts of betrayal ever seen in Scottish politics."

Reaction within the Convention was more measured but nevertheless in many cases expressed at least concern. Campbell Christie, the General Secretary of STUC for example, said, "I regret very much this about turn and I think it provides all sorts of mischief for those who will do almost anything to prevent a democratic Scottish parliament being established." The Liberal Democrats echoed this concern. Jim Wallace said that while they had always been in favour of a referendum in principle, they needed to be reassured that this was not simply a device to make progress more difficult. He said, "Tony Blair must fully and unequivocally commit himself, if he becomes Prime Minister, to establish a Scottish parliament, taxation powers included, according to the letter of the Convention plans."

Even within the Labour Party there was substantial anguish. By Friday June 28th, John McAllion MP, the Labour front bench spokesman on constitutional affairs, had resigned claiming not to have been consulted about the change. Even more shattering for the Convention was the resignation of Lord Ewing of Kirkford, one of the two co-chairs along with Sir David Steel of the Constitutional Convention. Lord Ewing, known to all of us as Harry Ewing, made it clear to me that he had no quarrel of any kind with the Convention or with the Convention's scheme but that his reasons for resigning were twofold: there was a lack of consultation which amounted to a slight of the Convention, and there was the policy itself with the proposal of a separate referendum question on tax-raising powers which opened up at least the possibility of that being ditched. He said, "I want to give the Convention a much higher profile to draw to the attention of the Scottish people the importance of constitutional reform, and that is why I decided to resign. The Convention does not belong to the Labour Party or to the Liberal Democrats, it belongs to the Scottish people. Almost every commitment that the late John Smith made has now been reversed."

There were strong feelings at many points within the Labour Party. The Scottish Party Treasurer Bob Thomson said that "the way the whole thing has happened has been very unfortunate. On the road to Dunblane or the road to Damascus – that is not where we make party policy. It is made at party conference." His reference to the road to Dunblane is to the claim made by George Robertson that he had been the originator of the new proposal for a referendum, at the time when Tony Blair was visiting Dunblane after the tragedy there.

The Labour leadership moved swiftly to counter this barrage of criticism and even outrage. George Robertson, in the course of a lengthy telephone call on Thursday June 27th, sought to reassure me that the Labour Party's change was purely one of tactics. Their commitment to the Convention's scheme remained firm and unchanged, but they saw the referendum as being the best way to get the proposals through Parliament as easily as possible, and to ensure the entrenchment we all wanted, i.e. that it would be difficult if not impossible for the plans to be later altered. He invited me to a private meeting with Tony Blair and himself the next day in Edinburgh.

Meanwhile, even before Tony Blair came to Scotland, the big guns of the Labour Party faced a sceptical and cynical press corps in Glasgow. No fewer than four senior leaders, all of them now Cabinet Ministers, George Robertson, Donald Dewar, Robin Cook and Gordon Brown lined up to support the new strategy. The *Herald* humorously commented on their body language which was "as restrained as that of a maiden aunt at a prayer meeting. The result was a line-up as exciting as yesterday's cold porridge under the distinct feeling that they were all aware that shuffling makes you look shifty." Be that as it may, George Robertson repeated his claim that he had personally recommended the new course and set it out clearly. He said, "As soon as Labour is returned to power, a white paper will be published, setting out the details of our plans. The people of Scotland will be asked to endorse the proposals in an early referendum to pave the way for legislation. There will be no tricks, no fancy franchise. The test will be a straightforward majority of the votes cast." He went on equally to defend the second question, saying, "There is a clear difference between the power of an institution and a pledge from a political party to exercise that power. In the event of the Scottish people voting yes to the taxation power, political parties will still want to think long and hard before entering into an election pledge to raise taxes. What matters is to establish firmly and explicitly the principle and we believe Scotland will back it." He concluded by repeating yet again the promises so often made: the pledge that a devolution bill will be on the statute book within the first year of a Labour government will be honoured – "Labour will deliver a new deal for the Scottish people which will be firmly based on the work of the Scottish Constitutional Convention."

Neither George Robertson's statements, nor the backing given by his three fellow members of the Shadow Cabinet, convinced everybody. A *Scotsman* editorial of June 28th voiced the cynical view that the whole proposal might be some Machiavellian tactic to avoid a tax-raising parliament by virtually anticipating a No vote on the second question. They said, "It is an unworthy interpretation, but an insistently niggling one. Tony Blair speaks in Scotland this afternoon; we can but hope that his words and subsequent events prove us wholly wrong."

It is my own belief that they were certainly wrong. That has been denied in words. It must be denied in events. The words were spoken in a small room in Edinburgh City Chambers which looked out over the sunny city to the Firth of Forth beyond on Friday, June 28th when I met Tony Blair and George Robertson. The definite impression I received was that the leader of the Labour Party was somewhat surprised and stunned by the vehemence of reaction in Scotland to the Labour Party's referendum proposals, and was anxious to reassure us of Labour's commitment to a Scottish parliament

The central point of our conversation was a direct request on my part that he give me a clear reassurance on four crucial points. To my considerable relief, he agreed without hesitation. These are best summed up in the minute of the July meeting of the executive committee at which George Robertson was present. That minute noted the assurances given to me by Tony Blair MP:

> a. the Labour Party's commitment to the proposals in
> *Scotland's Parliament; Scotland's Right* remained firm
> and unchanged;
> b. the Labour Party's commitment to the timetable
> also remained firm and would not be allowed to slip
> because of the referendum and all that it entailed;
> c. the Labour Party would campaign strongly and
> unequivocally for a Yes vote on both questions; and
> d. the Convention would be consulted on the precise
> framing of the two questions to be put.

The new Government's determination to act swiftly, which we

fully endorse, has ruled out any lengthy or detailed consultation, but the promise to consult was kept before the details of the Referendum Bill were announced.

Tony Blair pointed out to me that the referendum, far from delaying the timetable, would make it much easier to keep, since a clear Yes vote in a referendum would make opposition more difficult. I was particularly pleased to receive the fourth of these reassurances – since the exact way in which the questions are framed in any referendum is of particular importance and can greatly influence the outcome. There is of course no question of framing questions in a prejudicial way, but the second question on the tax-varying powers is of particular significance. If, no matter the precise wording, that question even appeared to be asking 'Do you wish to pay more tax?' (an interpretation that certainly would be put on it, if possible, by our opponents) then the outcome would be more in doubt. Even then I have a feeling that the majority of Scots would be willing to do so given good reasons. If however, the question more realistically and accurately, whatever its precise framing, is seen to be asking 'Do you trust Scotland's parliament with this power?' which is after all a power held by Westminster to an unlimited extent, then I believe we would get a fairer representation of Scots' true position.

The meeting with Tony Blair was refreshingly straightforward and helped to convince me that the Convention's trust in the Labour Party would not be betrayed. On Saturday June 29th I received a handwritten note from Tony Blair which he must have penned not long after our meeting in Edinburgh. He wrote: "Thank you for seeing me and for being so considerate. I hope we have acted for the best. That was certainly my intention. I look forward to seeing you again."

I for one believe and trust him, as the people of Scotland and the United Kingdom have so clearly done. That conviction, however, did not prevent me from resolving that the Convention must remain in being, as the consensus voice of Scotland, in order to maintain a watch on all that happens. We remain the guardians of *Scotland's Parliament; Scotland's Right.*

At our meeting I had assured Tony Blair that I would do my best to persuade Lord Ewing to reconsider his resignation from the Convention. Indeed I pointed out to Harry Ewing on more than one occasion, that his quarrel was not with the Convention, but with the policy of the Labour Party. He made it clear that that was the case. Speaking in the House of Lords on July 3rd he told the peers that there was indeed an argument in favour of the referendum. He said, "My complaint is that that argument never took place. The Scottish Constitutional Convention should have been consulted. We were not and I took the view that it was time that someone protested in order that our voice be heard."

My own position was that while I too regretted that there had not been wider consultation which might well have led to agreement and certainly muted much of the reaction, I felt we had to be politically realistic, and provided the Labour Party's commitment to the Convention's scheme was firmly restated, as it was, we should accept the position with good grace.

The debate was kept very much alive by two further developments at the beginning of July. Jim Wallace, the Scottish Liberal Democrat leader, called openly for a cross-party campaign to ditch Labour's second question on whether a Scottish parliament should have tax powers and criticised Blair's leadership on this as "dishonest and dangerous". There was certainly a hardening of opinion in the Liberal Democrat Party, and indeed some evidence of growing opposition within the Labour Party itself. *Scotland on Sunday* reported on July 7th that "less than half Labour's Scottish constituency chairman and chairwomen are in favour of asking a separate question on tax, according to our exclusive survey." Wallace, reflecting the growing anger of the Liberal Democrats, warned that Labour in government could not depend on Liberal Democrat backing for any referendum Bill: "We won't rubber stamp a Bill that has the second question in it."

The second development in early July, was the publication by the Labour Party of its *Scottish Road to the Manifesto* document, which laid out the core policies for the coming General Election. On the question of devolution its wording was identical to that which had been published the previous week at the UK level. It committed the party thoroughly to "a parliament with lawmaking powers, firmly based on the agreement reached at the Scottish Constitutional Convention." It also promised to "seek the people's approval for giving the parliament defined financial powers to vary revenue."

Throughout the next two months of that hot summer, the debate raged on, and was seldom out of the Scottish press. It was a testing time for me, as I strove to hold together the Labour Party on the one hand, and those in the Convention from the Liberal Democrats and trade unions on the other, who were determined to fight against the two question referendum. The line I took was quite simply that we must accept in good faith the Labour Party's firm and constant assurance that this was purely a tactical move designed to facilitate the whole process and that it did not in any way diminish either their commitment to the Convention's scheme in its entirety, nor their resolve to legislate within a year of gaining power. This meant that the Convention itself should take no particular position on this matter, leaving it to the individual organisations and parties to fight it out as they wished to do.

In practice, the fight went on mainly within the Labour Party itself with the public sector trade union UNISON, launching a campaign in Scotland to force a change in policy from a twin question to a simple single question referendum. Significantly, UNISON's national executive in London backed the stance of the Scottish leadership on this issue and their General Secretary Rodney Bickerstaffe personally supported the launch of the campaign by the associate Scottish Secretary of UNISON, Bob Thomson, who was also treasurer of the Labour Party in Scotland. By the time the Convention was due to meet again on July 26th, the STUC had lined up behind the dissent. Its finance and strategy Committee had told its delegation at our executive to urge Labour to "withdraw the proposal that a pre-legislative referendum be held," claiming that the question on tax-varying confused rather than clarified the debate. Campbell Christie said publicly, "If the proposal cannot be overturned, our position is that a referendum should contain one question which asks people if they want a Scottish parliament with tax-varying powers."

This position was also backed by a number of constituency Labour Party branches in Scotland and the press had a field day with our disunity, while Michael Forsyth and his colleagues in the Conservative Party were cock-a-hoop.

A few days before the executive meeting on July 26th, I circulated a confidential memo to all members of the executive, which to the annoyance of some of them, was leaked to the press. In this I pointed out that whatever the differing views on the referendum issue the consequence was to enhance the role of the Convention. I said, "Both before the General Election and now potentially more clearly after it, the Convention has an enhanced role both in education and persuasion on the one hand, and in the careful monitoring of the implementation of our proposals on the other." I referred to the fundamental difficulty that there had been a real "erosion of trust" and that we must rebuild that trust as a matter of urgency. I made two assertions which many members of the executive could not accept. I argued that political reality dictated "not only that we must accept this change, but that we should interpret it as a positive move, fully in tune with the Claim of Right which asserts sovereignty of the people." The second statement, to which at that stage much less notice had been paid, referred to the statements that Tony Blair had made in Edinburgh about sovereignty of parliament remaining secure. I argued that these could "be understood as tactical references – a recognition of a pact that we have never denied, namely that the unwritten British constitution allows in theory for no possibility of real and entrenched shared power. Personally, I would be willing publicly to accept this, provided it is clear to all concerned that there could be no retreat from the signing of the Claim of Right – and indeed

I hope and believe that one of the firsts act of Scotland's parliament will be to reaffirm the Claim of Right and the sovereign right of the people." The debate about sovereignty was to be raised shortly before the General Election by Tony Blair's further references, but I had in that paper in July 1996 suggested a compromised position.

The executive meeting on July 26th was one of the most difficult I have chaired. Paradoxically, it also showed the Convention at its best, for we came clearly resolved to hammer out these questions and come to a common mind. There was plain and honest speaking on all sides with George Robertson and Jack McConnell robustly presenting the Labour Party's position and Jim Wallace, Sir David Steel, Campbell Christie, Moira Craig of the Campaign for a Scottish Parliament, and others with equal vigour expressing doubts as to whether this could be regarded as purely a tactical matter, as the Labour Party claimed, or whether the second question did not in fact raise at least the danger of the integrity of the Convention's scheme being broken. I strongly presented the view in my paper that we were not in a position to express any consensus view on the referendum issue and that we should not divert our attention as we had done for so long, from the central task of campaigning and monitoring implementation of the scheme.

In the end we did it again – contrary to the fears of many and the hopes of some, we reached consensus and passed a unanimous resolution. It took note of the four assurances given to me directly by Tony Blair as quoted above and went on to reassert "full commitment to the Claim of Right for Scotland and the acknowledgement of the sovereign right of the Scottish people to determine the form of government best suited to their needs." It then asked the coordinating committee to plan a campaign strategy and in perhaps the most significant part, requested the coordinating committee of the Convention,

"in the event of a referendum becoming a reality;

a. to clarify with the political parties and the Labour Party in particular, exactly what the mechanism for drafting the White Paper and Referendum Bill would be, and what the Convention's role would be in determining its contents;

b. to begin preparations for effective lobbying to secure the speedy passage of the Referendum Bill in its agreed form without amendment;

c. to give urgent consideration to rules governing the conduct of any referendum including the question of finances;

d. to begin preparations for the establishment of a Yes to Scotland's Parliament campaign."

Once again we thought we had laid the matter to rest. We knew of course the debate would go on inside the Labour Party and elsewhere and that the Scottish executive, due to meet at the end of August, would have a hard decision to make. But we thought the Convention's stance was now clear and accepted by all. Yet again our expectation that peace had broken out was to be rudely shattered. Throughout August the debate rumbled on. From our point of view it was a wasted summer. Instead of making it a "long hot summer for John Major" as we had promised, the attention of the chattering classes at least was almost entirely on the differences over the referendum, and the battle to see which way the Scottish Labour Party would move.

When it finally did move at its executive meeting on the August 31st, it managed to turn a quarrel into a farce. In my diary I christened the week beginning on Saturday August 30th 1996, as 'the unholy week'.

The making of Scotland's parliament has been a prolonged and labyrinthine task, as any who have persevered in reading this book will realise, and there had been frequent storms and earthquakes along the way – but the fates had reserved their worst thunderbolts for this week. As the date of the Labour Party's

Scottish executive approached, there was evidence of a growing apprehension that the policy proclaimed by the leadership might not be supported in Scotland. On August 29th, the *Herald* reported that the executive vote was "beginning to look ominous for the party hierarchy, the possibility of a defeat by upwards of four votes on Saturday appears possible." George Robertson issued a solemn warning to the members of the Scottish executive that they should consider whether their decision would help Labour or the Tories. He said, "if Labour representatives put their personal anger before the interests of the Party and the chance of getting rid of the Tory government, then they will never be forgiven by the people of Scotland."

On the very eve of that fateful meeting, I spoke to George Robertson and Donald Dewar, who were still uncertain of the result, though they hoped for support for the Party's position. The press was even more uncertain. The *Scotsman's* headline on the day itself was 'Labour on Knife Edge.' That afternoon I was at home when George Robertson rang to give me the result. I am glad he did, for within minutes the correspondents of a number of newspapers were on the line to ask for comment. It seems that after a long period of intensive debate, in which both sides seemed fairly equally matched and the decision uncertain, a punch-drunk executive had voted for a compromise resolution cobbled together by a few of its members, which was greeted by most of the nation at first with incredulity and eventually with such scornful laughter that it had to be abandoned. The key passage in the resolution of the Scottish executive which caused all the trouble was "that the second question should ask for an endorsement of the detailed revenue varying powers outlined in the government's White Paper, but such powers will only be activated by a referendum called by the Scottish parliament itself."

Now, where did that leave us? It had always been my policy to be very careful in commenting to the press and not to feed their desire for controversial headlines and conflict. Indeed, I had been alternatively praised and damned by many in the press for being either "responsible" or "boring". On this occasion, however, I could only express my puzzlement by asking, "How is having a second referendum a concession to those who didn't even want one?" Others were blunter. John McAllion MP said, "Nobody expected this. It's a disaster. The public will be absolutely bemused," while Jim Wallace of the Liberal Democrats said, "When you leave the path of principle, heaven knows where you end up."

Scotland on Sunday the next morning exclaimed in its banner headline 'Oh no, it's two referendums' commenting, "Labour's devolution policy descended into farce last night – after a day of backroom deals between dissidents unhappy with Tony Blair's two question referendum and supporters of that U-turn led by George Robertson, the Shadow Scottish Secretary." Bill Speirs of the STUC echoed my own question when he said, "It is hard to understand how an argument between one question and two questions could have ended up with three questions." Over the next few days the Scottish press was virtually unanimous in its growing scorn for this new solution.

For the next few days I seemed to be almost constantly on the telephone trying either to find a solution, or to pacify angry or bewildered members of the Convention. Meanwhile the stream of scorn grew into a torrent. By Tuesday September 3rd, the *Scotsman's* banner headline read, 'Devolution Pact faces Collapse', as the Liberal Democrats expressed their anger and frustration, accusing the Labour Party of "doing something which is disastrously splitting the Home Rule movement."

George Robertson, to his credit, repeated again that "we are firmly part of the Constitutional Convention and we are fully committed to delivering the Scottish parliament that it agreed. Nothing we have decided in any way dilutes that plan or dilutes our commitment to that plan. What we are doing is getting involved in an exercise to ensure that plan becomes a reality."

A meeting of the Convention's coordinating committee had been planned for Thursday September 5th, but it became clear to me that no useful purpose would be served by it, except to allow people to let off steam which they were doing in any case publicly. However, I did reread carefully the resolution that had been passed by the Labour Party's Scottish executive and saw a way out of the dilemma. The resolution was clearly worded as a statement of belief rather than policy, i.e. it said that the executive "believes" certain things should happen. On this basis I put to Party general secretary, Jack McConnell on Thursday September 5th a series of proposals that seemed to me to offer a possible way out of this damaging public display of division. My suggestion was quite simply that if the Labour Party could not find a way of setting aside this resolution, it should be regarded as a proposal only, to be discussed with Labour's partners in the Constitutional Convention. It seemed to me that a line must be drawn very quickly under this whole episode, or we would never be able to get on with the real task of selling our scheme to the Scottish people and ensuring its implementation.

Throughout this 'unholy week' George Robertson had been touring the country and had clearly become convinced, not just by the press coverage, but by his conversations with people in all parts of Scotland, that the Labour executive's new position was basically untenable. On Friday September 6th, the Scottish press announced, again in banner headlines, that Labour was about to drop its commitment to a second referendum in Scotland. Indeed, Jack McConnell was reported as saying, "there would be no unilateral changes in Labour's policy. Any speculation to that effect is completely groundless. Clearly we have to discuss our position with our partners in the Constitutional Convention. Our top priorities are for maximum unity and the principle of consent for a Scottish parliament. These policies stand."

Clearly this went a long way towards calming the situation and diminishing, though by no means removing, the considerable annoyance and anger felt by some of the groups in the Convention, particularly the Liberal Democrats and the STUC. This was very widely welcomed, although there was still some scorn caused by the change of mind. In general there was a feeling that the right thing had been done and the crisis was over.

There is no doubt that this was one of the most difficult weeks in my period as chair of the Convention's executive. We might well have foundered and it took all my skill in negotiation and crisis management, to prevent the explosions blowing us apart. There is no doubt that the spotlight turned daily on our divisions and difficulties were a setback for the Convention and for the hopes for Home Rule. Officially, however, we were by September 6th back again where we had been on August 30th, i.e. with Labour's original proposal for a single two question referendum based on a White Paper and pre-legislative.

On Monday September 9th, I called a meeting of the Scottish Churches Constitutional Group at Scottish Churches House in Dunblane. This group which meets regularly, represents most of the major churches in Scotland and tries to maintain a common policy on these matters. We agreed on a common approach to the Convention, which was conveyed in a letter signed by the Rev Maxwell Craig, secretary of the group and general secretary of Action of Churches Together in Scotland. In this we said, "We attach great importance to the commitment we understand the Labour Party has given to consult the Convention on the form such a referendum will take." We went on to propose an early meeting of the executive, not to go over the past, but to reaffirm the Convention's commitment to *Scotland's Parliament; Scotland's Right* and to get on with the job.

This was not so easy. Over the weekend, my phone remained red hot. The Lib Dems, the Campaign for a Scottish Parliament and the STUC were all still deeply unhappy about the second question in the proposed referendum on tax-varying powers and were not ready to back down on that. They demanded a meeting of the coordinating committee as soon as possible to thrash this out. My own line was that such a meeting, especially after the last week, would be unhelpful since the Convention had no locus to pronounce on this matter and in any case could not achieve consensus. My view that there was nothing new to discuss and that such a meeting would not be wise. However, the fact that several leading bodies asked for this made it essential that I consult others. George Robertson informed me that he and Jim Wallace had agreed together that such a meeting would be unhelpful and should not be held just yet. Indeed the Labour Party secretary Jack McConnell said that he saw no point in the meeting, the purpose of which would simply be to try to persuade the Labour Party to change a policy it had now clearly announced, and that there would be no purpose in them even attending such a meeting. There was some confusion on the position of the Liberal Democrats, since some of their representatives were demanding a meeting but Jim Wallace, their leader, was reportedly agreeing with George Robertson that the meeting should not be held yet. I finally got through to Jim Wallace who confirmed that he was "not pressing for a meeting." Indeed, he expressed his opinion that if such a meeting were to follow up a forward looking agenda, he would be happy, but that he saw no point in reopening the whole subject matter from our last executive. In other words, since the executive in July had discussed fully Labour's referendum proposals and come to a clear position, a meeting now would simply be an occasion for rancour and bitterness. I repeated to all members of the Convention executive, my conviction that while there had been a serious erosion of trust, it was time to rebuild that and move forward together to our real agenda.

The real tragedy of this entire referendum episode was that the Convention lost the whole summer of 1996. Instead of forging ahead with a campaign of public education and information, as we had planned, all attention was centred on this one single issue, and it was October, with just six months or so to a General Election, that we finally turned back to what should have been our primary task.

CHAPTER 24

Forging 'Partnership for a Parliament'

In October 1996 the Convention was approached by a leading Glasgow businessman, Nigel Smith, who had organised the Business Says Yes campaign prior to the 1992 election. Nigel had undertaken extensive, in-depth research on various referendum campaigns throughout the world and brought his conclusions to us. He was convinced that only a unifying campaign with well worked out slogans and an efficient organisation would be effective.

Given that in any referendum campaign after the General Election, we felt it likely the No campaign would be well-organised and very richly financed by sections of the Conservative business community, Nigel saw the need for a campaign which would be as broadly based as possible and at some distance from the political parties and indeed from the Constitutional Convention. He argued, therefore, that we should give our approval to the development of a freestanding independent campaign, which would seek adequate financial support from various sources including trade unions and the business community and which would be based on some authoritative research into the primary motivations of people in Scotland.

The executive accepted this argument and commissioned Nigel Smith, along with Esther Roberton our own coordinator, to develop a more detailed proposal for a serious and well-organised campaign. We also endorsed the commissioning of an immediate research programme to provide the basic information for such a campaign. The necessary pump-priming finance, to enable a detailed survey to be held by System Three and later to allow propositions to be tested in focus groups, was obtained through generous support from two unions, UNISON and the Educational Institute of Scotland (EIS) and by some support from Nigel Smith himself as well as a grant from the Joseph Rowntree Reform Trust. On this basis we were able to go ahead rapidly and by December, Peter Kellmer, the well-known political analyst, had sent us his analysis of the results of that extensive poll. It showed, as expected, that a large majority of Scottish voters claimed they would vote for a Scottish parliament while a smaller but still fairly substantial majority said they would be prepared to vote for the tax-varying powers. Perhaps most significant it demonstrated that any fears of taxation and other negative consequences of a home rule parliament were substantially outweighed with most people questioned, agreeing most strongly with what might be called 'the hope agenda'.

The greatest agreement was with statements such as 'It is time important decisions affecting Scotland were made by a Scottish parliament elected by the Scottish people rather than hundreds of miles away in London' and that 'Scotland needs to take more control of its own destiny and stop blaming other people for its problems.' From the point of view of developing a campaign there were many detailed findings which indicated what should be the major emphasis throughout Scotland by all organisations taking part. There was also an interesting confirmation of the fact that, while there is some relationship to views of support for a particular party, this not by any means monolithic. Thus, for example, thirty four per cent of Conservative voters favour a parliament for Scotland. It is thus clear that Nigel Smith was right in his contention that any Yes-Yes campaign must be as broad as possible and not based simply on the political parties within the Constitutional Convention.

By the time the executive met again on January 24th 1997, Nigel Smith was able to bring to us a detailed proposal based on the research findings. The executive then made an important decision, "To entrust to the proposed freestanding campaign the task of fulfilling the Convention's second objective namely 'to mobilise the support of the people of Scotland behind the Convention's scheme'." We also asked Nigel Smith to continue seeking the major finance that would be necessary for such a campaign and to bring back to us a list of potential members of a Board of Trustees which would be endorsed by the Convention and would be responsible for developing the independent organisation.

Originally there had been some hope that this campaign might get off the ground even before the General Election on May 1st, but this proved impossible. However, the basic organisation was put rapidly in place, sufficient funds were guaranteed and trustees appointed for a campaign which used the working title Partnership for a Parliament.

In the days after the General Election result, this is now appointing staff and preparing for an intensive Yes-Yes campaign for a referendum which is likely to be held in September or October. Entrusting this campaigning role to Partnership for a Parliament meant that the Convention itself will have a single and important continuing role until Scotland's parliament is secure.

The pre-election period did give rise to a few dramatic incidents. Michael Forsyth continued to go on about the tartan tax *ad nauseam* and on St Andrew's Day, 1996 he pulled off a spectacular coup of gesture politics by returning to Scotland the Stone of Destiny with great pomp and ceremony. Three of the original four conspirators who had spirited the Stone of Destiny away from Westminster Abbey on Christmas Day 1950 were present at the

Edinburgh ceremony marking its return. George Robertson, while welcoming the homecoming, called for the stone to be housed in a devolved Scottish parliament, presumably under the speaker's chair. Since the people of Scone also want it back, we will have to see where it ends up – but I warm to the idea of the speaker of Scotland's parliament sitting above that ancient symbol of sovereignty and power

As 1997 dawned I issued a New Year message to the people of Scotland that "1997 will be our year of destiny. Before this year comes to its end the long lean years of waiting and of hope so often dashed may well be over. We have before us the best chance for many generations to rise and be a nation again. It may well be our last chance for this generation. This time we dare not, we must not, fail."

This echoed the widespread feeling that failure yet again would be an unthinkable disaster. As we entered the final few months before the general election, there was a growing air of confidence and optimism, but a very strong feeling of restraint, that we must not count our chickens! Back in 1992 our confidence had been dealt a severe blow by the actual result. We therefore approached the election with confidence but without any exaggerated claims. When, on April 4th, Tony Blair returned to Scotland to ruffle a few more feathers, our caution appeared wise. In answer to the West Lothian question, on which the *Scotsman* had changed its view and was now presenting as a major flaw, Tony Blair said, "The way of dealing with this is to make it clear that what we are proposing is devolution and not federation. Sovereignty resides with the Westminster Parliament." He then went on, "As far as we are concerned, sovereignty rests with me as an English MP and that's the way it will stay."

Admittedly, this was an answer to a question as to what he might say to his own constituents, but it might have been better phrased. He was asked whether he would ever prevent a Scottish parliament from using its tax-varying powers. He said, "The powers are like those of any local authority; powers that are constitutionally there can be used but the Scottish Labour Party has no plans to raise income tax and once the power is given it's like any parish council that's got the right to exercise it. But the Labour Party can make tax pledges and we have. Our five year pledge is there and it applies to Scotland as it does to England."

I have quoted this in full because it has been greatly misrepresented and misunderstood. It was perhaps a tactical mistake to use the comparison with an English parish council, but it is manifestly clear that the only thing he was saying was that if such a parish council can have both a power and the right to use it, how can it be denied to Scotland's parliament. Equally, he was clearly not saying that there would be any veto on Scotland's parliament's powers – purely that the Labour Party in its own policy would tell the electorate it would not use these powers, at least for the first parliament. That is a position the Constitutional Convention has always respected and understood. It was Michael Forsyth and his cronies alone who consistently and deliberately confused the power and the policy, by implying that taxes would inevitably and automatically rise.

So the election drew closer, in the longest campaign of modern times, one fought on the basis of sound bites, spin doctors, personal attacks and one which frankly scunnered most of the population! All the evidence is that people had already made up their minds and that changed little, if at all, through the campaign. One wonders whether all the millions spent on weeping lions, bulldogs, littering placards and all the rest, could not have been saved for a better purpose?

CHAPTER 25

Surprised by Joy

"The inaccessible Pinnacle is not Inaccessible"

Friday May 2nd 1997 was a beautiful sunny day in Edinburgh. I walked from the Parliament House down Regent Street and Princes Street. Outside one of the upmarket cafes was a blackboard, usually carrying the specials of the day. Today it read simply in large chalked capitals: "SUN OUT: TORIES OUT: WHAT A GRAND DAY."

The city seemed alive with new hope. The sun shone; birds sang in the flowering cherry trees in the gardens; above all, every face seemed to wear a smile that conveyed a mixture of relief, surprise and joy. Strangers stopped to shake my hand, or give an ecstatic hug. Everything had changed. The long night was over. Scotland's day had dawned at last.

My mind went back to another day more than five years before. That too was the day after a General Election, but no sun shone. The palpable air of gloom and depression owed nothing to the dreich day – Scotland's hopes lay shattered, in a nation condemned to five more years of the arrogance of a Government that neither listened nor cared. The writer William McIlvanney had called on us then to learn "never to tolerate an intolerable situation", and the joy of 1997 proves that we listened to his voice.

The new Labour Government has hit the ground running, the speed with which it has moved has proved that it means business – and high on the priority list of that business is Scotland's parliament. Our euphoria must not blind us, however, to the road that still must be trod if we are to see the parliament we have planned for so long, become a reality. The new Government is committed to producing a White Paper firmly based on the Constitutional Convention's scheme, and then to a two question referendum. A clear 'Yes' vote would both confirm Scotland's "settled will", and make the passage of the legislation through Parliament that much easier, and any opposition, already weakened by the scale of the election defeat, even less effective.

What can we now expect in Scottish politics? There are signs that the Conservative Party may finally come to terms with what they have been told for many years, namely that their collapse was not due to some failure to communicate, but had three profound causes. First, they were perceived as the party of English nationalism. They have never been able to rid themselves of the legacy of Thatcher's strident inability to understand Scotland and the Scots. Second, they have suffered from an image as an arrogant Government, unwilling to listen to anybody but its friends, always ready to lecture Scots on what was really good for us and imposing on Scotland, not just unpopular policies, but a market ideology alien to our community. But third, the most important reason for their failure has been their refusal to understand Scotland's deep cry for democracy and home rule.

In 1955, the Tories were the only party ever to win more than 50% of the vote in Scotland (and half of the 72 seats). Their slide to electoral oblivion coincides with the change of policy, in the hardening of their opposition to any real sharing of power. This was rubbed in, by the way in which power was obsessively centralised, by the weakening of local government and the cancerous growth of powerful quangos accountable only to the

"Governor General", the Secretary of State appointed by Westminster. In a perverse way, the eighteen years of Conservative Government may well have done Scotland a great service in the long run. It has proved to us beyond any doubt, that what we need is not just a change of government, which one day will inevitably change back again – but rather a fundamental change in the system, which will safeguard us for good. Mrs Thatcher and John Major have taught us something we will never forget: that the problem is not just *who* governs us, but *how* we are governed.

The growing demand in the Scottish Tory Party for greater democracy, for a Scottish identity, and above all for a new attitude to home rule and shared power are developments we should encourage and welcome. It surely cannot have escaped their notice, that the Tories' best and earliest chance of recovery lies in the electoral system for Scotland's parliament, which would, even on their present showing of some 17% of the vote, give them about twenty seats in the 129 seat legislature.

The SNP will certainly continue to argue that it can only spell out its attitude when the White Paper is published, and will also press for a multi-option referendum. Given that this is politically impossible, I am sure that in the end the Nationalists, and certainly most SNP supporters, will vote for a double Yes in the referendum, in the awareness that failure here would set back any real chance of change for another generation.

The Liberal Democrats will oppose the proposal for a referendum, and especially the second question on tax-varying powers as being unnecessary, but they will continue to give their strong and consistent support to the Constitutional Convention as guardians of our scheme, and will campaign vigorously for a Yes-Yes vote when the time comes.

What of the Constitutional Convention itself? What is our achievement and where do we go from here? The Convention's astonishing success is in danger of being ignored. We have set the agenda to which all parties are now reacting. We have demonstrated over eight years, a new way of doing politics. Against all the odds, and the constant cynicism of our opponents, we have shown that consensus is possible. We have not left politics to the politician, the whole of Scotland's society has been directly involved in the broadest coalition in living memory. We have produced a plan for Scotland's parliament which will be powerful and radically different from Westminster. It will be elected by a system that gives all parties fair representation and brings government closer to the people. We have secured the firm commitment of the Labour Party, now the Government, to legislation based on our scheme in *Scotland's Parliament; Scotland's Right*.

If this is now achieved, we will have transformed Scotland for good. If this is, as promised, the first step in a great programme of constitutional change, we will have pioneered the transformation of the United Kingdom into a modern democracy, fit for a new millennium. Not bad for eight years work!

So much for the achievements of the past, the series of minor miracles that brought us to this great day. What now of the future? What is the Convention's role? Our central task is to remain the guardian and guarantor of *Scotland's Parliament; Scotland's Right*. We hold in trust, three key documents, which together embody the commitments and promises made by us all. The first is the *Claim of Right* itself, bearing the signatures of John Smith, Gordon Brown, Donald Dewar, Robin Cook, George Robertson and virtually all Scotland's Labour and Liberal Democrat MPs in 1989, along with the senior representatives of local government and of Scotland's civic society. We also hold *Scotland's Parliament; Scotland's Right*, the definitive scheme of 1995, again bearing the signatures of us all. Finally, we hold in trust the *Electoral Agreement*, in which the two major parties in the Convention undertake to field equal numbers of men and women in winnable seats.

One of the fears most often expressed – and sometimes cultivated – is that the Labour Party in Government will retreat from its wholehearted commitment, and somehow fail to deliver the strong entrenched parliament they helped to frame in the Convention. I believe that fear to be wrong, for several good reasons. Successive Labour Shadow Secretaries of State – Donald Dewar, Tom Clarke, and George Robertson – have spent long and demanding hours in negotiation to achieve our result. Their commitment is proved by the real concessions they made on such issues as the electoral system, as others did too. More important, the new Government was elected with such a huge majority, on the platform of trust. Tony Blair said repeatedly that he would keep his promises and would make none he would not keep. I have just listened to his voice again, saying, "I vow that with the consent of the people, we will have devolved power to Scotland, Wales, and the Regions of England. This is my covenant with the people. Judge me by it. The buck stops here."

The promises in Scotland – "the 10 commitments brought down from the Mound" as given at the end of this book – were made by Labour as part of the Convention. We stand together as the guarantors they will be kept.

For these reasons I believe the widespread fear of betrayal to be unsustainable, but there is one major risk that we must face honestly. Tony Blair will be one of the most powerful Prime Ministers in history. He inherits enormous powers given by our unwritten constitution and especially by the so-called royal prerogatives: powers greater than any other democratic leader in Europe, all of whom have the checks and balances our system lacks. In addition his huge parliamentary majority and his iron control over his party combine to make the power of the office enormous. The danger is obvious. In Lord Acton's words, "Power tends to corrupt; absolute power corrupts absolutely."

The test of this Government's ability to resist that corruption will be its readiness to carry through a programme of constitutional reform that will change our system of government for good – in so doing, they will effectively ensure that neither they, nor any future UK Government, will ever again exercise such absolute unanswerable power. This is about the readiness of the most secretive and centralised government system in European democracy to share power and empower its people.

That the Convention has in fact provided the Government with its central policy for constitutional reform will be seen to have been the decisive change on which all others ultimately depend. I believe our gift to the new Labour Government could be the Big Idea, the central, coherent and powerful concept that could catch the mood of the nation, the vision that could provide a renewal of our society. That concept whose time has come is, I believe, that of Empowerment, which includes strong notions of Participation, Stakeholding, Democracy and Community.

In a society sick of the centralising of arrogant power and of the selfishness of a market force ideology, the principles underlining the commitments of the Convention are surely the simple but powerful ideas that could serve to undergird the reforms and to provide the coherent moral foundation for a truly great reforming Government. These ideas offer the hope of transforming and renewing our nation and community irreversibly. They have sustained the Convention and led us through the fire of our trial, to the success we have not just talked about in theory, but demonstrated in practice.

To these central ideas, I would add another which flows naturally from them – that of Sustainable Development. If the Government, both at UK and Scottish levels, can show that a truly participative democracy can produce long term strategies that combine economic, social and environmental goals in an integrated series of policies, then we will lead the way for Europe into a new millennium that really will offer hope and a better quality of life to all our children. These are our hopes.

So is there any continuing role for the Convention? Two of our three original aims are still to be fulfilled. We have still to "secure the approval of the people" through the referendum, and then to "assert the right of the people to secure the implementation" of our scheme. The second aim has been fully entrusted to an independent freestanding Campaign, which has got off to a good start, under the working title, Partnership for a Parliament. The final name will be Scotland Forward! The Convention has been assured that this body will mount an effective campaign and that it will be firmly based on a double Yes vote for the Convention's scheme. On that basis, we were happy to "entrust" this task to them, and to encourage all our members to support this financially and in all other ways.

This leaves the Convention, as the guardian of the scheme, with the third aim, to ensure implementation. We have already identified three major steps in keeping our promise that the Convention would remain in being "until Scotland's parliament is secure." The first is participation and scrutiny of the legislative process. This must of course have limitations. The Government is primarily responsible and the very tight timetable rules out any lengthy consultation. The Convention's interest is limited to ensuring that the White Paper reflects all the major principles in our scheme and does not significantly depart from them. We also received a direct promise from Tony Blair in July 1996, that we would be consulted in the framing of the referendum questions.

Our second task is to stimulate and monitor the discussion on the Standing Orders for Scotland's Parliament. These are the rules by which it will work, and it is of critical importance that we create a new kind of parliament rather than a pale imitation of the rejected and outdated Westminster model. We hope that there will be widespread discussion on this and that we will be able to recommend to the parliament when it meets, a set of Standing Orders that will make it one of the most advanced, open and truly democratic legislatures in the world. Finally we intend to continue the programme, Preparing for Change, which has already been very successful in teasing out what Scotland's parliament could actually do with its powers to change the things that matter in Scotland – health, education, housing, local government, employment and so on. This should involve the participation of people throughout Scotland and demonstrate the difference our own parliament could make in every major area that affects our lives. Under the new title, Partnership for Change, this programme will be carried out by a wide variety of organisations, with the

Convention in the role of catalyst and stimulator. Nobody can tell a democratically elected parliament what to do – but the aim of this programme would be to produce an intelligent consensus on the options open to the legislators, and the likely consequences of the various policy options.

When these tasks are complete, when Scotland's parliament meets at long last, after nearly three hundred years, the Scottish Constitutional Convention will, with joy and gratitude, hand the torch over to the new guardians.

This book has been both a political and a personal testimony. I have been publicly called, to my embarrassment, the Father or the Architect of Scotland's parliament. I do not deserve those titles, for I have been rather the catalyst that has enabled a large number of honest men and women to work together and to learn together that minor miracles still happen! There have been many moments of doubt along the way, but it is now clear that our work, imperfect though it is, will form the basis for the way forward for Scotland. If we now achieve a new parliament within a reformed United Kingdom, we will have laid better foundations than even we expected.

Hugh McDiarmid wrote in *Lucky Poet*,

"Let what can be shaken, be shaken,
And the unshakeable remain.
The Inaccessible Pinnacle is not inaccessible."

At the beginning of the Convention's long pilgrimage, I asked, "What happens when that other voice we all know so well says, 'We say No, and We are the State.' Well, we say Yes and We are the People." That other voice is silent. The State listens at last. The people say Yes, and their voice prevails. The making of Scotland's parliament will ensure that the voice of the people is never ignored again.

The Ten Commitments

We can summarise the ten major commitments, to which the people of Scotland will want to hold their politicians. I call them the Ten Commitments Brought Down From The Mound. They form the basis of the Scottish Constitutional Convention's contract with the Scottish people.

1. THE PROMISE THAT THE PEOPLE HAVE THE RIGHT TO DECIDE
   We signed the *Claim of Right*, acknowledging the sovereign rights of the Scottish people to determine the form of government best suited to their needs.

2. THE PROMISE TO IMPLEMENT OUR SCHEME
   In the *Claim of Right*, we also promised "to assert the right of the Scottish people to secure implementation of that scheme." After eight years of hard-won consensus-building, and of a new way of doing politics, we are committed to legislation firmly based on our common proposals.

3 THE PROMISE TO LEGISLATE WITHIN A YEAR
   There is a firm promise, often repeated, to ensure legislation, based on the Convention's scheme, within one year of a change of government.

4 THE PROMISE TO SECURE SCOTLAND'S PARLIAMENT AGAINST UNILATERAL ABOLITION OR INTERFERENCE

We stated that "we are adamant that the powers of Scotland's parliament, once established, should not be altered without the consent of the Scottish parliament, representing the people of Scotland." While recognising that legal entrenchment is not possible, we stated our belief, which even our opponents accept, that the future unilateral repeal or amendment of the Act would be "practically and politically impossible". We therefore "strongly recommend" that there be "a Declaration of the Parliament of the United Kingdom . . . that the Act founding the (Scottish) parliament should not be repealed or amended in such a way as to threaten the existence of Scotland's parliament, without the consent of the Scottish parliament and of the people of Scotland.

5. THE PROMISE TO ENSURE LONG-TERM STABLE FINANCES

Our scheme proposes that Scotland's finances will be assured, not by a block grant at the whim of Westminster, but by an "assigned budget" based on the continuing principle of equalisation coming to Scotland's parliament "as of right". This is far more important as a means of long-term stable income than the marginal powers over income tax variation, though these powers should be firmly assured whatever the policy decision of each party on their use.

6. THE PROMISE TO USE A FAIRER SYSTEM FOR ELECTIONS

The electoral system to be used for Scotland's parliament of 129 members will ensure fairer representation of parties and of all parts of the country. All members of the Scottish parliament will be elected by the people. None will be appointed by the political parties, whose role, as at present, will be confined to the selection of candidates.

7. THE PROMISE TO ENSURE GENDER BALANCE
FROM THE START
Labour and the Liberal Democrats have signed an Electoral
Contract, held in trust by the Convention, in which they
promise to "select and field an equal number of male and
female candidates . . . equally distributed with a view to the
winnability of seats." Other parties will be challenged to do the
same, making Scotland's parliament unique from the start.

8. THE PROMISE TO STRENGTHEN EFFECTIVE
LOCAL GOVERNMENT
The Act will commit Scotland's parliament "to secure and
maintain a strong and effective system of local government and
will embody the principle of subsidiarity." We believe that the
parliament should go further and adopt "the principles
contained in the European Charter of Local Self-Government
to safeguard the powers and competence of local government.
Power will be decentralised in a participative society.

9. THE PROMISE TO WORK BETTER THAN
WESTMINSTER
Scotland's parliament will be "very different from the
Westminster model." Its standing orders and procedures should
make it open, accessible and accountable, strengthened by a
charter protecting "fundamental rights and freedoms within
Scots law", and by an expected Freedom of Information Act.

10. THE PROMISE OF RENEWAL, HOPE AND VISION
FOR A NEW CENTURY
The most important commitment of all is that the interests of
the people "shall be paramount" and that Scotland's parliament,
with power in all major areas that affect the quality of life in
Scotland, will offer new hope, confidence, prosperity and justice
to our nation as we enter a new millennium.

These are the promises we made together to and for the people of
Scotland. They will be kept.